LATINO AMERICANS

ALSO BY RAY SUAREZ:

The Old Neighborhood: What We Lost in the Great Suburban Migration
(FREE PRESS, 1999)

The Holy Vote: The Politics of Faith in America
(RAYO/HARPERCOLLINS, 2006)

INCLUDING RAY SUAREZ

The Oxford Companion to American Politics
(OXFORD UNIVERSITY PRESS, 2012)

What We See: Advancing the Observations of Jane Jacobs
(NEW VILLAGE PRESS, 2010)

Social Class: How Does It Work?
(RUSSELL SAGE FOUNDATION, 2010)

Brooklyn: A State of Mind
(WORKMAN PUBLISHING, 2001)

About Men
(POSEIDON PRESS, 1987)

LATINO AMERICANS

THE 500-YEAR LEGACY THAT SHAPED A NATION

RAY SUAREZ

A CELEBRA BOOK

For my children—

Rafael, Eva, and Isabel—

three of my life's greatest joys

Celebra
Published by the Penguin Group
Penguin Group (USA), 375 Hudson Street,
New York, New York 10014, USA

USA | Canada | UK | Ireland | Australia | New Zealand | India | South Africa | China

Penguin Books Ltd., Registered Offices: 80 Strand, London WC2R 0RL, England
For more information about the Penguin Group visit penguin.com.

First published by Celebra,
a division of Penguin Group (USA)

First Printing, September 2013

LIBRARY OF CONGRESS CATALOGING-IN-PUBLICATION DATA:
Suarez, Ray, 1957–
Latino Americans / Ray Suarez.
p. cm.
ISBN 978-0-451-23814-6
1. Hispanic Americans—History. I. Title.
E184.S75S83 2013
973'.0468—dc23   2013015502

Printed in the United States of America
10 9 8 7 6 5 4 3 2 1

Set in ITC New Baskerville Std
Designed by Pauline Neuwirth

PUBLISHER'S NOTE
While the author has made every effort to provide accurate telephone numbers and Internet addresses at the time of publication, neither the publisher nor the author assumes any responsibility for errors, or for changes that occur after publication. Further, publisher does not have any control over and does not assume any responsibility for author or third-party Web sites or their content.

CONTENTS

TELLING
OUR STORY:
AN INTRODUCTION

THIS STORY is different from other conventional histories you may have read. For an author, recounting a story of one people in a particular place at a particular time is challenging enough, but this book sets out to tell how numerous peoples, from regions and continents flung across the globe, came together to become one people.

The Latino Americans come from Europe, Africa, Asia, and from the ancient nations of this hemisphere. They are the offspring of Spain's New World Empire. They arrived in the United States by jet aircraft this morning; they crossed a dusty, empty stretch of desert just yesterday; or long years after arriving here to work, they raised a right hand in front of a federal judge and swore to renounce all other allegiances to any other country. And most important, alongside those whose American story is a recent one are the generations of Latinos whose families have been in this country far longer than there has been a place called the United States, even longer than the arrivals from the British Isles who would go on to invent the United States.

They . . . we . . . are all those things at once. We are at once a new people on the American landscape and an old and deeply embedded part of the history of this country and continent. The Spanish names of saints, heroes, captains, and kings dot the landscape of much of the country . . . all the way from "the flowery place," Florida, at the southeast corner, to the San Juan Islands just off the Canadian border in sight of British Columbia. Because restless Americans have steadily moved south and west since World War II, shifting the population away from the Northeast and Great Lakes, millions more Americans unwittingly speak Spanish every day, heading into a Luby's luncheonette in El Paso, "the pass," sitting in traffic in San Diego, "Saint James," or taking that third card in hopes of hitting twenty-one in that "snow-covered place," Nevada.

At its height when the nineteenth century began, the Spanish Empire stretched from the islands scattered at the mouth of the Caribbean to the southern tip of South America, up through the Andes and the western Amazon to the continent's northern coast, through the slender arm of Central America to the vast landmass of Mexico and into North America, including at various times all or part of the territory of twenty-three U.S. states. The first European language heard in these vast territories was Spanish, the first Christian prayers followed the Roman Catholic rite, and the earliest surveys and land titles were granted to Spanish families.

Like the British Empire, the Spanish Empire had a shifting, often cruel and exploitative relationship with the hundreds of nations and peoples already in place when it arrived. Ultimately, however, the history was different in British and Spanish America over long centuries. This is not to minimize or underplay the horrifying tales of genocide, expropriation, and involuntary servitude brought to its enormous empire by the Spanish crown, but only to note that the two stories are different. As the British Empire and its successor governments in the United States

Mexico in the early years of independence from Spain. This 1837 map shows the vast extent of Mexican territory, including all of what is now the southwestern United States from Louisiana and Arkansas west to the Pacific Ocean. Above what is now California lay the vast Oregon Territory, under joint occupation of the United States and the British Empire during the 1830s. CREDIT: LIBRARY OF CONGRESS

pushed Native Americans west from the Atlantic seaboard until there was no more room left to push them into, the descendants of the Maya, Aztecs, and Incas remain very much present in their home countries, fully represented in the gene pool of the people who have come to the United States from the rest of the hemisphere in the last two centuries.

You cannot understand more than fifty million of your fellow Americans without knowing this history. More important, you won't be able to understand the America that's just over the horizon if you don't know this history. Latino history is your history. Latino history is our history.

The bright lights are scanning the yard. The sirens are wailing in the night. Worried guards with flashlights make their panicky rounds. This is an intellectual prison break. Too many Americans have been taught a siloed American history. The core narrative, the story at the heart of the story, is a grand procession of white guys on white horses, with the "oth-

Massive proimmigrant demonstrations filled the streets of American cities in 2006. CREDIT: STEVE SCHAPIRO/CORBIS

We Serve Whites Only. CREDIT: THE DOLPH BRISCOE CENTER FOR AMERICAN HISTORY, THE UNIVERSITY OF TEXAS AT AUSTIN

ers"—black Americans, women, religious and ethnic minorities—confined to their own separate areas. This book insists that the history of more than fifty million Latinos in the United States is your history too, no matter where in the world you or your ancestors came from.

Our country is changing. Latinos are in the same moment among the newest and oldest kids on the block. Juan Ponce de León was tramping around Florida in the sixteenth century and made it part of the Spanish Empire for centuries to come. Today, Spanish-speaking newcomers are inheriting and revitalizing Florida's twenty-first-century culture, and many Floridians are ambivalent about those changes. That is part of our story too.

In more than 235 years since the Declaration of Independence, an essential truth has often been overlooked by the generations who look on anxiously as new immigrants arrive by air, sea, and land. The United States has constantly been transformed by immigrants, and it has transformed them too. Immigration anxiety is fueled when too much attention is paid to the first part, and not enough to the second. Talk to anyone who has come to live in the United States from somewhere else in the world. With each successive year they are in our country, these immigrants become less a part of the place they came from, and more of an American.

Keep that in mind as you read this book. The situation in schools, workplaces, neighborhoods, on TV, in the armed forces, in church—in all the places that make the country what it is—breathtaking change is under way. At some point in the 2040s, a slim majority of Americans will trace their ancestry to people who arrived in this country from someplace other than Europe. For the first time in centuries, people who descended from the European empires that captured the continent, and people who descended from the generations of immigrants from Ireland, Germany, Italy, czarist Russia, and places large and small between Dublin and Moscow will be a minority of Americans.

Yeah. It's a big deal for people in the old and new majorities alike.

By the conclusion of this book, you should be thinking about the United States, its history, and its people in a slightly different way. There are now so many ways to get cozy with a book—with ink on paper or in dots of light on dark on the screen of an e-reader or sitting behind the wheel of your car listening to a recorded text. However you consume this work, I haven't done my job properly if you don't say (and regularly), "Hey, I didn't know that!"

This book is a handbook for getting a better perspective on that next America. There's going to be some stretching involved, and getting used to new ideas. It's going to be fascinating. It's going to be exciting for some . . . and uncomfortable for others.

Let's begin.

1

THE CONVERGENCE BEGINS

(LA CONVERGENCIA COMIENZA)

EVERY NATION has an origin story. It's the story they tell themselves, about themselves, to understand who they are.

Americans are no different.

In many ancient civilizations, the origin story ties a people so intimately to the land that they are made out of it, molded by a creator from the literal soil of the place. The Japanese, the Menominee Indians of the Great Lakes, the Yoruba of West Africa, all have creation stories that tie the people and their history directly to the land. There is no memory of another place. In their telling, they have existed along with the land, and had no life apart from it.

Americans are very different.

Our origin story has to bring almost all of us from someplace else on the planet. So where does the story of the United States of America begin? Some of you might say Plymouth Rock, the spot on the damp New England shores where the Pilgrims are said by tradition to have come ashore from the *Mayflower* in 1620.

Others might say Jamestown, some six hundred miles to the south, where in 1607 Englishmen in search of fortune, not fleeing religious persecution, began probing the sandy inlets and started spinning gold from tobacco.

This country was not just a creation of the British Empire, however. There were five hundred nations in North America before a European ship ever dropped anchor off the Eastern Seaboard. Once Europeans started coming over in ever greater numbers, the territory that is now the United States became home to many colonies.

The Dutch made their way up the Hudson River and settled in the breathtakingly beautiful valleys of what is now Upstate New York. At the mouth of the river, Dutch farms and trading houses spread over the tracts of land around the great harbor that became New York City. The Swedes tried to make a go of colonization in parts of what is now Delaware and Pennsylvania. Even the Scots, before becoming part of the United Kingdom, attempted to plant colonies in what is now Maritime Canada, New Jersey, and the Carolinas.

France's North American empire stretched across a vast and rich swath of the continent many times the size of the parent country, including what is today half of Canada, and the U.S. Midwest, Great Plains, and Pacific Northwest. In the far northwest, the expanding Russian Empire pushed east, crossing the Bering Strait, colonizing Alaska, and moving down the coast of what is now Canada's British Columbia toward what would one day be Seattle. The Russians began to probe even farther south to what is now northern California.

The Genoese sailor sent west by Ferdinand and Isabel of Spain, Cristoforo Colombo in Italian, Cristóbal Colón in Spanish, and Christopher Columbus in English, made multiple trips to the Caribbean, and began

Álvar Núñez Cabeza de Vaca. The Spanish explorer was one of a handful of survivors of a sixteenth-century Spanish expedition that set out from what is now the Dominican Republic and headed west through the Caribbean, Gulf of Mexico, Texas, and Mexico. He wrote detailed accounts of his wanderings and later made extensive journeys through South America. By the time of his death he had seen more of the Spanish Empire firsthand than anyone. CREDIT: COURTESY PALACE OF THE GOVERNORS PHOTO ARCHIVES (NMHM/DCA), 071390

four centuries of Spanish presence in the hemisphere. Looking for "Cathay," China, he began the creation of an enormous New World empire for Spain.

The empire belonged to Their Most Catholic Majesties the king and queen of Spain. Pull out a map and take a look at South America, where Spain's possessions included virtually all the continent outside Brazil, all of today's Central America and Mexico, and all or part of Texas, Arkansas, Missouri, Kansas, Nebraska, Oklahoma, New Mexico, Arizona, California, Oregon, Utah, Nevada, Wyoming, Colorado, and Idaho, North and South Dakota. At its height in the last years of the eighteenth century, Spanish territory stretched as far north as the southern lands of what are today the prairie provinces of Canada, Manitoba, and Saskatchewan.

So where does the story of the modern United States begin? On Plymouth Rock, sure, but not *just* there. . . .

In Virginia, sure, but not *just* there. . . .

It turns out there are many candidates for the origin point, a place to visit like the coasts of Virginia or Massachusetts and say, "It all starts here."

Forty-two years before the men of the Virginia Company of London began to pound the fort at Jamestown into place, and fifty-five years before seasick Protestant refugees stepped onto dry land from the *Mayflower*, a Spanish sailor named Pedro Menéndez de Avilés dislodged French Protestants from their settlement on the Florida coast and established St. Augustine.

The Florida city is today the oldest continuously occupied European city in the United States. From 1565 to 1821, St. Augustine, *San Agustín*, was a Spanish-speaking city. As European empires fought their wars in the New World, the Florida city lived under different flags, but it was essentially a Spanish place for three centuries. The next time a tense local controversy breaks out in Florida over the use of Spanish, take a second to recall how much longer that tongue has been at home in the state than that relative newcomer, *inglés*.

Across the face of this vast continent, the empires moved and probed and jostled and searched. They spent more than two centuries moving their frontiers toward each other, and fighting wars over the bountiful land. The boundary lines shifted and crossed, and eventually disappeared. By the mid–nineteenth century, as the dust cleared from the Mexican War, the shape of the modern continental United States emerged. What had been French and British and Spanish territories now flew under the flag of the United States.

But I'm getting a little ahead of myself.

IF YOU WALK out of the church of San Esteban del Rey on the Acoma Pueblo in New Mexico, it will take a moment for your eyes to adjust to the intense sunlight. Your skin will immediately mark the extreme change from the cool and intensely colored interior of the church to the blast of dry heat rising from the tiny plaza at the edge of the pueblo. A vast valley falls away from the lip of the steep mesa where the Acoma Pueblo stands perched on top.

You can see for miles in every direction. The dry, scrubby landscape dominated by brown and gold and flecked with green stretches out from where you stand to the mountains in the distance.

Here, another American story began. The Acoma people had lived in this place since the thirteenth century. They were here three hundred years before the Spanish arrived, and began an encounter that would remake their world. There were no straitlaced Puritans dressed in black

The Church of San Esteban del Rey, Acoma Pueblo, New Mexico. Built in the 1630s by native people under the direction of a Spanish friar, the church still stands on a butte in central New Mexico. The Acoma Pueblo was the scene of a battle between Mexican settlers and Acoma Indians that eventually led to the Pueblo Revolt of 1680, the single most successful act of resistance of European rule by Native Americans. CREDIT: LIBRARY OF CONGRESS, PRINTS AND PHOTOGRAPHS DIVISION, DETROIT PUBLISHING COMPANY COLLECTION

and white, bundled up against the cold and damp. There were no Elizabethan adventurers hoping to find a way to get Indians to part with land, tobacco, and gold to pay off the investments of shareholders back in London.

In today's New Mexico, and in Texas, Florida, California, and Arizona, soldiers and priests pushed their way north and west from the first places they made landfall from Spain. For decades, small groups of men—explorers, not colonizers—threaded their way through what would become the Southwestern United States, extending the authority the Spanish monarchs exercised from faraway Mexico City in the longer-settled parts of New Spain.

Shield your eyes from the midday sun and try to imagine traversing this landscape in outfits of wool, linen, and leather, with metal armor to protect shoulders, arms, chests. Wearing heavy leather boots on their feet and gleaming metal helmets on their heads, small groups of Spanish soldiers conquered Indian nations.

The church of San Esteban is a reminder of the oppression wrought by these strange men from far away. Inside, heavy forty-foot-long beams frame a particularly beautiful Spanish colonial church. Yet run your eyes over the vast landscape again and you will see no trees of any size. There are also no roads, no wheeled carts, and no machines. Indians carried those massive beams more than twenty miles across the land and to the top of the mesa. Tons of earth, stone, and clay were similarly hauled up from the valley floor over thousands of hours of Indian labor. It took fourteen years to build the church.

Juan de Oñate was a New World man. Unlike the earliest conquistadores—conquerors—who were Europeans, he was born in Zacatecas in New Spain, to a wealthy and influential family. The Oñate family was made minor nobility by an ancestor's victory over an Arab army in Spain, and they owned a silver mine in Mexico. Young Juan continued the arc of his family's upward mobility by marrying Isabel de Tolosa Cortés, granddaughter of the conqueror Hernán Cortés, and great-granddaughter of the Aztec emperor Moctezuma.

The Spanish king Philip II ordered Oñate to colonize the northern reaches of New Spain. The Spaniards' announced intention was to establish the Catholic religion and build new missions north of the Rio Grande. The young soldier, however, also had dreams of finding new silver deposits, a path to the pearls of the Pacific, and also to Quivira, one of the legendary Seven Cities of Cibola and, according to legends, a place where Indians covered in gold ornaments toasted one another with goblets of gold.

Along with souls for God and gold for Spain, the Spanish Empire moved north for solid security reasons, according to Professor Stephen Pitti of Yale University. "Spain is competing with England in particular and Portugal and the Dutch eventually," he said. "The Spanish are interested in securing parts of North America for their own national and imperial advantage. The Spanish are looking for the security of holding places like San Francisco Bay, or the Florida or Texas coasts."

Oñate crossed the Rio Grande at today's El Paso, Texas, and declared it a possession of Philip of Spain. He headed north, and established his capital by what he called the San Juan Pueblo, having extended the Camino Real, the Royal Road from Mexico City, another six hundred miles. (The San Juan Pueblo reverted to its original name of Ohkay Owingeh in 2005.) Construction on new missions began, sinking roots for the Roman Catholic faith that still thrive in that land four centuries later.

The soldiers who came north with Oñate had a problem. So far, they had found Indians, deserts, salt deposits, and not much else. The young captain was facing mutiny because the promised riches had not been discovered, and the colonists expected to head up from New Spain had not arrived in the new settlement either. Oñate punished rebels, ruled his small domain with an iron fist, and sent his restless men radiating out from his headquarters in search of silver and gold, water and game.

Oñate was now a full-fledged colonial governor of the province called Holy Faith of New Mexico. He visited the Indian pueblos now under his control. He hoped to find a shortcut to the Pacific and supply Mexico City with much-prized salt. He and his men hunted buffalo after failing to capture them, returning to the young settlement with plenty of meat and hides. Today what a buffalo looks like is such a common piece of knowledge, and it is hard to remember that people like Oñate were the first Europeans to see such animals, to draw and describe them in letters.

In a report to the king's representative, the viceroy back in Mexico City, Oñate's secretary, Juan Gutierrez Bocanegra, writes of the bison, "Its shape and form are so marvelous and laughable, or frightful, that the more one sees it, the more one desires to see it, and no one could be so melancholy that if he were to see it a hundred times a day he could keep from laughing heartily as many times, or could fail to marvel at the sight of so ferocious an animal."

In the autumn of 1598, shortly after taking control of the pueblo, Oñate's soldiers, under the command of his nephew Juan de Zaldívar, took sixteen captured Acoma men to the mesa and demanded supplies be delivered to the pueblo for their use. The Acomas' leader, Zutacapan, had abandoned his earlier intention to attack the Spanish forces in the belief that the Europeans were immortal. When the Acomas refused the Spanish demands for supplies, fighting began that, if nothing else, proved the rumors about Spanish immortality unfounded. Oñate's nephew was killed in the fighting along with eleven of his men. The governor sent Zaldívar's brother Vicente toward Acoma on a punitive expedition.

It was not the first example, and it would not be the last: Spanish soldiers were able to bring superior technology and firepower to bear. They attacked the pueblo atop the mesa with a small force, and a cannon. Vicente Zaldívar's attackers were able to inflict large numbers of casualties and widespread damage, even as they took terrible casualties in fierce combat with the Acomas. Zaldívar wrote in his diary that after the Indians surrendered, "Most of them were killed and punished by fire and bloodshed, and the pueblo was completely laid waste and burned."

But the Spaniards were not satisfied with mere victory. Hundreds of Acoma men were seized as slaves and dispersed to Spanish possessions in the New World. Originally, the governor decided to enslave them for twenty years, and amputate the right foot of every man over twenty-five years old. He relented, to a certain extent, and cut the right foot from just two dozen men. He enslaved many more men, along with girls and women over twelve years of age. Oñate had shown the colonists and the colonized that he could be a cruel man when he needed to be. Now it was time to show his own people he could deliver on the promises of riches.

The stories of great wealth in seven cities north of New Spain had been circulating for decades, since a Franciscan priest told officials in Mexico City that he had seen Cibola, the City of Gold, in what is now New Mexico. When Fray Marcos de Niza wrote about his journey in 1539, he said he first saw Cibola in the distance. It was, he wrote, a city larger than Mexico City, with fine houses. His story continued: "At times I was tempted to go to it, because I knew that I risked nothing but my life, which I had offered to God the day I commenced the journey; finally I feared to do so, considering my danger and that if I died, I would not be able to give an account of this country, which seems to me to be the greatest and best of the discoveries. When I said to the chiefs who were with me how beautiful Cibola appeared to me, they told me that it was the least of the seven cities, and that Totonteac is much bigger and better than all the seven, and that it has so many houses and people that there is no end to it."

The Spanish monarchs had already taken fabulous wealth out of Mexico in gold and silver. Nothing was bound to get their attention like the promise of even more riches. Earlier explorations headed to modern Kansas, Nebraska, and Missouri looking for the cities of gold. They found Indian nations peaceably farming corn, beans, and squash, but no golden goblets.

Oñate headed out in 1601 looking for two things: gold and a route to the sea. He brought 130 soldiers and a dozen Franciscan priests, and used Jusepe Gutierrez as a guide, the lone survivor of an earlier, ill-fated voyage in search of the Seven Cities. Oñate roamed far from his home province of Santa Fe de Nuevo Mexico. He followed the meandering Canadian River through northern Texas (near today's Amarillo), into

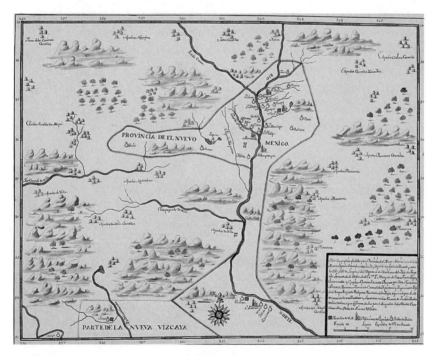

The Spanish province of Santa Fe de Nuevo Mexico. The land corridor leading north from Mexico across the Rio Grande at El Paso connected New Spain to a string of Spanish missions and Indian pueblos in this 1727 map. CREDIT: THE DOLPH BRISCOE CENTER FOR AMERICAN HISTORY, THE UNIVERSITY OF TEXAS AT AUSTIN

Oklahoma, and then north into Kansas. He and his men were received peaceably in the Quivira settlements. There was no gold.

Instead Oñate became the first European to describe the tallgrass prairie, which covered much of the Midwest before agriculture and European colonization.

Back in New Mexico, as the governor ranged over the continent, things were not going well. There were no promised riches. The land was hard to farm. The Indians clearly did not want the settlers there. When Oñate returned from Kansas he found many of the settlers had returned to their hometowns south of the Rio Grande, and only his strongest supporters among the colonists hung on in his makeshift capital.

Ranging far from his arid capital, Oñate saw well-watered land capable of supporting large settlements. Emboldened by what he had seen in the future Amarillo and Wichita, he decided to mount another expedition. This time Oñate, soldiers, priests, and a few Indian translators headed west.

The diaries kept by priests, officers, and, through secretaries, by Oñate himself provide thrilling reading, filled with all the wonder of men seeing unimagined things for the first time and having the rare privilege of being the first Europeans to experience these early contacts with the people scattered across the Southwest.

One of the priests heading west with Oñate, Fr. Gerónimo Zárate Salmerón, describes the people of one pueblo this way: "The men are well-featured and noble; the women are handsome with beautiful eyes, and they are affectionate. These Indians said that the sea was distant from there twenty days' journey. . . . It is to be noticed that none of these nations was caught in a lie."

Time and again, the witnesses to these early encounters illustrate the assumption that the Indians should understand that there were new bosses in town. At one point the Spanish column took a local chief hostage, and there was surprise and offense when the chief's own warriors launched an assault, freeing their leader unharmed.

Many of the languages spoken by Indian nations across this vast region came from different linguistic families and were mutually unintelligible; it is from the distance of four centuries impossible to know who was able to understand what and when. The diaries note that the Spanish expeditions all took Indian translators along with them, but at a time when people were not likely to travel many hundreds of miles from their homeland, the confidence that "our" Indians could talk to "those" Indians must often have been misplaced.

Father Francisco de Escobar's accounts of the trip west to the Gulf of California tells of energetic gesturing, pointing, and describing done by men encountered near the Colorado River: "They almost convinced me beyond all doubt there were both yellow and white metals in the land, though there is no proof that the yellow metal is gold or that the white is silver, for of this my doubts are still very great." Father Escobar may have had his doubts, but the feverish speculation was to go on for a hundred years.

When enthusiastic Spaniards animatedly asked about a large lake and deposits of gold, were Indians humoring them, passing along their own legends, or trying to describe a large and faraway body of water they themselves had never seen but only heard about, like the Puget Sound?

Indians told the Spaniards about a *laguna de oro,* a lagoon of gold surrounded by rich communities. Antonio de Espejo explored the Southwestern deserts in the 1580s, and was told by inhabitants of the Zuni Pueblo of "a large lake where the natives claimed there were many towns. These people told us there was gold in the lake region, that the inhabitants wore clothes, with gold bracelets and earrings, that they dwelt at a distance of a sixty days' journey from the place we were."

Espejo looked over a greater distance for the lake of gold than any Spaniard before him, but all he could find were copper deposits flecked with a little silver in modern-day Arizona.

Espejo's own exaggerated stories of potential treasure waiting to be found in the arid Southwest overwhelmed all the years of failure and what has been taken as proof that there were no cities of gold. Espejo's chronicles reinvigorated the rumor mill, and led in part to the eventual commissioning of Juan de Oñate to head north to New Mexico.

After all that search and struggle, maybe the Spanish should have seen a pattern emerging. Wherever they heard these Indian tales, the amazing lakes, peoples covered in gold were always a long journey from where they were at the moment. Oñate and his men also heard the stories of the lake of Copalla and gold. In Zarate's telling, the faraway Indians "wore bracelets of gold, on the wrists and on the fleshy part of the arms and in their ears, and that from there they were fourteen days' journey."

Oñate's expedition kept heading west, and reached the Gulf of California, the inlet that separates the Mexican mainland from Baja California. However, Oñate did not follow the gulf all the way up to its end,

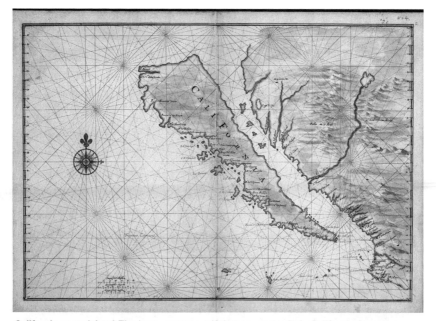

California as an island. The long, narrow gulf that separates Baja California from the Mexican mainland long led explorers and mapmakers to assume the territory was an island. The name came from a sixteenth-century adventure novel, *The Adventures of Esplandián*. The author, Garci Rodríguez Ordonez de Montalvo, told of an island at "the right hand of the Indies" inhabited by a race of black women. He called his "rugged island" California, the name that has stuck for 600 years. CREDIT: LIBRARY OF CONGRESS

where the Colorado River flows in. It was assumed the water continued northward, contributing to the idea that would persist for decades that California was a long island off the western shores of the North American continent.

Oñate headed back home to New Mexico and attempted to make up for what he lacked in gold with persistence. He petitioned the viceroy for more soldiers, more settlers, and more supplies to take another run at making a success of Santa Fe de Nuevo Mexico.

What he got instead of more help was a summons to return to court. Word had made its way to Mexico City of Oñate's treatment of Indians in general, and in particular his handling of the conflict at the Acoma Pueblo. King Philip II of Spain had issued a royal ordinance thirty years earlier governing the treatment of Indians by Spaniards. The use of violence against Indians was outlawed, which afforded them some protection from the casual assault and theft that marked so many encounters with Europeans. Standards were put in place for priests and monks, colonists, and military people.

It was five years before Oñate was finally called to New Mexico to face charges of cruelty to the Indians in connection with the Acoma uprising, and when he did the indictment significantly underplayed the carnage at the pueblo. He was also charged with executing mutineers and deserters, and adultery. He was fined, expelled permanently from New Mexico, and banished from Mexico City for four years.

Historian Marc Simmons concludes that given the charges, the sentence eventually handed down was a lenient one. "In the career of Juan de Oñate, we find a summation of the motives, aspirations, intentions, strengths and weaknesses of the Hispanic pioneers who settled the Borderland." The man often called "the Last Conquistador" died in Spain in 1626.

Founder of what became an American state. Witness to the founding of the oldest capital in North America, Santa Fe. Explorer of half a dozen American states covering a vast slice of the United States from Oklahoma to California. Whose name are you more likely to hear in an American history class? Captain John Smith, admiral of New England, saved from beheading by Pocahontas? Henry Hudson of the Dutch East India Company? Or Don Juan de Oñate, founder of the first European settlements north of the Rio Grande?

AS TRIBES ALONG the Eastern Seaboard, through the Great Lakes, and throughout South America learned all during the sixteenth and seventeenth centuries, defeating a few white men, or giving them what they wanted and sending them on their way, settled nothing. There would always be more.

In the decades that followed the death of Juan de Oñate, the Spanish viceroys in Mexico City continued to work to solidify their control of the vast, dry territories that stretched deep into the continent they maintained Spain owned. Roads poked their way into New Mexico, and eventually into Colorado, connecting routes of commerce and communication between the small cities and the sparsely settled European families heading north to take possession of land deeded by the Spanish Crown. Today, there are hundreds of thousands of descendants of these early families living in the Southwestern United States, including the actress Eva Longoria, and the former U.S. secretary of the interior and U.S. senator Ken Salazar.

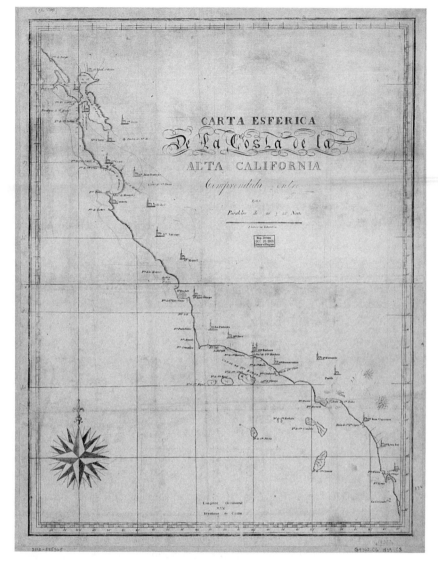

The California Pueblos. This network of religious and military settlements consolidated the weak Spanish control of its northern possessions. These missions later grew into many of the largest cities in California and the United States. On this map you can see missions that are today the cities of San Diego, Los Angeles, Santa Barbara, San Luis Obispo, Carmel, Santa Cruz, Santa Clara, San Jose, San Francisco, San Rafael, and others. CREDIT: LIBRARY OF CONGRESS

Along with bringing Catholicism to the pueblos, the priests brought Indians into the new missions, communities that blended Spanish economic and religious ambitions. Native people were moved from their land and traditional systems of land tenure to live and work in complexes that included fields, factories, and churches. This system also made it easier for relatively small groups of soldiers, civil servants, and priests to govern and tax Indian populations many times their size.

In California, exposure to European microbes unintentionally brought suffering and death to long-settled Indian communities. The fact that germs benign in the mouths and guts of Europeans were deadly to Indians has long been understood. What is less remarked upon is the social chaos widespread death and illness caused, leaving many Indians prepared to give up their destabilized ways of life and move in with the priests.

The Spanish mission system no longer exists in the United States, but, remarkably, many of the largest cities in the country, and major cities across the once-Spanish lands in the American Southwest, began their existence as missions. The cities include Los Angeles, San Francisco, and San Diego in California, and San Antonio, Texas.

Indian settlements that remained far removed from the expanding Spanish footprint maintained relatively peaceful relations with the Crown. In places where the mission system and Spanish claims for agriculture and mining impinged on existing boundaries and ways of life, the encounter was a source of growing tension. Defenders of indigenous religions deplored the growing number of priests settling in the region, and resented the forced labor used to build the churches.

In New Mexico, a religious leader from the San Juan pueblo called Popay saw the growing resentment of the Spanish colonists. At the same time, clashes between the native people of the Eastern Seaboard and British colonists were growing in frequency and ferocity, tensions were rising between Spanish colonists and native people in the West. Native people resented the system of forced labor pressed on them by the Spanish, and the pressure to abandon their religion.

In 1675, Popay was one of a group of forty-seven Indians convicted of sorcery in a trial in Santa Fe. The men had continued the rites and rituals of their own religion and refused to convert to Catholicism. Four were hanged; the remaining men were condemned to flogging and imprisonment. The Indian settlements across the colony sent a delegation to the capital to protest to Governor Juan Francisco de Treviño the treatment of Popay and the others. Fearing war, the governor released the prisoners and sent them home with a warning to stop the practices that had brought them to trial.

After a meeting of indigenous leaders in Taos, Popay emerged as a leader of the resistance to Spain. In 1680, he organized a revolt in pueblo communities across New Mexico. Unlike the struggles between the English and native nations in New England and the middle Atlantic states, this one succeeded.

Ask yourself for a moment how diverse groups speaking different languages, spread out over four hundred miles of territory, might organize a revolution. Popay sent runners to each pueblo carrying knotted deer-skin strips. Each day a knot in the strip was to be untied. The revolt would begin when the last knot was undone. It was a clever plan, but the Spanish caught two runners on their way to the Tesuque Pueblo, revealing the plan. So the war began two days early, on August 10, 1680. The Spaniards were caught by surprise, and fell back to Santa Fe.

The uprising struck at the spiritual and political authority of Spain. When the uprising began, the strategy was for each pueblo to demolish its mission church and kill its resident priest. Then the rebels were to move to the surrounding areas and kill the Spanish settlers. Once those objectives were achieved, the Indian forces were to move on Santa Fe. The first phases were quickly accomplished, and by August 15, thousands of pueblo Indian fighters were massed outside the capital preparing to attack.

The Spaniards launched a counterstrike to drive the Indians back from the city. They were, however, cut off and made a careful retreat from Santa Fe, but not before destroying much of the city. They headed to El Paso del Norte, today's El Paso and the southernmost city in New Mexico. It was the only successful revolution by native people against European colonialists anywhere in the New World. The pueblo Indian revolutionaries kept the Spaniards out of New Mexico for another twelve years.

During that time Popay tried to extinguish every sign that the Spanish had been in their country. Most of the pueblos destroyed the churches, but eighty years of Spanish rule in New Mexico had left behind an indelible deposit on the land. Some Indian families had been Christian for decades. Many spoke Spanish. Others had kinship links with Spanish settlers. The colonists had left behind European agricultural techniques, tools, and building styles.

Drought plagued Indian country. Quarrels between the different settlements and rivalries over leadership of the loose confederation marked the years of returned self-rule. When a column of Spanish soldiers arrived in 1692, the Indians were promised clemency and protection from nearby native nations if they would swear allegiance to the Spanish king and return to the Catholic faith. The pueblo leaders met in Santa Fe and agreed to terms.

Spain was back. Other attempted uprisings would follow, and were put down with uncompromising retribution by the new governor, Diego de Vargas. The process begun nearly a century earlier by Juan de Oñate would continue. Proximity and the passage of time would continue the work of melding the cultures, making modern New Mexicans. The thinly settled, arid land would become the center of the North American wool industry from the Spanish colonial era through the Mexican period into the area's entry into the United States.

Like colonists around the world, Spaniards set multiple goals for their overseas empire. The colonial lands had to sustain themselves economically, protect the political interests of the sovereign (in this case, act as a buffer against the expansionist ambitions of other empires), and advance the cause of the Catholic faith, which could count generations of Spanish monarchs as staunch defenders.

Decades later, in the far west of New Spain, more pioneer columns would come north, and begin our next story.

A LONG, THIN line of missions threaded its way up the California coast by the end of the eighteenth century. From San Diego in the south to San Francisco Solano in the north, more than twenty communities under the administration of the king were built by Indians and run by priests. Many of them planted the seed that continues to thrive today as a modern city. Others are archeological or historical sites, tucked away in less welcoming or less developed parts of the massive state.

It had been centuries since Mexico City was built on the foundations of the Aztec capital Tenochtitlán. California was called "the last corner of the Spanish Empire," according to Trinity University historian Arturo Madrid. Again, it was worries about the encroachment of other European empires that drove Spain to put a more permanent stamp on land it had claimed for generations.

The eighteenth-century Franciscan brother Junipero Serra is known as the founder of the California missions, and as such is one of the founders of modern California. "Part of Father Serra's mission was to Christianize, evangelize the peninsula all the way up," says historian Rose Marie Beebe, of Santa Clara University in California. "The missions in the presidios [fortified military bases] were founded to stop incursion from the Russians and the British. So there was a military reason and a religious reason for establishing *presidios* with the missions. They would have an *escolta*, a squad to protect the padres."

From this distance in time, it might seem odd that aside from Popay and similar anticolonial leaders, the indigenous people, living in old and established communities, would willingly submit themselves to the mission system, or could have been easily forced to do so by numerically smaller groups of priests and soldiers. Many of the Indian communities were collapsing from the effects of diseases brought by the Spaniards against which Indians had no immune defense. Stephen Pitti describes the tribes as "struggling to hunt, to collect acorns, to fish, to keep themselves going as communities that had lasted for centuries. The missions offered something which is not just spiritual but material. They offered Indian communities the opportunity to have bread on the table. Indians entered the missions with their own ideas about what they wanted out of those places."

The very priests who came offering a new way of life and a new way of belief unwittingly brought death and suffering in the diseases they transported in their bodies. The survivors found structure, comfort, and safety in the proselytizing and unpaid labor of the priests.

As the nineteenth century began, these young communities, constantly under construction, must have seemed like they sat at the end of the world. "These are still very small places that seemed rustic, like backwaters to visitors coming from Europe or Mexico City," writes Professor Pitti. "These are places in which Spanish-Mexicans feel themselves to be isolated, vulnerable." To Pitti, there is another important consideration. "Spanish-Mexican men in Alta California looking for partners find themselves partnering with indigenous women in these regions in part because there are so few Spanish-Mexican women who are coming from Mexico or coming from Spain in this period. So what happens in the frontier area is much more racial mixing than we see in some other parts of New Spain."

Even with the archipelago of missions strung along the California coast, few Mexicans took the chance to move to the northern colonies.

Some new arrivals did not make the trip voluntarily. In 1800, twenty-one youngsters, many of them illegitimate children who made their way to a home established for that purpose, were transported to California from Mexico City. During the journey—first by land, then by ship—one of the children died. Two of the girls were married to Spanish settlers before the end of the year. The others, who ranged in age from early childhood to adolescence, were distributed among California Spanish families. As an old woman, Apolinaria Lorenzana, the youngest of the children, dictated her memoirs and recalled, "On our arrival, the governor distributed the children like little dogs among various families." Life on the edge of the empire was hardscrabble enough to allow women to rise by being useful. Many of the diaries of nineteenth-century Spanish women in California revealed a society made more open by the chronic shortage of labor.

Lorenzana was to make a life that defied the restrictions colonial life elsewhere in New Spain normally held for women. She started out as one of the *niños expósitos*, abandoned children, and over her long life saw Alta California, Upper California, move from its days as a network of Catholic missions to a booming state in the expanding United States.

She tells the man who recorded her memories toward the end of her life, "When I was a very young girl, before coming from Mexico, I had been taught to read. And so when I was a young woman in California, I taught myself to write, and encouraged by the books I saw, I imitated letters on any piece of paper I could find—such as empty cigarette packets, or any sheet of blank paper I found discarded. In that manner I learned enough to make myself understood in writing when I needed something."

The young girl who arrived in the California missions was further schooled in the domestic arts—child care, cooking, sewing—and became a diligent worker in missions up and down the coast. "This is a child who is expected to contribute to Alta California society, to be useful in the society," Professor Beebe writes. "How is a seven-year-old child supposed to understand what the future holds? She must have been terrified in her heart, but she was a very strong child as is evidenced by all the things she did after she moved from Monterey to Santa Barbara to San Diego."

Professor Pitti reminds us that even for a foundling child, the move would have been bewildering. "Mexico City by the end of the eighteenth century is a major hub of urban life in the Americas, and for anybody to have moved from a place like that, a place that has real commercial life, that has various class strata, the sort of a city one could get lost in during this period the way one could have gotten lost in London or any of the great metropolises of that period . . . to move from that setting to the furthest remove of the Spanish Empire must have been a tremendous shock for a young girl."

It is unlikely that the young girl came to California expecting a life of greater ease and comfort. The abandoned children's home was an austere place to live. The day began early with prayers, breakfast, and then instruction, followed by more prayers, classes, and prayers again. Life in the home turned out to be good preparation for life in the missions, which ran on a similar schedule of bells, meals, and prayers.

She looked up at mission society just one rung removed from the very bottom. As a girl, she was even more vulnerable than a woman. As an orphan, she was even more exposed to the fragility and potential cruelty to which children could be exposed, because there were no family associations to give her status or promise her protection. She had no existing attachment to land, family, or tenure as both an orphan and an outsider, born elsewhere and transported to Alta California. The only weaker members of society in mission California were the longest tenured and most numerous, the native peoples of the North American coast.

Young Apolinaria Lorenzana's life was built on a series of accidents. After the children came north, she was placed with one of California's leading families, that of soldier and presidio leader Raymundo Carrillo.

Even her new protector was not so sure transporting the foundlings was good policy. He wrote the viceroy's court in Mexico City and asked that no more be sent: "I do not believe that there are any advantages to be gained by sending more children as these. The inhabitants do not want to take them in, because they have growing families of their own. These children are so unhappy, it seems pointless to take them away from the capital and expose them to hardship. They are too young."

Lorenzana followed the Carrillos from Santa Barbara to San Diego, and over time began teaching children to read. During a long illness, she was taken in by a priest at the San Diego mission, a Father Sanchez. From teaching she moved on to nursing, and then to teaching Indian women to sew.

"She becomes the glue that keeps mission San Diego together. The fathers trust her so much. They love this young woman," Professor Beebe writes.

She became so useful and so beloved at the San Diego mission, she was eventually called *La Beata*, the Blessed One. Professor Beebe's work with Lorenzana's own diaries, and those of her friends and coworkers in San Diego, reveals that "Apolinaria was so well trusted the fathers would allow her to go to the ships when they docked in San Diego harbor. She would go to the ships with the list of goods that the fathers felt were needed at the mission. But she had the permission to buy anything that she thought they needed."

By acquiring skills, working steadily, and, critically, by not marrying, Lorenzana attained a usefulness and independence rare for women in Spanish colonial societies of the day, who were often defined by their roles as mothers, wives, or religious sisters.

Lorenzana tells her chronicler she dodged the marital bullet: "When I was a girl, there was a young man who often entreated me to marry him. But I did not feel inclined toward matrimony [knowing full well the requirements of that sacred institution], and so I refused his offer. He then told me that since I wouldn't marry him, he was leaving for Mexico."

Try to imagine a tiny, elderly woman telling this story to an American man decades later, and adding, almost with a shrug, "Well, so he left." There is no regret expressed anywhere in the story she tells of her life that she had no children or husband. Over time, she would go on to have a hundred godchildren.

Apolinaria Lorenzana's long life covered California's decades of transition from Spanish colony to part of Mexico's independent nationhood to the arrival of the Stars and Stripes. As California sped into modern America, fewer and fewer people in the state had personally experienced the early, hardscrabble days of the mission system. Scholars began to collect oral histories, and historian and author Thomas Savage notes that he was steered to Lorenzana again and again.

"On my visit to San Diego this year [1878], many of the native Californians of both sexes spoke of [Lorenzana] in the highest terms of praise. She was known by many as *Apolinaria la Cuna* [the foundling] and by most as *La Beata*. She appears to be a good old soul, cheerful and resigned to her sad fate, for in her old age and stone blind she is a charge on the country and on her friends, having by some means or other lost all her property. She was loath to speak on this subject, assuring me she didn't want even to think of it."

Lorenzana remained in service to the mission friars for decades after her arrival, through the end of the Spanish colonial period and into the early years of Mexican independence, which was achieved in 1821. Her industriousness and compassion won her many friends and admirers, but little in the way of material possessions. In middle age, she asked the church for land at a time when the Alta California missions were being secularized—that is, taken from church control—by the young Mexican government.

The mission lands were first promised to Indians—to the neophytes— the people who had converted to Catholicism and become acculturated subjects. The Indians were stiffed, and instead the land transfers created a new aristocracy among the settler descendants, the Spanish families who had come north with the priests and soldiers to set down roots in this impe- rial backwater. Instead of becoming farmers and ranchers cultivating their own land, the Indians became a landless workforce for the new gentry.

The mission priests saw secularization as a simple land grab, in which the government in Mexico City would reward the often anticlerical new aristocracy. Some missions stopped maintaining their buildings in an- ticipation of a seizure; others started to slaughter the large herds accu- mulated over decades and sell the hides and rendered cattle fat to brokers from the United States.

The San Diego mission priests gave Lorenzana three big tracts of graz- ing land in the Jamacha valley in what is now San Diego County. The missionaries gave her the papers confirming the transfer, and in 1833 she turned to the government to affirm her ownership. In 1840, she was granted two square leagues of land (roughly nine thousand acres, or twenty-four square miles). She began to improve the land, invest in struc- tures, and plant crops near the Sweetwater River. Now a woman of means, Lorenzana hired a manager to oversee the ranch while she continued to live at the mission.

When the United States invaded Mexico in 1846 and American troops occupied San Diego, Lorenzana moved north to San Juan Capistrano in what is today Orange County. Her ranch was, for a time, left behind.

When California became part of the spoils of war and Mexico's vast northern territories passed to American sovereignty, Rancho Jamacha was seized by Americans. The Treaty of Guadulupe Hidalgo of 1848 ended the war between the two countries, but left thousands of Mexican citizens behind in a new country. Their future was unclear, despite the firm and unequivocal assurances made in the treaty to Mexican nationals now living in U.S. territory:

> Mexicans now established in territories previously belonging to Mexico, and which remain for the future within the limits of the United States, as defined by the present treaty, shall be free to continue where they now reside, or to remove at any time to the Mexican Republic, retaining the property which they possess in the said territories, or disposing thereof, and removing the proceeds wherever they please, without their being subjected, on this account, to any contribution, tax, or charge whatever.
>
> Those who shall prefer to remain in the said territories may either retain the title and rights of Mexican citizens, or acquire those of citizens of the United States. But they shall be under the obligation to make their election within one year from the date of the exchange of ratifications of this treaty; and those who shall remain in the said territories after the expiration of that year, without having declared their intention to retain the character of Mexicans, shall be considered to have elected to become citizens of the United States.
>
> In the said territories, *property of every kind, now belonging to Mexicans not established there, shall be inviolably respected. The present owners, the heirs of these, and all Mexicans who may hereafter acquire said property by contract, shall enjoy with respect to it guarantees equally ample as if the same belonged to citizens of the United States* [emphasis mine].

Despite the guarantees of the treaty, the Land Act of 1851 set up a U.S. Land Commission to establish which Mexican Californian land claims were legitimate. Unfamiliar with U.S. legal processes, unable to argue their claims in English-language proceedings, many landowning families took mortgages to pay their court costs, and ended up losing their land. A group of American military men who began to work as developers and land speculators after the Mexican War took control of Rancho Jamacha.

Through a series of transactions that were at the very least ill-advised, *La Beata* began to take mortgages on her ranch, and sell parcels of it outright. By the mid-1860s Lorenzana no longer retained any rights to the land, but for years to come she would insist it had been stolen from her, and until 1880 she would occasionally seek legal relief. Under its new Yankee owners, Rancho Jamacha became a profitable and productive agribusiness. To her dying day, Lorenzana would maintain that she was swindled out of her ranches, though the record would indicate otherwise.

Her chronicler asks extensively about the ranches, and recounts the old woman telling him, "It is a long story and I don't even want to discuss it. The other two ranches they somehow took from me. So, that's the way it turns out, that after working so many years, after having acquired an estate, which I certainly didn't dispose of by selling or by any other means, here I find myself in the greatest poverty, living only by the grace of God and through the charity of those who give me a mouthful to eat."

A foundling becomes a heroine in colonial California, a landowner in republican Mexico, and then a poverty-stricken public charge of the United States of America. Lorenzana was a symbol for the losses experienced in the transition, as people poured into the newly annexed territories from points east. With the burden of proof placed on her and the other ranch owners after the Mexican War, she ended the process of awarding title as a landless person, long before her legal rights were finally recognized.

Apolinaria Lorenzana died in 1884. She had been born in 1790, so she lived a remarkably long life for the time, a life that stretched from the early days of the Spanish missions to the closing of the American frontier and California's fourth decade as a state of the union. Her life would also become a cautionary tale, a reminder of the difficulty of making the transition from life in Mexico to life in the United States, even if you never emigrated to a new land, but a new land came to you.

THE NINETEENTH CENTURY saw the creation of the manifest destiny–driven "sea to shining sea" continental territory of the United States. Much of the Latino population of the United States is a legacy of the encounters and clashes between the young nation pushing west from the Atlantic and the Spanish Empire and Republic of Mexico.

The hundred years from 1800 to 1900 were a time of constant challenges to the peoples of North America, demanding their reimagination as individuals, as they were transformed, often by events beyond their control. An Indian in Texas, baptized a Roman Catholic and called by a Spanish name, might have begun the century as a Spanish subject, had children who became Mexicans, grandchildren who would mature to adulthood in the Texas Republic and the state of Texas, and great-grand-children who spent brief years living in the Confederate States of America.

Many of the American citizens who made their way to the Pacific Coast went "native," marrying into Mexican families, converting to Catholicism, and learning to do business with their neighbors in Spanish. Yet as we saw with Apolinaria Lorenzana, just a few decades after their arrival, the same *Californio* families who welcomed their immigrant American neighbors soon found themselves foreigners in their own homeland.

The welcome mat rolled out for the English-speaking immigrants from the East may have been fueled by the ambivalence felt by the northernmost of Mexico's citizens about the preexisting ties to a country and a polity that could seem very far away. "They felt California was the bastard child of Mexico, that they were forgotten," says Rose Marie Beebe. "Their *antepasados* [ancestors] were Spanish. They had children born in California, so they are *Californios*. They are a mix of people. They view themselves as Mexican but not Mexican. They live in an area far away from Mexico City, far away from the central government.

"And then, when the Americans come in, and the whole situation with the Mexican War, we lost part of ourselves. We were under Spanish rule and then under Mexican rule and now under American takeover. I think what comes out in the testimonials is the fear, the foreboding, of what is going to come next."

Even today the descendants of the Spanish, then Mexican families who inhabited what is now the Southwestern United States will say, almost ruefully, "We didn't cross the border. The border crossed us!"

To grow up in the North America of the twenty-first century is to live in an orderly, territorially stable country whose national borders are fixed and immutable. American states entertain no realistic speculation that they might become independent nations. Mexican states and Canadian provinces do not and will not flirt with switching their allegiance from Mexico City or Ottawa to Washington, D.C.

The nineteenth century was one of steady, repeated change that often caught whole populations off guard, wondering where, and to which people, they really belonged. One flashpoint on the continent was to be Texas, where the United States and Mexico bumped into each other west of the Mississippi River. As with California, Texas was important to Mexico not as much for the tiny settlements dotted across the province as it was as a bulwark against other empires: France, and Britain, and then the United States of America.

The two countries were both young. Mexico accomplished its break from Spain in 1821, the United States not even a half-century earlier. However, Mexico was made weak and directionless by factional battles that kept it perennially on the verge of civil war, while the hardening constitutional order in the United States brought about increasing wealth, size, and security.

It was Mexico's historical misfortune that the two states' interests would collide when they did, in an era of coups and military strongmen, while Americans were preparing to pounce and simply take what they wanted.

JUAN NEPOMUCENO SEGUÍN was born in San Antonio de Bexar, the largest Spanish settlement in the province of Tejas. The Seguín family arrived in the San Antonio River valley in the 1740s, making it one of the oldest Spanish families in that part of the empire. The valley was the locus for Spanish settlement in the region.

Juan's father, Erasmo Seguín, was an influential officeholder through Juan's childhood. In 1821, Erasmo informed American settler Moses Austin that Austin's petition to the Mexican central government to establish an American colony in Tejas had been accepted. Moses did not live out the year, but Erasmo began a friendship with Moses's son Stephen F. Austin— the American "Father of Texas"—that would last for the rest of his life. Austin began his life in Tejas wanting to work within Mexican law. The Austins counseled their fellow Americans against any overt Protestant practice that might draw the ire of the government-established Roman Catholic Church, and settlers were advised not to antagonize Mexican authorities.

Erasmo Seguín served in the Mexican congress, was a delegate to the constitutional convention, and was one of the three Texas representatives elected to present the province's grievances to the central government in Mexico City. Erasmo later joined the political opposition to the military strongman General Antonio López de Santa Anna.

Thus one of Erasmo's three children, Juan, came by example to the tumult of revolutionary Texas, and a life lived with feet in two countries. The Seguín family's American journey would symbolize the triumphs and tragedies of the nineteenth century for Tejanos, the Spanish-speaking Mexicans of Texas.

In his early twenties, Juan was already showing an interest in public affairs. At twenty-two, he was elected a San Antonio alderman. In the coming years the battle between the two main factions of Mexican politics was coming to a head: One faction, the Federalists, wanted a loose confederation with a high degree of self-rule in the provinces; the other, the Centralists, wanted a central government with a strong hand in the farthest reaches of the country.

In May 1834, when Santa Anna dissolved the Mexican congress that elected him president, and suspended the constitution, several parts of the country moved into open revolt. Of the states that used the constitutional crisis as a chance to break away, only the Republic of Texas, the Tejas portion of the Mexican state of Coahuila y Tejas, managed to establish its independence. That was not the end of the story. Santa Anna wanted Texas back.

Juan Seguín, like his father, was publicly critical of Santa Anna's decision to suspend the constitution and declare himself president under a new, centralized governor. Like Erasmo, Juan believed the future prosperity of his home relied in part on the presence of colonists from the United States.

Juan Seguín, one of the most prominent Mexicans to take the side of the American settlers in the battle for Texas independence. Mayor of San Antonio under Mexico, he led Spanish-speaking soldiers in the critical Battle of San Jacinto. Seguín became a senator in the new Republic of Texas but later headed south to live in Mexico. CREDIT: SEGUÍN, JUAN NEPOMUCENO; ACCESSION ID: CHA 1989.096; COURTESY STATE PRESERVATION BOARD; ORIGINAL ARTIST: WRIGHT, THOMAS JEFFERSON / 1798–1846; PHOTOGRAPHER: PERRY HUSTON, 7/28/95, POST CONSERVATION

Davy Crockett (1786–1836). When the ruins of an old mission church called the Alamo became a myth factory in March of 1836, one of the biggest legends to come from the doomed fortress was Crockett. The politician and soldier headed west to join the growing American community in Texas after losing his reelection bid to the U.S. House of Representatives. He was one of the last Americans to die in the battle as Mexican forces breached the walls and entered the compound. Already famous before the war in Texas, Crockett's folk hero status was only further burnished by his fight to the death in San Antonio.
CREDIT: LIBRARY OF CONGRESS

Under the old government, Juan Seguín had risen to the rank of colonel in the territorial militia, and had become the *alcalde*, or mayor, of San Antonio. He now openly organized against the Santa Anna government and helped establish a constitutional convention for Texas. In their earliest forms, the wars for Texas independence are really understood as a battle against the Centralists, who wanted to run the vast country from Mexico City and defend the power of the Roman Catholic Church.

Seguín's first goal was probably not the establishment of an independent nation, or to cease to be Mexican. When he organized a Tejano militia in 1835 he rode to the aid of the Mexican governor of Tejas, a Federalist, who shared his opposition to Santa Anna. Seguín took a commission as a captain in the Texas Army from Stephen F. Austin in early 1836. With his company of thirty-seven men, Seguín rode scouting and resupply missions for the revolutionary army. Was he still a Mexican? What did he seek when entering combat against his political foes in the Mexican Army? The politician and soldier invested his future completely in the success of the republic. In his memoirs, Seguín declared, "I embraced the cause of Texas at the report of the first cannon which foretold her liberty."

He holed up in the Alamo with its doomed defenders when the advance guard of Santa Anna's troops were spotted as they headed toward San Antonio to take back the city. Seguín fought with William Travis, Jim Bowie, and the famed American-born fighters in the old mission. Before the climactic assault by Santa Anna's army, the Spanish-speaking officer was dispatched as a courier to deliver news of the siege at the Alamo to Texan forces. By the time Seguín returned to San Antonio, Santa Anna and his forces had already wiped out the Alamo garrison.

Seguín fell back to Gonzales, where the Texan revolution began, and combined with American-born commanders to prepare for another battle with Santa Anna. It came just a few weeks later in the Battle of San Jacinto, where Juan Seguín was the only Texas Mexican to lead troops in battle on the side of the American settlers. His participation was militarily unimportant, but deeply symbolic at the same time. Seguín and his men were singled out for their bravery by the two senior American commanders, Sam Houston and Edward Burleson. San Jacinto was the pivotal battle in the war against Mexico, and has been called the "Yorktown of Texas." Seguín's unit ratified the idea that Tejanos were ready to risk their lives for the new country.

When the smoke cleared, Seguín was an officer in a victorious army. He had been an early adopter of the Texan cause and a community leader in his old country, and he sought to serve his new one. If the Texas revolt had been successfully turned back by the Mexican army, the U.S.-born rebels could have easily headed home. Seguín, one could argue, had taken a bigger risk, making war on his home country and his own government.

First, Seguín monitored the retreat of Mexican troops, escorting them back to the Rio Grande. He then headed home to San Antonio, where he supervised the burials of the ashes of the Alamo defenders, and became the military commander of the city. At first, he hoped the native-born Tejanos would make common cause in building a new country with the newcomers from the United States. He had, as he writes in his memoirs, "a wish to see Texas free and happy." Seguín was shocked by the resentment and racism that confronted a fellow Texas patriot and comrade in arms. Though they were still a majority of the residents of the new country, most Tejanos were peasants, and came to be viewed as outsiders, a problem to be overcome.

It is important to remember what many of the new arrivals saw when

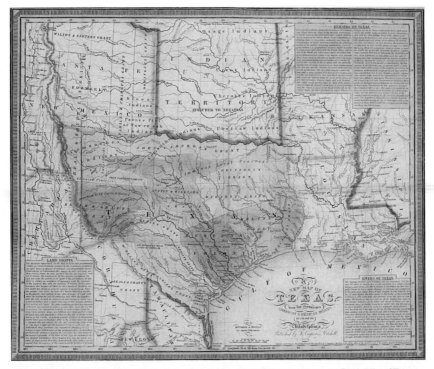

Map of Texas in 1836. After the successful war against Mexico, the new Republic of Texas was much smaller than the later state of Texas. More land seized from Mexico in the later Mexican-American War would be added, along with territories that would become the states of the American Southwest. CREDIT: THE DOLPH BRISCOE CENTER FOR AMERICAN HISTORY, THE UNIVERSITY OF TEXAS AT AUSTIN

they looked at Texas. They saw a place where they could bring the cotton economy of their native American South—not just the plants of the genus *Gossypium*, but the accompanying slavery that made King Cotton so profitable.

When they looked at the Mexicans who already lived on the land, the newcomers did not see new partners in making their fortune, just more nonwhite people. South Carolina senator and defender of slavery John C. Calhoun recoiled from the idea of annexing Mexican territory in 1848: ". . . we have never dreamt of incorporating into our Union any but the Caucasian race—the free white race. To incorporate Mexico, would be the very first instance of the kind of incorporating an Indian race . . . I protest against such a union as that! Ours, sir, is the government of a white race."

Putting Mexicans on an equal level with citizens of the United States, Calhoun further said, would have been an "error" of the kind that had "destroyed social arrangements" in other countries.

However much the settlers across the Southwest might have invoked their Spanish heritage, Calhoun like many Americans had no question that they were not white. As nonwhites, Mexicans, even in their own country, deserved little consideration: ". . . in the whole history of man, as far as my knowledge extends, there is no instance whatever of any civilized colored races being found equal to the establishment of a free popular government, although by far the largest portion of the human family is composed of these races. . . . Are we to associate with ourselves as equals, companions, and fellow-citizens, the Indians and mixed race of Mexico? Sir, I should consider such a thing as fatal to our institutions."

The long-settled Tejano families living on land wrested from Mexico now faced uncertainty that would not be solved by simply switching allegiance from the flag of one nation to another. Ultimately, it would not matter to many of their new neighbors and fellow citizens how they saw themselves. The newcomers saw them as not all that different from Indians, who had been aggressively pushed off their land by English-speaking North Americans for two centuries. It would be another 150 years before we would call what was happening to Tejanos by another name: ethnic cleansing. The land hunger before the American Civil War, and the widespread social chaos after it, put the needs of English-speaking Americans ahead of the rights of the original Tejano families.

Not that the Mexican observers of the nineteenth century thought highly of the riffraff, freebooters, and rootless adventurers drifting into Mexican lands from the United States. Jose Maria Sanchez was a surveyor sent by the Mexican government in 1828 to take a look at the U.S. settlements and report on what he saw. The ambassadors of Anglo-Saxon civilization did not receive a rave review from Sanchez, who said of one settlement, "Its population is nearly 200 persons, of whom only ten are Mexicans, for the balance are all Americans from the north with an occasional European.

"Two wretched little stores supply the inhabitants of the colony: one sells only whiskey, rum, sugar, and coffee; the other rice, flour, lard, and cheap cloth. The Americans from the North, at least the greater part of those I have seen, eat only salted meat, bread made by themselves out of cornmeal, coffee, and homemade cheese. To these the greater part of those who live in the village add strong liquor, for they are, in my opinion, lazy people of vicious character. Some of them cultivate their small farms by planting corn; but this task they usually entrust to their negro slaves, whom they treat with considerable harshness." Slavery was illegal in Mexico, and the American settlers knew it.

In 1837 Juan Seguín was elected to the new senate of the Republic of Texas. He was the only Spanish-speaking senator, but managed to conduct his business using a translator, even chairing the committee on military affairs. At the very time Seguín was becoming a leader of the young republic, landless Americans were pouring into Texas, and town after town moved to expel its native-born Tejano Mexican residents. The senator moved into the land business himself, trying to make his fortune in the Wild West atmosphere of what was, after all, the Wild West.

Another reminder of the fluid nature of nationhood and the malleability of national borders came with Seguín's support of the Federalist general Antonio Canales Rosillo, who was attempting to set up what would have constituted a buffer state between Mexico and Texas, the Republic of the Rio Grande. Canales would eventually fall back in line with the Mexican government, take up a commission as a general, and fight the Texans in the Gulf Coast border regions that now constitute south Texas. Another Mexican general, Mariano Arista, even contacted Seguín and tried to convince him to join with Mexico and help his homeland retake Texas.

Though he rejected the Mexican overtures and actively helped thwart a Mexican reinvasion that resulted briefly in the occupation of San Antonio by a Mexican army, whispers began that Seguín was not loyal to the Texas Republic. A Mexican general hinted that the mayor of San Antonio was still a loyal Mexican citizen. U.S.-born Texans began to accuse Seguín of treason. In his memoirs, he recalled how he was driven out of his hometown, with vigilantes hot on his trail: "In those days I could not go to San Antonio without peril of my life. Matters being in this state, I saw that it was necessary to take some step which would place me in security, and save my family from constant wretchedness.

"I had to leave Texas, abandon all, for which I had fought and spent my fortune, to become a wanderer. The ingratitude of those, who had assumed to themselves the right of convicting me; their credulity in declaring me a traitor, on mere rumors, when I had to plead, in my favor the loyal patriotism with which I had always served Texas, wounded me deeply."

Seguín resigned as mayor of San Antonio and fled to Mexico with his family. "I had determined to free my family and friends from their continual misery on my account; and go and live peaceably in Mexico. That for these reasons I resigned my office, with all my privileges and honors as a Texan."

• • •

JUAN SEGUÍN'S PROBLEMS were only beginning. Heading south meant confronting the army and the country he had so recently worked to defeat: "I sought for shelter amongst those against whom I fought; I separated from my country, parents, family, relatives and friends, and what was more, from the institutions, on behalf of which I had drawn my sword."

When the Mexicans offered him a choice between imprisonment for treason or military service, Seguín said he had no choice but to accept a commission in the Mexican Army. Before long he was headed back to Texas in the ranks of a force under General Adrian Woll, to fight the United States in the Mexican-American War.

After the war Seguín asked for permission to return to Texas. "After the expeditions of General Woll, I did not return to Texas till the Treaty of Guadalupe Hidalgo. During my absence nothing appeared that could stamp me as a traitor. My enemies had accomplished their object; they had killed me politically in Texas, and the less they spoke of me, the less risk they incurred of being exposed in the infamous means they had used to accomplish my ruin."

Before long harassment in the place he had fought to free forced him south across the Rio Grande again, and back to Mexico. "A victim of the wickedness of a few men, whose imposture was favored by their origin, and recent domination over the country; a foreigner in my native land; could I be expected stoically to endure their outrages and insults?"

Juan Seguín lived his last days in Nuevo Laredo, on the banks of the Rio Grande, just across from Texas and the United States. He died in 1890, at eighty-three. In 1976, his remains were finally brought home to Texas, for burial in the town that bears his name.

Across what became the Southwestern United States, moving the border, and finalizing the new relationship between the United States, Mexico, and America's new Mexican citizens, did not end the conflict over land, resources, and status. In the *Californio* newspaper *El Clamor Público* (the *Public Outcry*), an article published July 26, 1856, complained about continued violence against California's Mexicans: "It is becoming a very common custom to murder and abuse the Mexicans with impunity." The paper later charged that the English-speaking Americans who had been pouring into California in the years after gold was discovered subjected

Mexicans "to a treatment that has no model in the history of any nation conquered by savages or by civilized people."

The part-Cherokee popular novelist John Rollin Ridge collected the stories circulating about a Mexican who turned rebel after Americans beat him and raped his wife. His 1854 book *The Life and Adventures of Joaquin Murieta, the Celebrated California Bandit* mixed fact and fiction to create a dashing Mexican Robin Hood, whose guerrilla battles against Americans were justified by his people's treatment: "The country was then full of lawless and desperate men, calling themselves Americans, who looked with hatred upon all Mexicans, and considered them as a conquered race, without rights or privileges, and only fitted for serfdom or slavery. The prejudice of color, the antipathy of races, which are always stronger or bitterer with the ignorant, they could not overcome, or would not, because it afforded them an excuse for their unmanly oppression." As Mexicans do to this day, songs celebrating the exploits of Joaquin Murieta were composed and widely circulated. One of the Murieta *corridos* included these lyrics:

Yo no soy americano	I am not an American
pero comprendo el inglés.	but I understand English.
Yo lo aprendí con mi hermano	I learned it with my brother
al derecho y al revés.	Inside and out.
A cualquier americano	I can make any American
hago temblar a mis pies.	tremble at my feet.
Por cantinas me metí	From bar to bar, I've traveled
castigando americanos.	punishing Americans.
"Tú serás el capitán	"You could be the captain
que mataste a mi hermano.	who killed my brother.
Lo agarraste indefenso,	You caught him unarmed,
orgulloso americano."	you arrogant American."

In Texas, another brown Robin Hood arose in the lawless and disputed land between the Nueces River and the Rio Grande in the southern part of the state. Juan Nepomuceno Cortina Goseacochea, often called Cheno Cortina or simply Juan Cortina, led a Tejano militia in the 1850s and 1860s against the Anglo authorities in south Texas and the Gulf Coast. The raids and battles came to be known as the Cortina Wars or the Cortina Troubles, and pitted his soldiers (depending on the year and the circumstances) against the U.S. Army, the Texas Rangers, the French invaders of Mexico, Anglo militias, the Confederate Army, and Mexican national forces.

Cortina's keen interest in defending the interests of Juan Cortina was backed by what appears to be a sincere rage over the treatment of the people of northern Mexico and South Texas. The manifestos and pamphlets he issued during his military campaign ring with the romance and ardor of nineteenth-century rhetoric and a strong intelligence: "There is no need of fear. Orderly people and honest citizens are inviolable to us in their persons and interests. Our object, as you have seen, has been to chastise the villainy of our enemies, which heretofore has gone unpunished.

"These have connived with each other, and form, so to speak, a perfidious inquisitorial lodge to persecute and rob us, without any cause, and for no other crime on our part than that of being of Mexican origin. . . ."

Cortina was dubbed the "Red Robber of the Rio Grande." While opposed and pursued by the authorities of two nations, or enlisted to join them to fight the other country, Cortina could see himself as a fighter sacrificing his life for his people. "Innocent persons shall not suffer—no. But, if necessary, we will lead a wandering life, awaiting our opportunity to purge society of men so base that they will degrade it with their opprobrium. Our families have returned as strangers to their old country to beg

Mariano Vallejo. California military leader, politician, and rancher. His long life spanned three eras of California. He was born a subject of the Spanish Empire, came to prominence a citizen of Mexico, and ended his life an American. Like many of the landed *Californio* families, Vallejo extended a friendly hand to the first wave of American settlers heading west to Mexico's northernmost territories from the United States. He was imprisoned by American migrants, his properties looted. Vallejo would later be treated as a foreigner in his own homeland. CREDIT: THE BANCROFT LIBRARY, UNIVERSITY OF CALIFORNIA, BERKELEY

for asylum." Cortina goes on to slash at the greed and envy of his Anglo enemies, while expressing the quiet faith that nature would always provide. "Further, our personal enemies shall not possess our lands until they have fattened it with their own gore."

With his striking words, Cortina reminds his Tejano constituents what they already knew too well: That the political firestorms that swept through Mexico, Texas, and the United States left them vulnerable to Anglo-Americans who won through conquest what they could not buy. It was a time when "flocks of vampires, in the guise of men came and scattered themselves in the settlements, without any capital except the corrupt heart and the most perverse intentions.

"Many of you have been robbed of your property, incarcerated, chased, murdered, and hunted like wild beasts, because your labor was fruitful, and because your industry excited the vile avarice which led them." It cannot be known from the remove of a century and a half whether Cortina was blind to, or purposely ignored, the expropriation of native land, the original sin that gave Mexicans the land in the first place.

Perversely, two sets of stereotypes came to operate simultaneously in the minds of the Americans heading to lands taken in the Mexican War. On the one hand, says Stephen Pitti, large landholders, even ones like Mariano Vallejo, who extended a warm welcome to U.S. immigrants, were portrayed "as baronial state holders, kind of feudal lords from the Middle Ages who have landed in this nineteenth century but who are products of another time and therefore should be moved on to history and not made part of the modern world." At the same time, writes Pitti, "Latinos are seen as knife-wielding, as greasers, as dangerous, dirty, threatening figures in Gold Rush society who are also not ideal citizens, but for different reasons.

"How *Californios* would counter the stereotypes about them, how everyday Latinos would counter the stereotypes about them would be critically important for the way in which others would understand them in the nineteenth century."

Following the Treaty of Guadalupe Hidalgo, hundreds of thousands of Mexican families became a permanent part of America's future. That the United States was able to conquer Mexico so easily in the 1840s served to confirm Mexican inferiority in the eyes of many Americans. Pitti maintains that this was one wound that time would not heal. "Anglos in places like Texas and New Mexico and California continued to affirm the basic terms of the U.S.-Mexico war: That an inferior people had been conquered by a superior people. That democracy had won out over feudalism and backwardness. That progress was in the hands of the Americans and Latinos in places like California were destined to extinction. Latinos in California were simply destined to go away in the face of a superior American culture."

BACK IN NEW Mexico, even after their terrible suffering at the hands of the Spanish, the Acomas did not destroy the mission church of San Esteban del Rey, as ordered by Popay. Today the church stands as a reminder of the New World culture created by the encounter between Spain and the native people of the pueblos. The church includes one of the most extensive and intact seventeenth-century buildings in New Mexico. Its original hand-hewn staircase, altar screen, and communion rails are now almost five hundred years old.

Don Juan de Oñate was remembered by New Mexico and in 1991, a large equestrian statue was erected just outside Española. In 1998, on the four hundredth anniversary of Oñate's heading north from Mexico City to establish the new colony, a group of Acomas quietly headed to the site and "amputated" the right foot from the bronze—boot, stirrup, and spur. The Acomas sent newsrooms a statement: "We took the liberty of removing Oñate's right foot on behalf of our brothers and sisters of Acoma Pueblo. We see no glory in celebrating Oñate's fourth centennial, and we do not want our faces rubbed in it."

The statue was repaired.

Don Juan's foot was never returned.

SHARED
DESTINIES . . .
MADE MANIFEST

2

Americans and Mexican Americans. In parts of cities like Los Angeles and San Antonio, Mexican culture was alive and thriving. At the same time, this culture could be turned into a consumable experience for other Americans, who traveled to places created for the tourist trade to eat Mexican food, hear music and buy crafts. CREDIT: LOS ANGELES PUBLIC LIBRARY

THE STATUE of Liberty has a name.

Not Augusta, though the artist, Frédéric Auguste Bartholdi, did base the giant figure's face on that of his own mother. The sculpture erected on an enormous pedestal in the New York Harbor is called *Liberty Enlightening the World.* The tablet cradled in Liberty's left arm carries the inscription, *July 4, 1776*, hammering home an important idea widely understood in the nineteenth-century world: that the Declaration of Independence unleashed something meant to be seen in the farthest corners of the world. Carrying the date of the U.S. break from Britain in her gracefully curved fingers, rays of light jetting from her crown, a torch held high, Liberty was meant to light up a world still largely unfree.

While some hoped American ideas and ideals would reach the ends of the earth, others had more concrete ambitions. In 1912, President William Howard Taft said, "The day is not far distant when the Stars and Stripes at three equidistant points will mark our territory; one at the North Pole, another at the Panama Canal, and the third at the South Pole. The whole hemisphere will be ours in fact as, by virtue of our superiority of race, it already is ours morally."

For more than a century after a group of farmers, lawyers, merchants, and investors signed their names to the Declaration in Philadelphia, its echoes reverberated around the world. Simón Bolívar and José de San Martín in South America, Giuseppe Garibaldi in Italy, and Charles Parnell in Ireland all took inspiration from George Washington, Thomas Jefferson, and the founders. While the deeds of America's leaders were often, like Taft's forecast, propelled by assumptions of white supremacy, the ideals of 1776 were easily exported, especially when they did not face close scrutiny from faraway freedom fighters who wanted to know how well the ideal lined up with the real.

Leaders of independence movements saw that a relatively small population could resist a larger, stronger imperial power, and have a chance of success. The comparative ease with which people could move from Europe to the United States during the nineteenth-century era of explosive economic growth led to the creation of organizations of foreign-born communities across America that could both raise money and assist in the running of revolutions "back home." Ramón Emeterio Betances of Puerto Rico, struggling to create a united front in Spain's Caribbean colonies, organized in exile in New York in the 1860s. The General Council of the First International, one of early Communism's most influential organizations, moved to New York from London in 1872. Garibaldi, in a lull between revolutions in South America and Europe, found a safe harbor in New York.

Even as the United States struggled throughout the nineteenth century to "form a more perfect union," American ideals about liberty did "enlighten the world." The century was one of constant cross-pollination between North America and the rest of the hemisphere.

One of the idealists inspired by the American Revolution was a twenty-seven-year-old Cuban named José Julian Martí Pérez.

You might have no idea who José Martí is just from hearing his name. Maybe his iconic face, that of a young, dreamy aesthete with a flamboyant mustache, would spark some recognition. Perhaps you have passed the famous image of Martí, dressed in a dark suit and holding the reins of a rearing horse, reproduced as a heroic statue at the foot of New York's Central Park. It is more likely you have heard some of Martí's poetry, in the stanzas of "Guantanamera," or "Woman from Guantánamo," arguably the best-known Cuban song in the world.

José Julian Martí Pérez: Often called "The George Washington of Cuba," José Martí struggled for Cuban independence from his teens. During long years of exile he wrote prodigiously: Poetry, essays, news reports, and political writing poured from his pen. CREDIT: LIBRARY OF CONGRESS

. . .

IN JANUARY 1880, Martí was one of the more than thirty million people who made their way to the United States from around the world. He had been arrested for sedition, jailed and abused back in Cuba for his writing and for having contact with other men who wanted to send the Spanish packing and start a republic. He was deported, and wandered from Spain to Central America, to Mexico, and then to New York.

The poet, philosopher, and essayist liked what he saw in the North. For one thing, the young man was relieved to no longer be on the run: "Elsewhere they make men flee; but here they welcome the fleeing man with a smile. From this goodness has arisen the strength of a nation."

His early years in the United States were marked by repeated admiration for the young and powerful nation, as he notes in an arts and culture magazine called *The Hour*: "I am, at last, in a country where everyone looks like his own master. One can breathe freely, freedom being here the foundation, the shield, the essence of life. One can be proud of his species here."

Historian C. Neale Ronning does what we sometimes have to rely on historians to do: point out the obvious. José Martí was hardly a revolutionary leader from central casting. "How can we explain the emergence of Martí as the authoritative leader of the Cuban Revolution? He was young, chronically ill, nervous, small of stature, intellectual, and hopelessly romantic. These are not the qualities usually associated with the charismatic leader of a war for independence. They are hardly the qualities we might expect to have appealed to the veteran leaders of the earlier wars for independence." In reply to his own query, Ronning cites Martí's charisma, as observed by his contemporaries, and his fierce intellectual energy.

During the American years, Martí wrote at a furious pace about every aspect of American life. He felt the power, the energy, and the pace of nineteenth-century New York. In his essay "North American Scenes" he writes of the workers' playground of Coney Island in Brooklyn: "Nothing in the annals of humanity can compare to the marvelous prosperity of the United States of the North. Does the country lack deep roots? Are ties of sacrifice and shared suffering more lasting within countries than those of common interest? Does this colossal nation contain ferocious and terrible elements? Does the absence of the feminine spirit, source of artistic sensibility and complement to national identity, harden and corrupt the heart of this astonishing people? Only time will tell.

"For now it is certain that never has a happier, more joyous, better equipped, more densely packed, more jovial, or more frenetic multitude lived in such useful labor in any land on earth, or generated and enjoyed greater wealth, or covered rivers and seas with more gaily bedecked steamers, or spread out with more bustling order and naïve merriment across gentle coastlines, gigantic piers, and fantastical glittering promenades."

Martí's reflections on nineteenth-century America echoed those of some of the first Europeans to see the North American continent, and Old World intellectuals who never actually made the journey, who gobbled up everything they could read about the prodigiously gifted continent across the sea.

During the New York years, Martí hitched his intellect to his energy and his powerful curiosity and got to work. He wrote poetry. He wrote essays. He translated novels into Spanish and edited a Cuban independence newspaper *Patria—Fatherland*—and helped found the Cuban Revolutionary Party. He traveled widely, in the United States and throughout the Caribbean, rallying Cuban émigré communities around the anti-imperial cause.

The young Cuban covered the trial of President James A. Garfield's assassin, Charles Guiteau, for a Mexico City newspaper, *La Opinión Liberal.* After a long passage describing Garfield's killer in monstrous terms, as subhuman, Martí pivots and makes this paradoxical plea: that Guiteau's life be spared. Martí asks for Guiteau's life not for the killer's sake, but for society's. "Reason demands that his life be spared, because of the futility of his horrendous act and because killing the monster is an inadequate way of ending nature's power to grow monsters—for, in the end, moved by prolonged solitude and fear watered by tears, the gnawed-away man may revive deep within his body, and in these days of wrath justice might appear to be vengeance. One should not kill a wild beast at a time when one feels oneself to be a wild beast."

WHEN JOSÉ MARTÍ arrived in the United States, Cuban nationalists were making very little headway in their struggle to be free of Spain, and the island was still in the midst of a protracted transition from slavery to emancipation. The Cortes, Spain's parliament, had just approved an emancipation law, but it set out an eight-year path to freedom for most of the island's enslaved workers that included years of *patronato*, patronage, or instruction that would prepare black Cubans for citizenship.

From his youth, Martí was a fierce opponent of racism and slavery. When the Ten Years' War, an unsuccessful fight for independence, began in 1868, slaves were enlisted in the struggle. Today the scene of the ringing of a plantation bell, the farm called La Demajagua, is a national monument in Cuba, intended to preserve the memory of the summoning of the slaves and free men from the sugar fields by grower Carlos Manuel de Céspedes. The plantation owner asked all his field hands and foremen, slave and free, to join him in a war to liberate Cuba. The Mambises, the rebel soldiers, did not prevail. In 1878 a peace treaty with Spain ended the fighting, with slavery still widespread on the island and colonial rule intact.

Though still just a teenager, Martí would attract renown and the attention of the Spanish authorities with his writing. He was arrested and branded a traitor. In much the same way as the Ten Years' War set the stage for eventual Cuban independence, Martí's deportation created the conditions for him to become an international figure, not just a Cuban one. The long-established Cuban exile groups got a leader who could rally them with his passion, his vision, and his pen.

Reading Martí today, from more than a century's remove, it is fascinating to see the author's strong attraction, admiration, and at the same time the revulsion for the United States that would feature in the observations of so many Latin American intellectuals in the coming decades. The economic dynamism and personal freedom they saw in America was what they wanted for their own societies, while at the same time some of the downsides of that freedom—the casual racism and stark inequality— forced them to reconsider their own feelings.

In many of his writings, Martí reflects on the differences between North Americans of the English-speaking world and the people he called "Hispanoamericans." In his powerful essay about Coney Island, after riffing on the tremendous wealth and productivity demonstrated even on what was a day trip for everyday New Yorkers, he includes this aside: ". . . the traveler goes in and out of the dining rooms, vast as the pampas, and climbs to the tops of the colossal buildings, high as the mountains; seated in a comfortable chair by the sea, the passerby fills his lungs with a powerful and salubrious air, and yet it is well known that a sad melancholy steals over the men of our Hispanoamerican peoples who live here. They seek each other in vain, and however much the first impressions may have gratified their senses, enamored their eyes, and dazzled and befuddled their minds, the anguish of solitude possesses them in the end. Nostalgia for a superior spiritual world invades and afflicts them; they feel like lambs with no mother or shepherd, lost from the flock, and though their eyes may be dry, the frightened spirit breaks into a torrent of the bitterest tears because this great land is devoid of spirit."

Martí saw the North American view of the Spanish-speaking countries as condescending, ignorant, and self-congratulatory. Toward the end of his New York years, as U.S. disdain for Spanish presence in the hemisphere and Cuban speculation about an American protectorate grew, he wrote the editor of the *New Evening Post*: "There are some Cubans who, from honorable motives, from an ardent admiration for progress and liberty, from a prescience of their own powers under better political conditions, from an unhappy ignorance of the history and tendency of annexation, would like to see the island annexed to the United States.

"They admire this nation, the greatest ever built by liberty, but they dislike the evil conditions that, like worms in the heart, have begun in this mighty republic their work of destruction. They cannot honestly believe that excessive individualism and reverence for wealth are preparing the United States to be the typical nation of liberty. . . . No self-respecting Cuban would like to see his country annexed to a nation where the leaders of opinion share towards him the prejudices excusable only to vulgar jingoism or rampant ignorance."

The worries about the United States and speculation about the larger country's territorial ambitions in Cuba were grounded in reality. American leaders talked about Cuba frequently during the nineteenth century. That defender of American liberty, Thomas Jefferson, sounded like a stone-cold imperialist when he wrote in 1809, "I candidly confess that I have ever looked upon Cuba as the most interesting addition that can be made to our system of States, the possession of which (with Florida Point), would give us control over the Gulf of Mexico and the countries and isthmus bordering upon it, and would fill up the measure of our political well-being."

In 1823, President James Monroe declared that any efforts by European powers to expand their Western Hemisphere colonies would be regarded as an act of aggression and trigger resistance from the United States, a declaration called the Monroe Doctrine. That same year Jefferson wrote to President Monroe that adding Cuba to American territory "is exactly what is wanting to round out our power as a nation to the point of its utmost interest." In other letters to Monroe that year, the third president spoke of taking Cuba as not only being desirable for U.S. interests, but also essential to keeping Britain and France from seizing it first.

John Quincy Adams, who served as Monroe's secretary of state, speculated that "annexation of Cuba to our Federal Republic will be indispensable to the continuance and integrity of the Union itself." Adams sounds like an expansionist and an anticolonialist in the very same passage when he writes, "Cuba, forcibly disjointed from its own unnatural connection with Spain and incapable of self-support, can gravitate only toward the North American Union, which by the same law of nature cannot cast her off from its bosom."

In midcentury, American ambassadors meeting on the Belgian coast (including the future president James Buchanan, then serving as the U.S. ambassador to Britain) wrote a notorious document called the Ostend Manifesto, recommending, among other things:

> 1. The United States ought, if practicable, to purchase Cuba with as little delay as possible.
>
> 2. The probability is great that the Government and Cortes of Spain will prove willing to sell it, because this would essentially promote the highest and best interests of the Spanish people.
>
> Then, first. It must be clear to every reflecting mind that from the peculiarity of its geographical position, and considerations attendant on it, Cuba is as necessary to the North American Republic as any of its present members. . . .

It must be clear to every reflecting mind. It is hard to get more overtly grasping than that. Getting Cuba one way or another had become by the 1850s a particular ambition of American Southern planters and politicians, who craved the island as an additional slave state. Northern politicians and abolitionists passionately opposed the move, but Southerners dreamed of maintaining the balance of power in the U.S. Senate by adding two proslavery senators and as many as nine members of the House of Representatives. Whether by what President Polk called "amicable purchase" or by what the minister to Spain William Marcy described as "detachment" from Spain, growing numbers of Americans were crafting rationales for taking Cuba.

At least twice in the mid–nineteenth century, American presidents tried to purchase the island outright: In 1848 James K. Polk, who was already absorbing much of Spain's former North American empire by defeating Mexico in war, offered $100 million, and Franklin Pierce raised the offer to $130 million. Both times the offers were rebuffed by Spain.

In the political pressure cooker of 1850s America, race played a major role in the feverish speculation over Cuba. You may remember in chapter one the misgivings expressed by influential South Carolina senator John C. Calhoun, who worried about U.S. annexation of Mexican territories containing so many new residents who might upset the racial mathematics of American society.

The Ostend Manifesto of 1854 was written by three diplomats, the U.S. ministers to France, Spain and Great Britain, to the U.S. Secretary of State, William L. Marcy. The manifesto maintained that the United States was fully justified in seizing Cuba if Spain would not sell it, in order to prevent the island from following Haiti into slave revolution against white masters. "We should, however, be recreant to our duty, be unworthy of our gallant forefathers, and commit base treason against our posterity, should we permit Cuba to be Africanized and become a second St. Domingo [Haiti], with all its attendant horrors to the white race, and suffer the flames to extend to our own neighboring shores, seriously to endanger or actually to consume the fair fabric of our Union." A slave uprising in Cuba was an approaching "catastrophe," according to the manifesto, that justified "wresting" Cuba away from Spain.

The Cuban-born Martí was himself the son of European immigrants to the island, and thus had no long-standing familial history there. Yet he embraced the mixed-race history and contemporary reality of his homeland and the vast Latin lands of the hemisphere. He loathed racism at home in Cuba and in his U.S. sanctuary. Martí chronicled the mistreatment of native peoples and the descendants of black slaves across the hemisphere and went out of his way to credit non-European peoples for their significant and undeniable cultural legacy that made them the Caribbeans, Central, and South Americans they were.

In his landmark essay *"Nuestra America,"* "Our America," Martí is determined not to let his brothers and sisters of European ancestry from across the hemisphere run away from their own families' pasts. "These sons of carpenters who are ashamed that their father was a carpenter! These men born in America who are ashamed of the mother that raised them because she wears an Indian apron, these delinquents who disown their sick mother and leave her alone in her sickbed!"

On the political and military sides, the Cuban fight against Spain was multiracial. Martí and rebel military leader General Calixto García were white. Juan Gualberto Gómez, journalist, revolutionary leader, and politician, was born to slaves on a sugar plantation, and bought his freedom. Another key rebel leader, General Antonio Maceo, called the Bronze Titan, *El Titán de Bronce*, was mixed-race, the child of a Venezuelan trader and an Afro-Cuban.

To make sure Cubans got the point, Martí did not shy away from discussing race on either side of the Florida Straits. Writing in *Patria* in 1893, in an essay called "My Race," Martí insisted the fate of the revolution would not rise or fall by race: "Cubans are more than whites, mulattos or Negroes. On the field of battle, dying for Cuba, the souls of whites and Negroes have risen together into the air.

"In the daily life of defense, loyalty, brotherhood and shrewdness, Negroes have always been there, alongside whites. Negroes, like whites, are divided by their character—timid or brave, self-sacrificing or selfish—into the diverse parties in which men group themselves."

In "Our America," Martí alternates between hardheaded political observation and romantic evocation of the America dreamed of in European salons during the Age of Discovery, when in the fifteenth and sixteenth centuries the big empires sent small expeditionary fleets across the Atlantic. "Our feet upon a rosary, our heads white, and our bodies a motley of Indian and *criollo* [Creole, native-born children of white colonists] we boldly entered the community of nations. Bearing the standard of the Virgin, we went out to conquer our liberty. A priest, a few lieutenants, and a woman built a republic in Mexico upon the shoulders of the Indians. A Spanish cleric, under cover of his priestly cape, taught French liberty to a handful of magnificent students who chose a Spanish general to lead Central America against Spain. Still accustomed to monarchy, and with the sun on their chests, the Venezuelans in the north and the Argentines in the south set out to construct nations."

Martí was a cofounder and organizer of the Cuban Revolutionary Party. The party's manifesto, written by Martí and published in his newspaper *Patria*, identifies Puerto Ricans as brothers in the struggle, and again reaches across lines of class and color to declare that the party, and its aims, do not belong just to European-descended elites. He reached back to the Ten Years' War, its triumphs and tragedies, and exhorted his countrymen inside and outside Cuba to do better this time.

From the safety of New York, Martí expressed his compassion for, and his solidarity with, his people back home. "By 'adversary' the free Cubans do not mean the Cuban who lives in agony under a regime he cannot shake, or the established foreigner who loves and desires freedom, or the timid Creole who will vindicate himself for today's laxity with tomorrow's patriotism." Perhaps "expressed his compassion for *some* of his people back home" might be more accurate.

Florida, home to well-established Cuban communities from the nineteenth century to today, was an important center for organizing for Martí and the Revolutionary Party. Martí was a frequent visitor to Tampa's Ybor City, speaking to cigar workers at their benches and writing to their local papers from the road. As the start of a new insurrection began to draw closer in 1894, Martí went to Cayo Hueso, or Key West, the American town closest to Cuba and home to an old émigré community. The purpose of the Revolutionary Party, he told a mixed Cuban and American audience, "is not to bring to the country a victorious group who considers the island its booty or domain, but to prepare abroad, by every means possible, the war that is necessary for the good of all Cubans."

In a sadly prescient passage of the speech, he told his audience of his belief that one could "play with one's own death, but not with the death of others." His and the party's aspiration, he said, was to minimize blood and sacrifice, and never unleash Cuba "into a premature revolution for which the nation is not prepared."

He closed with a call to action: "May I continue to be confident in my people, whose patriotism reanimates me and whose voice encourages me to continue in the journey?" A reporter included an account of thunderous applause from the crowd, which "trembled" as Martí described Cuba's victimhood at the hands of Spain.

During a deep economic recession in the 1890s, Martí told the Cubans of Key West, "It is not the loss of confidence for independence that the Cubans of Key West lament. Today they need it more than ever, today they feel in themselves the agony and the solitude of their people. Today with more spontaneity and tenderness than ever, with more generosity and unity, they will give their warm loyal souls to those that swear to live and die for them, or to die of humiliation and pain if there would be no other way to die!"

A share of the wages of thousands of Cubans in the United States was being used to buy guns in preparation for a reopening of war with Spain. In January 1895, U.S. authorities intercepted ships loaded with weapons headed from Florida to Cuba, thwarting the planned assault. Martí responded quickly, drafting an order for the people of Cuba to rise up against Spain, signed in January 1895. The revolution began in February of 1895; on April 1, Martí and a roster of political and military leaders of the revolt headed for the island.

Six weeks later, on May 19, Martí was dead, killed by Spanish troops in his first engagement, the Battle of Dos Ríos. He was just forty-two years old. In a letter, unfinished at the time of his death, to his friend Manuel Mercado, Martí revealed how far he had come in his thinking about the United States from that dazzled young exile looking for a place of refuge:

> *My dearest brother,*
> *I am daily in danger of giving my life for my country and duty—the duty of preventing the United States from spreading through the Antilles as Cuba gains its independence, and from overpowering with that additional strength our lands of America. All I do and have done to this date is for that purpose.*

He came tantalizingly close to seeing the day Spain would leave his homeland. It is tempting to imagine the ambivalence Martí would have felt when that day did not come by Cuban force of arms, but by American invasion.

THE ANTI-SPANISH DRUMBEAT in the American press and American popular culture grew in volume through the 1890s. Martí might have found a tendency toward derision and condescension in Americans' attitudes toward Hispanoamericans, but as the decade moved toward a close, concern for the Cuban people led him to depict them as noble victims. They were portrayed as brave patriots, oppressed and exploited.

In Washington, New York, and elsewhere, U.S. anticolonialists, neoimperialists, and human rights advocates made common cause. Anticolonialists had wanted Europeans out of the hemisphere since the Monroe Doctrine was defined in 1823. Neoimperialists looked at the other great powers of the world and wondered why a growing power like the United States should not have its own foreign territories and spheres of influence to teach and guide colonized people in a civilizing mission. The mistreatment of Cuban independence forces by the Spanish authorities genuinely worried people who read the lurid tales of injustice and cruelty by decadent colonial officials.

Normally, these types of Americans did not agree on much. But this much was clear to them all: Spain had to go. This convergence of interests stood on a foundation of steady speculation about Cuba in previous years, speculation that we saw earlier raised a heated response from Martí.

During the tumult of the Civil War years and the conflicts of Reconstruction that followed, Cuba was a less present object of American desire. The Ten Years' War between Spain and Cuba, the weak or unfulfilled reforms promised in the treaty that ended the conflict, and the presence of a foreign army so close to America's shores all inflamed different segments of American public opinion. Take your pick: The troubles in Cuba ratified the justification of the Monroe Doctrine and the need to keep Europe out of the Americas, or the corruption and incompetence of Spanish rule meant the United States must take steps to expel Spain.

As Cuba's colonial master for four hundred years, Spain intended to hang on to its island. More than 150,000 Spanish soldiers sailed to Cuba in 1895, and in the coming two years tens of thousands were to die in action with the Cuban rebels and of disease. Valeriano Weyler, the newly appointed captain-general of Cuba, kept his well-equipped soldiers fighting against the ragtag Cuban army. Unable to fight back using conventional tactics, the Cubans resorted to guerrilla war, and Weyler clamped down even harder on the rebellious country.

However, things had changed in Spain too since the Ten Years' War. Putting down the Cuban revolt put a severe strain on the Spanish treasury. There were protests, even draft riots, the challenge to the Spanish government rising as casualties climbed in the Caribbean. This time the Cuban irregulars were better led, and better equipped as well.

Significant American investment in the production of Cuban agricultural exports suffered as Spaniards moved farmers from the countryside into the urban areas. Weyler believed support for the guerrilla army would dry up without civilians in the countryside. The privations of life for civilians in what were called "reconcentration camps."

There were also specifically American reasons for wanting the Spaniards out of Cuba. The United States was the single largest buyer of Cuban exports in the late Spanish period, and American interests suffered in the 1890s, with a 75 percent drop in value, from $60 million to $15 million.

The United States was actively searching for a place to build a canal in Central America to cut the long shipping times between Atlantic and Pacific ocean ports. A large European military presence in the Eastern Caribbean had the potential of threatening the sea-lanes leading to the site of a future canal. More and more influential Americans began to conclude that a friendlier government in Havana could be useful.

American officials urged Spain to grant Cuba independence and leave in a negotiated settlement, or at the very least arrange for autonomy—self-rule for the Cuban people. Goaded by dueling newspaper barons William Randolph Hearst and Joseph Pulitzer, U.S. public opinion built steadily on the Cuban side. All this happened at the same time a new American president, William McKinley, arrived at the White House in March of 1897. Spain issued a declaration of autonomy in 1897 that granted limited self-rule to Puerto Rico, Cuba, and the Philippines. The Carta Autonómica de 1897 was not far-reaching enough to satisfy the aspirations of any of the island nations at this advanced stage of the breach with Madrid. Nor, as much as it mattered, did it satisfy the publishers of the *New York World* and the *New York Journal*.

For all the lionizing of brave Cuban freedom fighters and scorn for decadent Spanish oppressors during the run-up to war, most Americans still knew little of Cuba, or Cubans. The idealistic portrayal of brave rebel soldiers and the oppressed people of the island did not last long once American occupation began.

U.S. Undersecretary of War J. C. Breckenridge did not think highly of the people his armies were fighting to free. He wrote in a memorandum, "This [the Cuban] population is made up of whites, blacks, Asians and people who are a mixture of these races. The inhabitants are generally indolent and apathetic. . . . Since they only possess a vague notion of what is right and wrong, the people tend to seek pleasure not through work, but through violence. . . . It is obvious that the immediate annexation of these disturbing elements into our own federation in such large numbers would be madness, so before we do that we must clean up the country. . . . We must destroy everything within our cannons' range of fire. We must impose a harsh blockade so that hunger and its constant companion, disease, undermine the peaceful population and decimate the army. The allied army must be constantly engaged in reconnaissance and vanguard actions so that the Cuban army is irreparably caught between two fronts."

By the beginning of 1898, Spain was assuring the United States it would make some concession to the rebels, but would not quit Cuba. The U.S. consul in Havana, Fitzhugh Lee, told the White House about riots in Havana, and McKinley sent the USS *Maine* to Cuba, it was claimed at the time, to protect American lives and property during the Cuban unrest. From the start, the *Maine*'s reception was friendly enough. Cuban civilians greeted the ship, and American sailors mingled ashore with Spanish sailors from the *Viscaya*, sent to Havana at the same time as the *Maine*.

The crew of the American battleship the USS *Maine*. Of the 355 men on board when the ship exploded in Havana Harbor in February, 1898, 261 were either killed by the blast or drowned.
CREDIT: DETROIT PHOTOGRAPHIC CO.

The wreckage of the battleship *Maine* in Havana Harbor for viewing in a stereoscope, which made photographs appear three-dimensional.
CREDIT: NATIONAL ARCHIVES

After the *Maine* was in Havana Harbor for just three weeks, on February 15, an explosion destroyed it and killed almost everyone on board. Most of the battleship's crew was asleep belowdecks when the explosion occurred. The same newspapers urging the United States to free Cuba from Spanish rule now kicked their coverage into a higher, more hysterical gear. The *New York Journal* sent famed Western artist Frederic

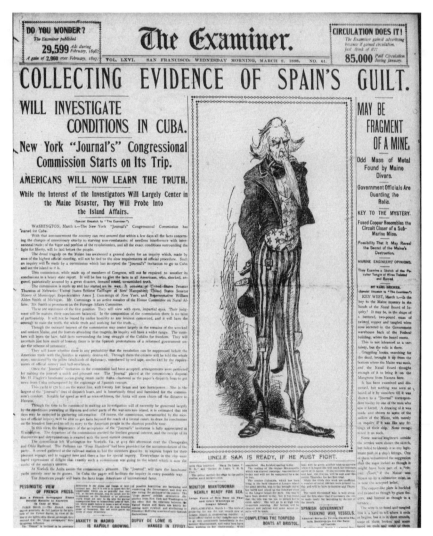

William Randolph Hearst pushes America toward war with Spain. Hearst's chain of *Examiner* and *Journal* newspapers told lurid tales of Spanish decadence, and cruelty toward the brave and freedom-loving Cuban people. Here on the front page of the *San Francisco, Examiner* readers saw an angry Uncle Sam prepared for war and could read day after day about the newspaper's own investigations into the explosion of the *Maine*.
CREDIT: LIBRARY OF CONGRESS

Remington to Cuba to provide illustrations for the paper, and Hearst, the *Journal*'s owner, offered a $50,000 reward (a fortune in 1898) for information that would lead to the conviction of whoever blew up the *Maine*. While his newspaper alleged almost daily that Spain destroyed the ship, the *World*'s Pulitzer privately heaped scorn on the idea, saying no one "outside a lunatic asylum" really believed the Spanish did it.

The *Maine* tragedy did not cause the American war with Spain, but it may have made the growing pressure to declare war impossible for the McKinley White House to resist. A few weeks after the *Maine* disaster, dueling reports declared the U.S. ship had exploded after hitting a mine—and after *not* hitting a mine, when armaments stored belowdecks exploded (the latter finding was ratified by repeated studies in ensuing

Joseph Pulitzer's *New York World* also pushed for war with Spain. Another press baron, Hearst's competitor Pulitzer, told his readers of a calm and confident American president, and a Spain with only two choices—give up, or fight. CREDIT: LIBRARY OF CONGRESS

years). The pace of events rapidly accelerated. Little more than a month after the *Maine* explosion, the U.S. minister to Spain demanded an end to war in Cuba and Cuban independence. The next day Spain refused the American demand. Just over a week later, McKinley asked Congress for a declaration of war.

On April 19, 1898, the U.S. Congress declared Cuba independent. Three days later, the U.S. Navy began to blockade Cuba. On April 23 the president called for 125,000 volunteers. The next day Congress declared war on Spain, but the House included a provision, the Teller Amendment, that forbade the United States from annexing Cuba.

Secretary of State John Hay might have called it a "splendid little war," but the Spanish-American War of 1898 should have signaled to American

"Suspended Judgment." The United States, represented by Uncle Sam, is not sure Spain belongs in the company of civilized nations. In the pages of the *World*, Spain is a dark and weedy little man, in fancy knee stockings, with a traditional hat, a guitar slung over his back, and a sword dripping blood. CREDIT: LIBRARY OF CONGRESS

leaders that for all its growth and potential, the country was hardly a world-class military power. The tiny U.S. Army was scattered across a continent-size country. Young American volunteers poured into recruiting stations to free Cuba, and found a War Department unable to properly uniform them for battle in the tropics, or arm them with the latest rifles.

Many soldiers were sent into action with Springfield rifles more than twenty years old, single-shot weapons using old-fashioned, smoky gun-powder. The more modern Norwegian Krag Jørgensen rifle was carried by a minority of American soldiers and marines, but even that newer firearm was inferior to the Mauser with which Spanish soldiers were armed. Today we remember the Battle of San Juan Hill as a glorious victory that helped make the national reputation of Theodore Roosevelt, and forget that some 750 Spanish regulars held off an American force twenty times larger, helped in part by their superior arms.

In short, the United States scored quick victories over naval and land forces it outnumbered, outspent, and eventually overwhelmed. The new kid on the world block beat up on a power in twilight, centuries past its days of imperial glory. Historian Maria Cristina Garcia of Cornell University describes the war as little, but something less than splendid: ". . . the navy really won the war, destroying powerful Spanish fleets in Santiago harbor and across the Pacific in Manila. Cubans had been fighting for independence for decades. The Americans put the last nail in Spain's coffin. But then the Americans made a blunder of their own." The U.S. Army entered Santiago de Cuba after the Spanish garrison surrendered

General Calixto García. A key leader of the Cuban forces in decades of struggle against Spain, he felt he was snubbed by the Americans once U.S. forces completed their victory. García died in Washington, D.C., while on a diplomatic mission, and he was temporarily buried in Arlington National Cemetery. An American warship, the USS *Nashville*, returned his body to Cuba for a hero's burial. CREDIT: LIBRARY OF CONGRESS

on July 17, 1898, and kept the Cuban forces camped outside the city. The U.S. forces managed to defeat Spain and insult Cuba in the same instant.

With carefully controlled anger embedded in the courtesy, General Calixto García protested to the American commander General William Shafter, "I have been until now one of your most faithful subordinates, honoring myself in carrying out your orders as far as my powers have allowed me to do it.

"The city of Santiago surrendered to the American army, and news of that important event was given to me by persons entirely foreign to your staff. I have not been honored with a single word from yourself informing me about the negotiations for peace or the terms of the capitulation by the Spaniards. The important ceremony of the surrender of the Spanish army and the taking possession of the city by yourself took place later on, and I only knew of both events by public reports.

"I was neither honored, sir, with a kind word from you inviting me or any officer of my staff to represent the Cuban army on that memorable occasion."

Having dispensed with the critique of his high-handed treatment by American forces, García got to the heart of the matter: "Finally, I know that you have left in power in Santiago the same Spanish authorities that for three years I have fought as enemies of the independence of Cuba. I beg to say that these authorities have never been elected at Santiago by the residents of the city; but were appointed by royal decrees of the Queen of Spain.

"A rumor too absurd to be believed, General, describes the reason of your measures and of the orders forbidding my army to enter Santiago for fear of massacres and revenge against the Spaniards. Allow me, sir, to protest against even the shadow of such an idea. We are not savages ignoring the rules of civilized warfare. We are a poor, ragged army, as ragged and poor as was the army of your forefathers in their noble war for independence. But like the heroes of Saratoga and Yorktown, we respect our cause too deeply to disgrace it with barbarism and cowardice."

The general closed his letter by resigning his command and informing his American counterpart his army would be moved elsewhere.

García knew Shafter's attitudes were not rumors at all. The American general neatly reflected his country's attitudes toward their Cuban comrades: "Those people are no more fit for self-government than gunpowder is for hell."

You've Earned Your Independence. A cartoon in the *World* shows Uncle Sam looking across the Florida Strait to a plucky little Cuban revolutionary, flying the *Cuba Libre* (Free Cuba) banner. CREDIT: LIBRARY OF CONGRESS

JUST A FEW years after historian Frederick Jackson Turner's 1893 lament over reaching the end of a wide-open continent and the closing of the American frontier, the United States was adding territory far beyond its shores, through war. The conflict with Spain was quick, relatively inexpensive in lives and money, and brought under the American flag millions of nonwhite and mixed-race citizens from the Antillean islands of the Caribbean to Guam and the Philippines clear across the other side of the planet. Perhaps there is a better word to describe the inhabitants of these new U.S.-occupied territories than "citizens." More on that later.

With the liberty of the Cubans being the stated reason for going to war with Spain in the first place, the question was widely asked in Havana and Washington, "What happens now?" It was unclear from the very moment the American defeat of the Spanish army in Cuba was complete, and remained so as the Spanish legislature approved the terms for ending the war, and the queen regent of Spain Maria Christina signed the treaty on behalf of her son, still a boy, King Alfonso XIII.

Congress had forbidden the annexation of Cuba by the United States, but had not specified a hands-off policy toward other territories. Both the Philippines and Puerto Rico had been home to active, and occasionally armed, anticolonial movements in the second half of the nineteenth century. Emilio Aguinaldo led the resistance to Spanish rule in the Philippines, and was proclaimed president of the First Philippine Republic in 1899, only to see the Americans take control of the island nation.

Aguinaldo maintained in the years that followed that U.S. diplomatic and military officials had urged him to return to the Philippines from exile to aid in the war against Spain and the transition to civilian control. Popular relief at seeing the Spanish leave was replaced by dismay at seeing the Americans stay. The Philippine guerrilla army once fighting Spain turned its fire on American forces in a bloody civil war with enormous Philippine casualties.

As the United States got a firmer grip on the Philippines and Puerto Rico, in the face of disappointment and armed resistance the puzzle pieces began to fall into place on Cuba. How do you control a place while providing a promised independence to a long-colonized people? Part of the answer came with the Platt Amendment, legal language drafted in Washington and attached to the new Cuban constitution. The amendment created an unusual kind of freedom for Cuba: an independence under terms directed by the United States. It read in part, "That the government of Cuba consents that the United States may exercise the right to intervene for the preservation of Cuban independence, the maintenance of a government adequate for the protection of life, property, and individual liberty, and for discharging the obligations with respect to Cuba imposed by the Treaty of Paris on the United States, now to be assumed and undertaken by the government of Cuba."

The Platt Amendment told the Cubans, if they had any doubt, that Uncle Sam was looking over their shoulder, and if the government of the day in Washington saw things it did not like, the United States could—

would—impose its will. The young government of Cuba would not be free to make its own mistakes.

In what came to be known as the Roosevelt Corollary to the Monroe Doctrine, the new president, Theodore Roosevelt, who'd served as the colonel of a volunteer regiment in Cuba and was catapulted to the vice presidency by the war, left no doubt about a future role for America: "It is not true that the United States feels any land hunger or entertains any projects as regards the other nations of the Western Hemisphere save such as are for their welfare.

"Chronic wrongdoing or an impotence which results in a general loosening of the ties of civilized society, may in America, as elsewhere, ultimately require intervention by some civilized nation, and in the Western Hemisphere the adherence of the United States to the Monroe Doctrine may force it, however reluctantly, in flagrant cases of wrongdoing or impotence, to the exercise of an international police power."

PUERTO RICO HAD been home to a resistance movement against colonial rule since the early 1860s. The first revolt came in September 1869, with the *Grito de Lares*, the Cry of Lares, an attempted armed insurrection crushed by Spanish forces in a matter of weeks.

As in Cuba, the leaders of the resistance to colonial rule also opposed slavery. Again as with Cuba, the Spanish authorities, tied down by fiscal problems at home and multiple revolutions across the Americas, had been leaning heavily on colonial cash to restock the treasury in Madrid, raising taxes and extracting cash. This led to growing unrest, especially among members of a European-descended intellectual elite with links in North America and Europe. Many of the leaders of the Puerto Rican independence movement, men like Ramón Emeterio Betances and Eugenio María de Hostos, were spared execution after the failed military uprising and, like Martí, would spend the years that followed in exile. Others like Mathias Brugman and Francisco Ramirez Medina, the president of the abortive Republic of Puerto Rico, did not survive the aftermath of the brief combat.

When you look at the leadership you see a microcosm of a cosmopolitan nineteenth-century Antillean elite. Teachers, physicians, small businessmen, they were the sons of parents born across the Caribbean world. Most were born in Puerto Rico, some in other Spanish possessions. They were fired up by the political and social revolutions rocking the rest of the Spanish-speaking world (even by events in Spain, which had just become a republic for the first time), and wanted the same for their adopted or native home.

The circumstances of their births and parentage also represented what was happening in the wider Caribbean world. In 1815 King Ferdinand VII of Spain issued the Royal Decree of Graces, opening his possessions to increased immigration from Europe. From this distance, nearly two hundred years, it is hard for us to grasp just what a shock wave the Haitian Revolution sent through the Caribbean, the young United States, and the colonial powers of Europe. The Spanish king, like other rulers of plantation colonies with large slave populations, wondered whether lurking in the slave cabins and fields there might be another Toussaint L'Ouverture, another Jean-Jacques Dessalines, men who created the first black republic in the New World.

Slave masters from Missouri to Rio de Janeiro slept just a little bit less securely after Haiti's spasm of horrifying violence on both sides sent France packing. Ferdinand VII's proclamation was designed to create more profitable colonies, but at the same time "whiten" the populations of places like Cuba and Puerto Rico. The Decree of Graces said European Catholics willing to pledge loyalty to the Spanish Crown could easily move to Puerto Rico and Cuba and receive free land, and hold slaves.

Both island colonies saw increased immigration in the first decades after Ferdinand's decree. However, later in the century, as instability stalked Europe, people poured in from France, Ireland, Germany, Corsica, and Italy. Slaves, people of mixed races, and free blacks made up a smaller share of the overall populations. Nearly half a million settlers came to Puerto Rico alone, "whitening" the population, paradoxically feeding both the allegiance and the resistance to Spanish rule.

By the 1850s, Spain had lost all its New World colonies except for Cuba and Puerto Rico. That might have strengthened her resolve to hold on. Negotiations with the Spanish Crown by delegations from Puerto Rico were fruitless, both in the efforts to end slavery and the demands to win a measure of autonomy for the island. Puerto Rico had not produced the riches of Cuba, nor fired the imaginations of imperial powers in quite the same way. Puerto Rico is about thirty-five miles from north to south, and some hundred miles from east to west, and at the time, the island's population was small, its infrastructure undercapitalized, and its economy providing little more than subsistence for the majority of its people.

Ramón Betances organized his independence movement from New York and the Dominican Republic, and served as a delegate to the Cuban revolutionary junta, and secretary of the Dominican League. During a long sojourn in New York, Betances applied for U.S. citizenship in the superior court of New York, in anticipation of the military revolt in Puerto Rico. The doctor wanted to protect himself from possible retaliation by the government of Spain, and believed U.S. citizenship would insulate him.

In these years the leaders of the Puerto Rican independence movement moved constantly among the Dominican Republic, Venezuela, Haiti, the United States, and Europe. The intellectual networks forged by these journeys lasted for decades. Orator, essayist, and motivator Ramón Betances was not stopped or slowed by the defeat of the Lares uprising. In 1869, Betances returned to New York to take up his work with the Central Republican Board of Cuba and Puerto Rico. The organization's aim was to encourage military action against Spain on both islands. Many of the anticolonial leaders hoped to one day join Puerto Rico, Cuba, and the Dominican Republic into an Antillean confederacy.

As we have seen, the war in Cuba continued, and gathered steam. In Puerto Rico, however, the efforts to win self-rule from Spain continued on the diplomatic track, with leading citizens agitating for concessions, and organizing Puerto Ricans in the young diaspora to maintain the pressure.

In the propaganda in the U.S. media, in debates on Capitol Hill and at the White House, Puerto Rico was not a lower priority than Cuba. It rarely came up at all. During the run-up to war there were no conversations about the relationship between the United States and a postcolonial Puerto Rico. Editorial cartoons prominently featured a representation of Cuba, a little brown man in the raggedy white clothing of a peasant. When Puerto Rico featured in these drawings at all, it appeared as an even smaller, often younger little brown fellow, in similar rags, topped by a *pava*, the straw hat of the farm worker.

It was only after the real prizes in the Spanish imperial crown, Cuba and the Philippines, were seized and secured in 1898 that the military turned its attention, and its fire, on Puerto Rico. First came a naval bombardment of San Juan, on the island's northern coast, then a July 25 land invasion by General Nelson Miles and eight thousand men at Guánica, on the southern coast.

Just a few weeks later, on August 9, the last major Spanish force on the island was defeated at Coamo, in the south central part of Puerto Rico. By then there were almost no Spaniards left to defeat. That same day, Spain formally accepted the terms for ending the war offered by President McKinley.

Little more than a month later, when the queen regent signed the protocol, the evacuation of Puerto Rico by Spain began, ending four hundred years of Spanish administration. Again, by far the most attention in Washington and the newly occupied island territories was paid to Cuba and the Philippines, and there was little evidence the new colonial power thought about what would happen next to Puerto Rico other than the fact that unlike Cuba, which was merely occupied and understood to be on its way to some form of self-government, Puerto Rico was to be occupied and possessed by the United States. It was still unclear what this was going to mean to the people of Puerto Rico, who at this time numbered nearly a million.

Puerto Rico began its American journey under military occupation, with its name officially changed in U.S. documents to "Porto Rico" (a usage that was changed to "Puerto Rico" in 1932), and its currency changed from pesos *puertorriqueños* to an unusual hybrid, Puerto Rican dollars.

The day the queen regent signed the final documents bringing an end to hostilities with Spain, and giving up all claims to a long list of long-held possessions, who were Puerto Ricans? Were they citizens of the Spanish Empire? Were they citizens of the United States? Were they citizens of Puerto Rico, an island just captured by a country that had not yet welcomed them in as citizens?

The Foraker Act, the popular name for the Organic Act of 1900, was the first step, but hardly a definitive one in declaring what Puerto Ricans were. It is significant that the act spent a lot more space defining the fate of pineapples and sugarcane, and the rate of exchange of Puerto Rican pesos and U.S. dollars, than it spent on the fate of the people of the island.

After setting out the duties and tariffs now collectible on agricultural commodities and manufactured goods heading from Puerto Rico to ports in the mainland United States, Article 7 stated, "That all inhabitants continuing to reside therein who were Spanish subjects on the eleventh day of April, eighteen hundred and ninety-nine, and then resided in Porto Rico, and their children born subsequent thereto, shall be deemed and held to be citizens of Porto Rico, and as such entitled to the protection of the United States, except such as shall have elected to pre-serve their allegiance to the Crown of Spain on or before the eleventh day of April . . . and they, together with such citizens of the United States as may reside in Porto Rico, shall constitute a body politic under the name of The People of Porto Rico, with governmental powers as herein-after conferred, and with power to sue and be sued as such."

That phrase "governmental powers, as hereinafter conferred" left the hard stuff, the political rights of Puerto Ricans, for later. It was the U.S. response to a people who had finally achieved a measure of self-govern-ment under a declining Spanish Empire, and now had new political mas-ters. "Hereinafter" was going to be years in length, and it did not take very long for the internal contradictions in America's new imperial proj-ect to emerge.

There were legislators in Washington who argued in the closing days of the war and thereafter that America's new Caribbean territory should be treated like Arizona, New Mexico, and Alaska, integrally part of the United States, its citizens fully and unquestionably citizens of the coun-try, and its products treated like products from anywhere else in the country.

For other Americans, Puerto Ricans were a people in need of educa-tion, in need of the kind of training for liberty that the United States could provide, and the Spanish colonial masters had not, in four centuries. In response to a report on the Senate debate on the future of Puerto Rico, the *New York Times* printed a letter from one S. S. Harvey, who wrote from Ponce, "Let us educate these people, and teach them what government of the people means. They do not know, and never will, unless the people of the United States teach them." Harvey insisted that if the preinvasion Puerto Rican elite were left in charge, the island would be "Spanish in all but name a hundred years from now." After dismissing the island's edu-cated elite as unsuited for and uninterested in U.S. democracy, he "praised" the common people as "light-hearted, simple-minded, harmless, indolent, docile people, and while they gamble and are fond of wine, women, music, and dancing, they are honest and sober."

ENTER ISABEL GONZÁLEZ and Samuel Downes.

Downes was a New York merchant. When he imported oranges from San Juan, he was charged $659.35 in duties. Downes sued the collector of tariffs in the Port of New York, pointing out that a similar amount of oranges brought into New York from Florida would have no duty collected, as guaranteed from the earliest days of the United States by the U.S. Constitution. In a narrow decision, the Supreme Court found that the people of America's new island possessions were not covered by constitutional guarantees in many cases, unless an act of Congress made those territories "an integral part" of the United States.

Justice John Marshall Harlan's dissent was a strong rebuke to the idea that there were places and peoples who were inside U.S. jurisdiction but outside the protection of the Constitution: "This nation is under the control of a written constitution, the supreme law of the land and the only source of the powers which our government, or any branch or officer of it, may exert at any time or at any place." Since all of Congress's authority came from the Constitution, Harlan wrote, it could not exert authority outside of that same Constitution. "Monarchical and despotic governments, unrestrained by written constitutions, may do with newly acquired territories what this government may not do consistently with our fundamental law. To say otherwise is to concede that Congress may, by action taken outside of the Constitution, engraft upon our republican institutions a colonial system such as exists under monarchical governments." Harlan dismissed the idea that the United States could take possession of Puerto Rico, or, as it appeared in federal documents, Porto Rico, imposing a currency, requiring the Puerto Rican government to report all its spending to the U.S. executive branch, subjecting Puerto Rico to U.S. tax laws, and holding the island outside the umbrella of the Constitution.

Isabel González was a young woman who headed to the United States to begin a life with her fiancé, who worked in Staten Island, New York. Just twenty years old, she left San Juan on the SS *Philadelphia*. While the ship was en route, the immigration commissioner for the U.S. Treasury Department issued a new regulation changing the status of travelers like González to that of foreigners, aliens. Under this regulation, González was no longer to be treated like a legal resident of North Carolina, let's say, deciding to relocate to New York. She was now to be treated like a new arrival from a foreign country, with discretion given to immigration authorities over whether the immigrant would be a desirable presence in the United States.

Instead of simply walking ashore in the United States, González and other Puerto Ricans on the *Philadelphia* were transferred to Ellis Island for processing. U.S. immigration law specifically excluded from entry into the country "all idiots, insane persons, paupers, or persons likely to become a public charge." In the case of González, pregnant with her fiancé's child, plenty of attention was paid to the likelihood that she might one day rely on public sources for support, that she would become "a public charge."

González had contacts and family waiting ashore, not least her fiance, and they were willing to attest to a network of support for her, and the child, if she was allowed to come into the country. Her first stop on a long legal journey into the United States was a special board of inquiry convened to take testimony on her fitness to enter as an alien national. The commissioner of immigration at Ellis Island, William Williams, had made it policy to pay special attention to unmarried, pregnant women who carried less than ten dollars.

The social assumptions of the day that looked down on single mothers were not confined to Puerto Ricans. Again, the debate over González's entry could be based on her desirability as a resident of the United States as long as she was defined as an alien national, as someone the country could take or leave. Even in the midst of one of the greatest immigration flows in world history, concerns over newcomers weakening the country were a permanent part of the debate. As Williams testified at the González

Isabel González. The petitioner in the landmark Supreme Court case for Puerto Ricans, *Gonzáles v. Williams.* The case affirmed the right of Puerto Ricans to move freely between their home island and the U.S. mainland.
CREDIT: COURTESY OF BELINDA TORRES-MARY

inquiry, "It will be a very easy matter to fill up this country rapidly with immigrants upon whom responsibility for the proper bringing up of their offspring sits lightly, but it cannot be claimed that this will enure to the benefit of the American people."

González's family members living in New York and New Jersey testified that they could assure the government the young woman would not become a public charge. Her cause was undermined by the absence of her fiancé, Juan Francisco Torres, who could not leave work. González was again denied entry to the United States. At this point she might have simply gone home, as provided by U.S. law, another person of modest means and little clout steamrolled by the power and indifference of the state.

González's uncle, Domingo Collazo, had been active in the Cuban Revolutionary Party, and knew many of the leading lights in the Antillean freedom movement. Collazo filed a habeas corpus petition, a legal demand that a prisoner be brought to court in order for the state to justify their continued detention. Through other Collazo contacts, prominent lawyers took interest in González's case. Another court, the U.S. Circuit Court for the Southern District of New York, sided with the immigration authorities, and affirmed González's exclusion.

All this was possible because under the seizure of Puerto Rico from Spain and the Foraker Act creating "citizens of Puerto Rico," Isabel González was not a U.S. national, and had no legally enforceable access to the country that now governed hers.

Again, fate intervened in a way that reflected New York's status as a crossroads, filled with interested onlookers who knew an important cause when they saw one. Federico Degetau was another man molded by the ferment of the nineteenth century. Degetau was the son of a German-Puerto Rican family, educated in Spain, an anticolonialist and editor, and in the 1890s, one of the commissioners who represented Puerto Rico in autonomy talks with Spain.

On the eve of the Spanish-American War, Degetau was the mayor of San Juan, and a member of the Spanish legislature, the Cortes. After the war, he was appointed a member of the first cabinet created by the new U.S. administration. Degetau was appointed or elected to jobs of increasing prominence and responsibility under the Americans, culminating in several terms as resident commissioner, Puerto Rico's delegate to the U.S. House of Representatives. As resident commissioner, Degetau had already protested the turn-of-the-century decisions regarding the legal status of Puerto Ricans.

After González exhausted her appeals through the immigration system, she and her legal team switched tactics, no longer arguing against the "public charge" clause of immigration law. González would now head back to court to argue that you could not exclude, detain, or block Puerto Ricans who wished to enter the United States for one very good reason: Once the United States took Puerto Rico in war, took control of her commerce, and appointed executives in Washington to run the place, Puerto Ricans were now living in a part of the United States and were American citizens. Degetau teamed up with González's lawyers, Paul Fuller and Charles LéBarbier, and Frederic Coudert Jr., who had just argued the *Downes v. Bidwell* case, and headed to the Supreme Court.

Degetau believed González provided a test case that would undermine the U.S. effort to hold on to the territory while excluding the Puerto Ricans themselves. The resident commissioner and the young migrant woman wanted the case to make law on behalf of all the residents of the island. The U.S. government's lawyers continued to argue against González's entry based on moral appeals, portraying the woman and her fiancé as unfit parents whose life choices should not win the approval of the federal government.

Ironically, González herself made the landmark case, which misspelled her first and last name as *Isabella Gonzáles v. William Williams*, moot, by marrying Torres and thus becoming eligible for entry to the United States through marriage. She pursued the case anyway, out of the conviction that all Puerto Ricans were citizens.

The justices agreed, sort of: They determined that González was not an alien, and thus could not be denied entry to the United States. At the same time, they refused to rule that González was an American citizen. The decision said that since the United States took control of the island from Spain, "The nationality of the island became American instead of Spanish, and, by the treaty, Peninsulars [people born in Spain], not deciding to preserve their allegiance to Spain, were to be 'held to have renounced it, and to have adopted the nationality of the territory in which they may reside.'" Thus, if Spaniards chose not to declare themselves Spanish after the war, they were now part of the United States.

The court noted that the resident commissioner, whose salary was paid by the United States, was chosen by voters in Puerto Rico, however limited the vote, given as it was to no one "who is not a bona fide citizen of Porto Rico, who is not thirty years of age, and who does not read and write the English language."

A door was pushed open by Isabel González, and as the young century progressed, more of her fellow islanders decided to improve their lot in life by walking through it. Between 1908 and 1916, seven thousand Puerto Ricans emigrated to the United States. Another eleven thousand came in 1917 alone. As free as they now were to move, however, they were still trapped in a legal limbo, now tagged with an ambiguous status, defined as "noncitizen nationals."

After decades of leadership in the Puerto Rican struggle for autonomy from Spain, writer and politician Luis Muñoz Rivera tried to prick the conscience of Americans with a challenge that made his people's predicament plain: "The United States has not been fair to us. We are a people without a country, a flag, almost without name. What are we? Are we citizens or are we subjects? Are we your brothers and our property your territory, or are we bondsmen of war, and our islands a crown colony?"

The Jones-Shafroth Act of 1917 was an attempt to clear up the ambiguity, but it continued the pattern of never granting anything without taking something in return. The act gave Puerto Ricans full and un-

Puerto Rico. The early decades of American presence on Puerto Rico brought little in the way of economic development. The Great Depression hit the U.S. hard, and it was devastating for the island territory. CREDIT: LIBRARY OF CONGRESS

equivocal citizenship. It also opened the men of the island to conscrip-
tion in the middle of the First World War. Twenty thousand Puerto Ricans
would serve in the armed forces during the war.

There was no way the early arrivals could possibly know what was waiting for them in New York. A relative few Puerto Ricans were sending
home the kind of intelligence immigrants often rely on to make up their
own minds. Many years later, a migrant named Bernardo Vega recalled
watching his homeland disappear in the distance from the deck of a ship
carrying him to Brooklyn. "I did not want to lose a single breath of those
final minutes in my country. I stayed up on deck until the island was lost
from sight in the first shades of nightfall." A young tobacco farmer, Vega
left his native Cayey, Puerto Rico, aboard the steamship *Coamo*. During
the trip he shared his immigrant dream with his fellow passengers. "The
overriding theme of our conversations was what we expected to find in
New York City. First savings would be for sending for close relatives. Years
later the time would come for returning home with pots of money." New
jobs. Remittances. The immigrant family dream would eventually lead to
a triumphant journey home. "Everyone's mind would be on that farm we
would be buying. All of us were building our own little castles in the sky."

Hailing from a small town tucked in the mountains of western Puerto
Rico, Vega was a *jíbaro*, a peasant who is an island archetype. The *jíbaro*
of folktales and national memory is stolid, wise, independent, and decent. At the same time, in jokes *jíbaros* are simple, uneducated, and sometimes gullible. Whether they were possessed of common sense born of
experience, or credulous hicks, nothing back home could have prepared
jíbaros and *jíbaras* for their new lives in New York.

A Puerto Rican farmworker.
CREDIT: LIBRARY OF CONGRESS

For a large number of Puerto Ricans, their first castle on the U.S. mainland was an aging tenement building in East Harlem. The neighborhood had been welcoming immigrants for decades: southern Italians, Germans to the south, African-Americans to the west in Central Harlem. Before long, corner groceries catering to Puerto Rican tastes appeared, along with *botánicas* selling potions, amulets, herbs, and statuary that featured in Puerto Rican folk religion. The heat of the summer streets was broken, a little, by *piragüeros*, shaved-ice men who rasped a metal scrape across the top of a shrinking block of ice, molded it into a cone shape, and topped it with flavored syrup. A bit of home, far away from home, eaten as familiar music drifted down from upper-story windows.

East Harlem was the core of a community that would eventually far outstrip San Juan in size. Though Spanish-speaking immigrants had come in small numbers throughout the nineteenth century, the growing barrios in Manhattan, Brooklyn, and the Bronx represented something new. These were the first major Spanish-speaking communities in the United States outside Florida and the Southwest.

Unlike other arrivals in New York, Puerto Ricans arrived as citizens, but they were still outsiders. "Like all those who live in another culture, the people of Spanish Harlem felt a little lost," says Juan González, journalist and historian whose parents brought him to New York as a little boy. "They were citizens, but citizenship didn't change the way Anglo-Americans looked at them, since most Americans didn't differentiate one group of Hispanics from another. New York felt so strange and so cold, but it had opportunities. So they were in a kind of nowhere land, not truly part of any nation. And yet they were at home in this one."

One of the restless Puerto Ricans who headed to Nueva York was Rafael Hernández. One day his name would be known across Latin America, his music emanating from radios and phonographs from Santiago, Chile, to the tenement streets of Spanish Harlem. After serving as a musician in the legendary Harlem Hell Fighters regiment in World War I, he moved to New York. The story often told is that during a snowy Harlem winter, while working at his sister's music store, he composed one of the most famous Puerto Rican songs of the twentieth century, "*Lamento Borincano* (Puerto Rican Lament)."

A happy task, well begun, was followed by disappointment and a foretaste of disaster. It may be only the slightest exaggeration to say every Puerto Rican knows this song. It reflects the want and pain of the island in the twenties and thirties, and the poverty that drove so many people to try to find something better in the United States. That the man widely celebrated as the greatest Puerto Rican songwriter of the twentieth century wrote this profoundly Puerto Rican song in New York deeply resonates with a people who sing of their island the way people usually sing about a lover. Puerto Ricans would go on to become the only Latin American people who created their most significant and best-known music on other soil, away from their homeland.

The United States, and New York in particular, would continue to both lure and confound Puerto Ricans for the rest of the twentieth century. After beginning the century with the possibility of self-government snatched away, and paradoxically continuing it with a fight to join America as citizens, Puerto Ricans would find in New York the stage for their greatest triumphs and the most profound heartaches.

MEANWHILE, BACK ON the border, the World War I era brought change and tumult to Mexico and Mexican-Americans. A giant Latino migration to the United States was under way, and the number of Mexicans, an estimated one million between 1900 and 1930, dwarfed the numbers coming from Cuba and Puerto Rico.

Porfirio Díaz. More than three decades of dictatorial rule in Mexico created the conditions that led to the Mexican Revolution of 1910. CREDIT: LIBRARY OF CONGRESS

By the end of the first decade of the twentieth century, Porfirio Díaz had ruled Mexico with gradually strengthening dictatorial powers for more than thirty years. Under Díaz, Mexico was crisscrossed with railroads that transported wealth pulled from the country's rich mines. His power was so complete that this one man lent his name to the era, the Porfiriato, but opposition had been gathering and was about to burst into action.

Díaz finally consented to elections in 1910. He jailed his opponent, Francisco Madero. When the results were finally announced, the Mexican people were told Díaz had gotten the vast majority of votes, with only a tiny number cast for Madero. The "defeated" candidate called for an uprising, and the revolution began. Díaz fled the country, but the beginning of war unleashed long-simmering conflicts in society that could not be put back in the box.

The Mexican Revolution of 1910 created modern Mexico, set in motion forces in Mexican life that would play out over the rest of the century, made enduring heroes of José Doroteo Arango Arámbula (better known as Pancho Villa) and Emiliano Zapata. However, the tumult of the nearly ten-year war disrupted millions of lives and sent hundreds of thousands of families fleeing to the United States.

One of them was a little boy, Salvador Villaseñor, who headed north in 1918. The war had stretched on for eight long years. Los Altos de Jalisco sat at Mexico's waistline, in Jalisco state on the Pacific Ocean. Author Victor Villaseñor, who has written extensively of his family's journey from rural Mexico to the United States, said his father, just seven years old, was one of the last survivors of fourteen children.

Though the war had taken a long time getting to his town, it came with horrifying violence. "One day the little boy, Juan Salvador, went out searching for some firewood. He saw some wild men shoot the horses out from under six people, then hack the riders to death with machetes, just to get some clothes and shoes. Juan Salvador was crazy with hunger; he tried to take a bite out of the hide of a dead horse. His teeth weren't big enough, he went hungry. But he survived, and my grandmother survived—because she relied on miracles. She always relied on the spirit world of miracles."

One of Díaz's economic development projects was the completion of a north-south railroad that tied Mexico together and linked the country's interior to the United States. When the revolution dragged on, the rail line became an escape route. In 1918, Victor Villaseñor's grandmother grabbed his father and Victor's uncle, Francisco, and headed to the train tracks. They would wait for days. "Finally, a train came," said Villaseñor. "Juan Salvador and his mother and brother got on the train with thousands of other people." The empty cattle car was full of manure, which had to be shoveled out by hand. Their goal was El Paso, still the destination to the north from Mexico it had been since Juan de Oñate crossed there more than three hundred years earlier.

"Juan Salvador's brother told him that in El Paso there was a big pond full of huge lizards the size of dragons, with big rows of sharp teeth. Every night these monstrous alligators were turned loose into the Rio Grande to eat Mexicans who tried to cross the border. So Salvador's brother taught him to practice these words: 'Hello, mister. Where's the alligators?'"

The boy saw no alligators. The Mexicans who streamed north with him, for all the long and difficult relationship between the United States, Mexico, and Mexican-Americans, still dreamed of *el Norte* as a place that promised riches and a better life.

The reality was often very different. Villaseñor remembered his father's first encounter with his new home. "That morning, as the train came into the El Paso basin, Salvador couldn't believe what he saw. He expected a luscious green valley; he saw nothing but dry earth, rock and sand. Not even one blade of grass. Nothing could live there except lizards and snakes. This was the end of the world. In El Paso, it got even worse. Everywhere Salvador saw crowds of poor, ragged, starving people. He woke his mother. She looked out at the dry country, then the mob of desperate people. 'What a beautiful day!' she said. 'See all those vultures in the sky over there? There's so much to eat here that even the vultures get their share.'"

Historian Gary Gerstle sees similarities with other immigrants. "In many ways Mexican immigrants were not so different from the Europeans who came at the same time. Italians fled from civil war. Jews came to escape oppression, war, and poverty. And Mexicans were faced with exactly these fears and crushing burdens. People today think of Mexicans as strictly economic immigrants, but the first great wave were generally refugees from a horrible, bloody war."

El Paso was Ellis Island for Mexicans, in the view of historian Vicki Ruiz. While New York was one of the continent's economic engines, El Paso was not. The new arrivals from southern and eastern Europe entered a densely populated, rapidly industrializing region hungry for labor, with a highly stratified economy. West Texas a hundred years ago had an operating economy, but hardly the same kinds of opportunity as existed in the northeast.

At the same time, Ruiz says, offers for work could come with the first steps into the country: "When a man crossed over Stanton Street Bridge to El Paso from Ciudad Juárez, he'd go past a line of labor contractors promising all sorts of things—you know, high wages, beer with dinner, benefits. But if it was a single woman or, God help her, a single mother, immigration inspectors would pull them aside and mark them, 'Likely to become a public charge.'"

The Villaseñor family made it from Texas to southern Arizona. "They had nothing. They slept on the street. You know that saying—'the sun is the blanket of the poor.'" Young Juan Salvador, Villaseñor recalled, saw something that changed his life. "One day he saw a wrinkled old bag of bones begging in the street—sick-looking, dirty, whining, crying, clawing at people as they went by. Then he realized it was his own mother. The shame was so great that he cried, and he swore to himself that his mother would never beg again." So in 1922 he went to work. He was twelve years old. There was plenty of work. Hard work. The Chinese immigrants heading east from the Pacific coast had done a lot of it in the mines and on the railroads, but American immigration law had shifted before the Mexican Revolution, with the Chinese Exclusion Act. There was work for the new guys, the Mexicans. Juan Salvador Villaseñor got a day-shift job at the Copper Queen Mining Company in Douglas, Arizona, then used an assumed name to get a job on the night shift.

He was caught trying to smuggle a small bag of copper out of the mine, and sentenced to six years in prison. He escaped, but Villaseñor said his father's time in prison had changed him: "His life became filled with jails, fights, brothels, gambling dens and pool halls. His world was the underworld."

By the mid-1920s, still a teenager, Juan Salvador was a bootlegger in San Diego's barrio. "My father always said that coming into the *barrio* was like entering a different country. The houses were tiny, run-down. There were no sidewalks or paved streets, but there were chickens and pigs and goats running loose. It never failed to amaze him how different his people were from the Anglos. *Los mejicanos* never wasted anything. Instead of grass in front of their homes, they had vegetable gardens. And they didn't fence in their livestock; instead, they fenced in their crops."

The immigrants' hard work, in factories, on farms, and down mines helped make their new home states wealthy places that attracted investment from other parts of the country, and attracted new Anglo-American migrants from the Midwest and eastern seaboard. But these new neighbors looked down on the *mejicanos* even as their labor made Anglo-American fortunes. While references in newspapers and popular culture were full of stories of laziness and lack of ambition, the barrios of the Southwest were humming. Ernesto Galarza recalled Sacramento in his autobiographical novel, *Barrio Boy*: "Every morning a parade of men in oily work clothes and carrying lunch buckets went up Fourth Street, and every evening they walked back, grimy and silent. Within a few blocks of our house there were smithies, hand laundries, a macaroni factory, places where wagons were repaired, horses stabled, bicycles fixed, chickens dressed, clothes ironed, furniture repaired, wine grapes pressed, lumber sawed, suits tailored, vegetables sorted, railroad cars unloaded. The barrio was an open workshop."

Living in a neighborhood with other immigrants is a time-honored first step in finding your way in America. The barrio was, at the same time, a construction made out of necessity. The other neighborhoods of Los Angeles, Phoenix, and Dallas were not open to the newcomers. According to Antonio Rios-Bustamante, author of Mexican Los Angeles, there was "widespread racial prejudice—Anglo-Americans often refused to rent or sell to Mexican-Americans. In Los Angeles, a new community arose, with a migration within the city—from the old neighborhood in central L.A. to the east side, across the river. But whether it was old or new, the *barrio* was a comfort zone, a place where you could associate with people who understood you."

In tradition-bound immigrant families, the home was often the place where the rules of the home country, religion, and custom were most strenuously enforced. Coming to America changed the rules outside the house, where employers often treated women and men equally, said Vicki Ruiz. "Women of the *barrio* often worked at home, taking in boarders, doing laundry, or sewing. Some women labored in canneries or garment factories. Or they worked in the fields—often just sleeping on the ground in the fields, just as the men did."

So many people came, and joined families already making a life in America, that gradually a distinctly Mexican-American daily life evolved in places like Los Angeles and San Antonio. It was enriched by constant replenishment, with new people traveling north from Mexico. It also evolved, however, into its own way of life quite apart from Mexico . . . cross-pollinating the culture from home with American popular music, movies, and fashions.

America's transformative power changed the people who came here, while the new arrivals in turn changed the places they arrived. In the barrios of Los Angeles you knew you were not in Guanajuato, Mexico City, or San Luis Potosí. Yet you also knew you were not in other places in America not touched by the large-scale Mexican presence.

While Mexicans were offered and were forced to accept lower wages for the same work as their Anglo neighbors, they also knew they were getting more—much more—money than they would make for that work back in Mexico. This economic reality would endure for decades to come, and in time would challenge people on both sides of the border, when farm owners would use the desperate poverty of Mexicans to undercut the wages of native-born and legally resident farmworkers.

People who never would have met one another in Mexico found one another in the United States, people like Villaseñor's parents. "One evening in San Diego Juan Salvador saw a woman standing outside a dance hall in the *barrio* in an orange dress, and he knew. This was Lupe, my mother, and this was love at first sight. She was an honest, hardworking girl, a *barrio* girl.

Lupe and Salvador Villaseñor's wedding day. After fleeing north during the Mexican Revolution, Salvador Villaseñor worked as a miner and a bootlegger during Prohibition. He was handsome and tough, but at his young wife's insistence he settled down to successful, legitimate businesses. CREDIT: VILLASEÑOR FAMILY

"I always say that the angels of destiny brought this woman through my father's *barrio* in a caravan of trucks. She was a migrant worker, following the harvest, and she was passing through, picking tomatoes. She had the most education of anyone in her family—she'd finished the sixth grade. Lupe was good, hard-working, and Salvador was, I have to admit, kind of a crook. But he convinced the priest that he wasn't a sinner, because Jesus himself had turned water into wine—just like a bootlegger!"

As Villaseñor remembers it, his mother, Lupe, somehow managed the opposite of Jesus's miracle. She changed Juan Salvador's wine into good clean water, and made an honest man out of him.

The family owned a series of liquor stores and pool halls, worked hard, and as Villaseñor tells it, "lived out a version of the American Dream. They had lives full of violence and desperation yet never without hope, you know.

"The U.S. was the place of good and wonderful possibilities. It didn't matter if you were a *bandido* or a bootlegger or a migrant worker or a president. It was always a challenge, always a rain of gold with God giving you the breath of life, giving you hope for a better day. The path was crooked. Yet there was a path."

A Mexican Independence Day celebration in 1920s Los Angeles. So many of the photos from this era have a touching "foot in each world" quality, as a young community figures out what to retain from the old country and what to adopt from the new. Mexican and American symbols are side by side as the crowd gathers to re-enact the *Grito* (shout) that marked the proclamation of Mexico's separation from Spain in 1821. CREDIT: LOS ANGELES PUBLIC LIBRARY

When the Great Depression hit the American Southwest, that path, for many, led right back to Mexico. Los Angeles itself was coming to a rough accommodation with its large Mexican population. Cultural appropriation was in full swing as Anglos traded intelligence on their "find," the best Mexican restaurant in this or that part of the city, and Spanish- and Mexican-style homes, furniture, and housewares were all the rage. This city with the Spanish name that was full of Midwestern migrants suddenly "rediscovered" its mission roots in 1930 by turning the center of the original pueblo and mission of Nuestra Senora de Los Angeles de Porciuncula, Our Lady of the Angels of Porciuncula, into the Olvera Street tourist attraction. The United States was preparing to solve its own employment problems by sending "foreigners" back to Mexico. The only problem? Many of those foreigners were as American as *empanada de manzana*, apple pie.

Young Emilia Castañeda remembers wearing her favorite dress for the journey. "I wore it because it was my favorite, and this was an important occasion. Because we were going away, we were leaving everything behind."

Emilia was from Boyle Heights, a Los Angeles neighborhood that had become home to many Mexicans and Mexican-Americans, not far from present-day Dodger Stadium. "I remember my Japanese-American girlfriends, Midoriko and Natsuko. We were like the United Nations in Boyle Heights—all kinds of people.

"I remember saying the Pledge of Allegiance to the flag of the United States of America, and to the republic for which it stands, standing up beside our desks, every morning at my school on Malabar Street."

The Great Depression was bankrupting countless people, destroying futures, and breaking up families. Many Americans believed low-paid immigrants were taking "American" jobs, and making Mexicans targets of particular resentment. As the job crisis got worse, unemployed Americans did not suggest that Italians or Germans should be put on ships and sent home.

At a time when America was in a heightening panic over foreign agitators, fifth columnists, and "alien ideologies," Vicki Ruiz suggests there is another reason it was considered desirable to send Mexicans home: "Growers initially felt that Mexican workers were attractive because they were 'naturally' docile. But their history proves that Latino Americans are very often willing to organize, and strike, when faced with intolerable conditions.

"In the Depression, that's exactly what they did—in garment factories, in canneries, in mines, in cigar factories. And in 1933 alone there were thirty-seven major agricultural strikes in California. Strikes were common enough that employers were ready to let workers go."

As in the heated debates in this century about how to handle immigration, families of mixed status were particularly vulnerable to the blunt instrument of the law. Emilia Castañeda and her brother Francisco were U.S. citizens, born after the family came to the country. "But my father, he was not. He had to go. The *migras* said my brother and I could stay if we declared that we were orphans. They would put us in an orphanage. But I wasn't an orphan.

"I had my father. I kept saying I had my father. So they sent us all away to Mexico. 'Back' to Mexico, they kept saying. But I had never been to Mexico." The Castañedas were packed onto a train with hundreds of other Mexicans and Mexican-Americans, and sent rumbling across the desert on that long ride back to Mexico.

Between 1931 and 1935, as American joblessness reached its Depression crescendo, some four hundred thousand Mexicans, more than half of whom were American citizens, were "repatriated" to a country that in many cases they had never seen. Carried on entirely without due process, the mass deportations were authorized by President Herbert Hoover, who gave the go-ahead to his secretary of labor, William Doak, to deport half a million foreigners. Gary Gerstle says the U.S. government and the coun-

Emilia Castañeda. U.S. born, raised in the Los Angeles barrio of Boyle Heights, Castañeda was one of the thousands of U.S. citizens sent "back" to Mexico during the Great Depression. "I never stopped thinking of myself as an American," she said. "The other kids [back in Mexico] teased me because I couldn't speak Spanish well, because we didn't belong there." CREDIT: CASTAÑEDA FAMILY

try's citizens lurched one way, then another, in their treatment of Latinos for a century. "The government was alternately welcoming and threatening, depending on the economy. In boom times, companies lured workers north; in hard ones, Latinos were harassed, attacked, and deported.

"These reverses are a powerful continuing theme in the story of Latino Americans. The deportations in the thirties came so close to the time when the need for Mexican labor was insatiable—it was the direct result of market forces in America. To the Mexican workers it seemed like Please-come-and-stay . . . now-go-away."

For young people like Emilia, "home" was not Mexico; it was East Los Angeles. "I didn't like the hard life in Mexico. Why did I have to carry laundry on my head and wash it by hand, walk miles for clean water? I was used to turning on a faucet in the kitchen, using a bathroom with a flush toilet. I never stopped thinking of myself as an American. The other kids teased me because I couldn't speak Spanish well, because we didn't belong there. We were outcasts, *repatriados*."

A family member found Castañeda's birth certificate in a box of papers sitting in a closet. She and her family now faced a painful choice. "I proved I was a U.S. citizen, and I could come back home. So I did. But my brother Francisco wouldn't come. He kept saying, 'Why go to a country that rejected me, that took away my homeland?' He wouldn't come, and my father also refused. So I came back here alone. I took the same train, from El Paso to Los Angeles—back again on the same train where they packed us together and sent us away."

Mexicans and Mexican-Americans wait to be sent to Mexico in Los Angeles' Union Pacific train station during the Great Depression. CREDIT: LOS ANGELES PUBLIC LIBRARY

Emilia Castañeda went back to night school to relearn English. The classes were held in her old elementary school. Looking back, she said the years in Mexico left her a stranger in her homeland, disoriented. "It was my world. But it didn't feel like home this time. I lost my place here, and I still don't know why they did this to us.

"They broke my family apart, you know. I couldn't go to my father's bedside when he was dying. This is a feeling I will have until I die."

ISABEL GONZÁLEZ, AMERICAN citizen, went on to live a long life. She married Juan Francisco Torres and moved to New Jersey. She continued to be an outspoken advocate for Puerto Rican rights back on the island and on the mainland. She sent a steady stream of tart, smart, and strongly argued letters to the editors of the *New York Times*, which published her views on Puerto Rico's U.S.-appointed governor, tariffs on coffee, and the efforts to displace the Spanish language on the island through the educational system.

José Martí became the rope in a tug-of-war between Cubans in postrevolutionary Cuba and Cubans who left the island to escape Communism. Poet, freedom fighter, martyr Martí's serious face with its exuberant mustache looks down on Cubans playing dominoes and sipping coffee in a sleepy provincial town on the island, and in a park that bears his name on a busy Miami street.

Victor Villaseñor's parents bore up under the terrible challenges of Depression America, and emerged, dreams intact, if maybe a little dented. "My mother and father journeyed through hell. They never expected anything. But spirits, the beings of the spirit world, guided them on to hope."

Depression would soon give way to world war once again. Latinos would again be asked to prove they had a right to a place in the American whole.

AT WAR:
ABROAD . . .
AND AT HOME

"The Fearless Mexican." Sargeant Macario Garcia was presented the Medal of Honor, America's highest military decoration, for bravery after suffering terrible wounds in a battle near the Belgian-German border. He was the first Mexican citizen ever given the Medal of Honor. Mexican citizens and Mexican-Americans have won a disproportionate number of the highest military honors in modern U.S. wars. CREDIT: NARA

LATINOS WERE given their rights as American citizens in law long before those rights were fully recognized by their fellow Americans. As it had been for African-Americans, it turned out that citizenship and full recognition of equality moved on separate tracks. One of the great catalysts in advancing the struggle for civil rights was the Second World War.

Boys barely men, and men already familiar with hard days of work in fields and factories, were swept up by a war that was fought in every corner of the globe. They would meet farm boys and laborers from across the world in North Africa, Europe, and Asia . . . schoolteachers and salesmen, auto mechanics and bus drivers . . . and try to kill them to save their own lives.

For many, the United States was their adopted country, a place they would now fight for after beginning their lives somewhere else. Others were from families that had been "American" for a century or more, but excluded from enjoying the same rights and aspirations many of their neighbors took for granted.

Men and women who in many cases rarely traveled much beyond the county line had been halfway around the world, been part of the most powerful and successful armed forces ever assembled in the history of the world. Young people from the Rio Grande Valley in Texas, cane plantations in Puerto Rico, and small county seats in California's agricultural belt fought well and suffered much. Commendations, decorations, and awards marched in orderly lines above their left breast pockets, in recognition of outstanding valor and sacrifice, or for just doing their part. They had rubbed shoulders with and fought alongside people from everywhere and taken their measure. They came home knowing they were equal to their fellow Americans. The second-class citizenship many had been forced to live with before the war would no longer be good enough.

The struggles of returning African-American servicemen, and how their fights for equal housing, schooling, and public accommodation spurred the civil rights era, have become a well-known part of our history. Perhaps less well-known is the fight for equality going on at the same time across the states bordering Mexico, on the West Coast, and in big cities like New York.

IN 1940, PRESIDENT Franklin D. Roosevelt ordered the first peacetime draft in American history. The secretary of war drew the first selective service number and it belonged to Pedro Aguilar Despart, a Mexican-American from East Los Angeles. Up to half a million Latinos would follow Pedro into uniform, including 375,000 Mexicans and Mexican-Americans, and more than 72,000 Puerto Ricans.

They volunteered for the most hazardous duties and military specialties. They won more than their share of decorations for bravery. A remarkable seventeen Latinos won Medals of Honor, America's highest military decoration. It had been only some eighty years since the first Latinos won the decoration "for conspicuous gallantry" during the Civil War.

Military units were often drawn from one geographical area, so the housing segregation in force in their hometowns often followed Latino servicemen and women into service. Many served in entirely Latino units: the 88th Infantry Division of the U.S. Army, called "the Blue Devils" in the Italian campaign; Company E of the 141st Regiment from El Paso, Texas; and from Puerto Rico the "Borinqueneers," the 65th Infantry Regiment. They fought ferociously. One general said of his Latino soldiers, "They were the first to fire and the last to lay down their arms."

The stories of Latino servicepeople both illustrate their evolving status inside American society, and remind you of the amazing—and sometimes peculiar—personal journeys that can happen only in America.

Rafaela Muniz Esquivel had trained as a nurse in San Antonio and started work in the last months before the war began. She joined the Army Nurse Corps as a second lieutenant and worked in a military hospital stateside. As the war moved toward its bloody climax, Muniz Esquivel moved toward the front. She treated mounting numbers of casualties in England, then France, then Luxembourg. In what was once the summer palace of the Duchess of Luxembourg, she received both American and German wounded. She recalled to an oral historian, "That was where they used to bring the wounded back by loads. We were always on the go. Most of the time we were dressed. We didn't have time. There was no way that we could really get undressed to sleep."

Patients arrived on litters, and were then placed on top of cots until a triage nurse could determine whether a patient needed to head right to surgery or into a ward. "It could have been beautiful before all those casualties were there," Esquivel says. "The grounds were big, but I never went on the grounds."

While it is easy to determine how many Puerto Ricans from the island were drafted and enlisted during World War II, it is harder to figure out how many Puerto Ricans served from families that had already migrated north. Eugene Calderon was one of them, and his strange story tells you something about the difficulties a legally segregated military had in dealing with Latinos.

Calderon was born in San Juan in 1919, and moved to New York as a boy with one of the earliest waves of Puerto Ricans in the 1920s.

Eugene Calderon. In the segregated military of the Second World War, white officers complained when the young Puerto Rican New Yorker was assigned to their unit. When he was moved to the famed Tuskegee Airmen, black soldiers and aviators did not understand why he was with them either. After the war, Calderon founded some of the institutional pillars of Latino New York. CREDIT: COURTESY OF CALDERON FAMILY

"My father was a gang leader in East Harlem," recalled his son Gene. "And the police in the area were cracking down. They got a hold of his group and were arresting them. They missed catching him by about three feet.

"The following day he enlisted in the military and that is how he began his military career." Calderon told the military he wanted to fly, and he was sent to Alabama. "When he landed in Tuskegee they put him in with the white officers, and the white officers complained that he was not white. So they moved him over to the black officers in the black barracks and they complained because he wasn't black. He ended up being in the third barracks, where he and another Latino were, and they were the only two in the barracks." Calderon became a company clerk for the now famed Tuskegee Airmen.

Calderon told his son the army used a subtle dodge to control the number of fliers of color by monitoring their flying hours. "And as soon as they got anywhere close to certifications they would transfer them to a different area and then they would have to start accumulating those hours again.

"When he got close to his hours they moved him [from Tuskegee] out to South Dakota in the middle of the winter. Here is this Puerto Rican from New York City in South Dakota in the middle of the winter. Then they sent him to the Midwest. Here he is trying to do something, wanting to contribute, and yet every time he came close it was like he was being tempted with a treat and as soon as you got too close it was taken away from you.

"In Tuskegee he had a real sense of what discrimination was all about. He never thought of it in New York, because in East Harlem there were Italians and blacks and Puerto Ricans and Jews and Irish. When he went down south they didn't have that kind of integration, so he got the full sense of, 'Why am I being separated?'"

Guy Gabaldon could trace his family's presence in America back to the arrival of Spanish soldiers in the American Southwest, some four hundred years before. Gabaldon was born and raised in the East Los Angeles neighborhood of Boyle Heights. At the age of ten, he was already earning his own money, shining shoes downtown.

Gabaldon was tough, and ready for whatever he might face. Friends like Lyle Nakano remember young Gabaldon as a wild boy: "Guy was always trying to prove he had a lot of guts. He used to jump out of second-story windows, hop trucks, ride freight trains on a dare and sometimes without a dare. But one thing: Guy always stood by his friends."

His life took a peculiar turn for a Mexican kid from Boyle Heights. A Japanese-American family took him into their home during his middle teen years. He didn't know it at the time, but the Nakano family was giving him life-changing gifts. "They taught me Japanese," Gabaldon said. "But mostly, they taught me how to love."

History intervened to make Gabaldon's novel life valuable to his country. Japan attacked the American naval base at Pearl Harbor, Hawaii, on December 7, 1941, and the next day, America was at war. California's place on the Pacific coast led to panic, and turned suspicion on tens of thousands of Japanese-Americans. Whether recent arrivals or second- and third-generation Americans, a hundred thousand ethnic Japanese were rounded up and sent inland to hastily built relocation camps.

Marine Private First Class Guy Gabaldon (*center in sunglasses*). After living with a Japanese family in the years leading up to the Second World War, Gabaldon watched his foster family sent to internment camps after Pearl Harbor. The Japanese he picked up along the way came in very handy after he enlisted in the Marines and was sent to the Pacific. He became the "Pied Piper of Saipan," convincing cornered, outnumbered, and desperate Japanese soldiers to surrender rather than fight. By doing so, he saved thousands of Japanese and American lives. He is seen here with civilians on Saipan.
CREDIT: STEVEN RUBIN

The Nakanos were sent to an internment camp in Arizona. Guy Gabaldon lost his friends and the people who had become his family. "I was left alone in L.A. All my buddies were gone." On his seventeenth birthday, in 1943, Gabaldon headed for a recruiting office. His new family would be the United States Marine Corps. An elite military force, the Marine Corps did not throw out the welcome mat to racial and ethnic minority recruits. Latino numbers were small, and the door was not opened to blacks until 1942, when a few all-black units were raised. But Gabaldon had one thing few men turning up in California recruiting offices did: He spoke Japanese. At the same time that Japanese-Americans were heading to internment camps, America was heading to war with Japan.

By 1944, U.S. forces, including Gabaldon's 2nd Marine Regiment, were heading west and tightening the noose on Japan's dwindling empire. Next in the chain of islands "hopped" by the marines was Saipan in the Mariana Islands. With each stepping-stone across the Pacific, American forces were closer to being able to mount regular and sustained attacks on the Japanese home islands. If Saipan was secured, enormous bombers, the B-29 Superfortresses, would be well within range of Japan.

As America drew closer to Japan, however, the already fierce fighting became even more savage. Gabaldon's commanding officer, Captain John Swabie, remembers the young marine's first impressions of Saipan: "When we landed and Guy saw for the first time wounded and killed Japanese soldiers he froze. It really bothered him."

He didn't stay frozen for long. His first night on Saipan, the young marine went off on his own—with no orders from his superior officers—and headed behind Japanese lines. Gabaldon remembered his early forays behind the lines: "I came back with a couple of prisoners. My commanding officer, he says, 'Don't you ever do that again.' He says, 'This is the Marine Corps and there will be teamwork here.'"

His early success did not win the argument. His commanding officer went on: "'You're not a prima donna. You're not working on your own.' I says, 'Yes, sir, very good, sir.' And that night I filled my pockets with ammunition, and I went back into Japanese territory."

His secret weapon? The Japanese language skills picked up living with the Nakano family in East L.A. Gabaldon went to the Japanese soldiers, cut off from resupply, fighting American forces growing stronger by the day, and told them fighting on was pointless. "At night I'd go to caves.

I'd get to one side of the mouth of the cave and say, 'You are completely surrounded. I've got a bunch of marines here with me behind the trees. If you don't surrender, I'll have to kill you.'

"And usually, it worked. Not always. I'd have to throw grenades in and kill. And I'd capture maybe ten or fifteen, twenty at a time."

He was taking prisoners. He was also saving lives. On island after island, American soldiers and marines were forced to flush out Japanese soldiers determined to resist to the bitter end, and kill them. Square mile by square mile, the Americans took more and more of Saipan, until, trapped on the tip of the island, Japanese troops began to launch suicide attacks. Many of the besieged men had concluded they had only two choices: kill or be killed. Guy Gabaldon offered them another option.

In July, weeks after the initial American landing on Saipan, marine patrols came upon a large group of Japanese soldiers. In their midst stood a single marine. Many of the Japanese were still armed, but no longer in combat. An American teenager was ordering them around—in Japanese. Gabaldon alone was bringing in eight hundred prisoners.

"I had them look out at the ocean and I said, 'The war is over. Look at all those destroyers and navy ships out there. This is pointless. Go home to your families.'" He was saving the lives of Japanese soldiers, but don't forget that by ending their resistance, he was also saving the lives of hundreds of his fellow marines who would have certainly died in brutal charges on fortified Japanese positions, manned by an enemy ready to fight to the death.

Guy Gabaldon was given the nickname "the Pied Piper of Saipan." That whimsical name undersold the magnitude of what a teenage marine had done. Acting on his own initiative, Gabaldon had captured half a Japanese regiment by himself. By taking more than a thousand enemy soldiers out of the action, he saved the lives of countless Americans. His commanding officer nominated him for a Medal of Honor. He was given a lesser honor, the still considerable Silver Star. Later he was given the Navy Cross, second only to the Medal of Honor, awarded for "extreme gallantry" and "going beyond the call of duty."

Years later, Gabaldon remembered success had a hundred fathers. "After the campaign we set up a rest camp and high-ranking officers came in and promotions and decorations were handed out to those who had earned them. Pretty much everyone in my company was promoted, except me."

Half a world away, in Europe, another Mexican, one who came to the United States as a little boy, was helping to bring victory for his adopted country within reach. Macario Garcia was born in Villa de Castaño in the Sierra Madre Mountains, one of ten children. The family moved to Texas to work as sharecroppers. Accounts differ as to how much schooling the young farmhand managed to get, but they agree it wasn't much.

Less than a year after Pearl Harbor, twenty-two-year-old Garcia was inducted into the United States Army. Less than two years after that, while Private Gabaldon was wading ashore onto Saipan, Private Garcia hit Utah Beach in Normandy. All along, he risked his life for a country still not his own.

Garcia was wounded in the fight to liberate Cherbourg, France. He helped capture Paris from the Germans, and was in the regiment that broke through the Nazis' defensive Siegfried line. In one battle Garcia destroyed a machine gun, took the gunner prisoner, scouted behind the German lines, and was once again wounded. By now a sergeant, the young Mexican had a Bronze Star and two Purple Hearts.

In November 1944, Sergeant Garcia led a squad as the U.S. Army fought its way into Germany. He and his men reached Grosshau, between the Belgian border and the German city of Cologne. Garcia found his squad held down by machine-gun fire. Macario's son Robert had heard the story many times. "It's an ambush. They're getting chewed up. They have no cover. The guy next to my dad is killed and my dad is hit in the shoulder and in the foot."

Garcia crawled through the grass, making his way around one of the machine-gun nests. He hurled grenades and charged the gun position, killing three Germans. Because Garcia was between the two lines, he was exposed to fire from both sides, friend and foe alike. He advanced on the second machine gun, catching seven Germans by surprise. He killed three, and took four others prisoner. Garcia's son recalls that Macario was seriously wounded. "My dad was covered in blood and in horrible pain. He couldn't move one arm. Couldn't feel his foot. But he refused medical treatment—flat-out refused—and kept fighting until the Germans had been decimated or ran away.

"Then he collapsed and lost consciousness."

The newspapers called him "the Fearless Mexican." He became the first Mexican citizen to receive the Medal of Honor. The citation accompanying the award told of Garcia's "conspicuous heroism, his inspiring, courageous conduct, and his complete disregard for his personal safety."

THE WAR PROVED to white America that the stereotypes about minority men and women in uniform were not just wrong, but outrageously wrong. A lot had changed while the servicemen and -women were away. Too much hadn't. After millions of men were taken from the civilian labor market, the United States experienced severe shortages of workers. Some of that gap was filled by women, who marched into factories and offices to take the places of fathers, brothers, and husbands now in the service. The lives of Latino workingmen and -women would move on two different and vital tracks during the 1940s: battlefront and home front. Developments in both would have unforeseen impacts on the other that would play out for years to come.

In the spring of 1942, the first alarms were sounded about farm labor. By harvesttime, it was threatened, the crops needed to feed the home front and soldiers around the world would be rotting in the fields with no one to pick them.

In August of that same year, the U.S. and Mexican governments signed an agreement for the supply of one million temporary workers to be transported and paid by Uncle Sam. Part of the agreement promised that Mexican workers in the United States would not be mistreated.

And so they came. *Braceros*, farmworkers (from the Spanish word for "arm," *brazo*), began to arrive by the end of September. They went to work in twenty-one states, harvesting sugar beets, plums, tomatoes, peaches, and cotton. Almost immediately, *braceros* went on strike in Stockton, California, after American farmers paid less than what had been promised in Mexico. The farmers backed down, and the *braceros* went back to work. With each year the numbers grew: By the end of 1943, 76,000; by the end of 1944, 118,000; by 1945, more than 300,000 Mexican men had worked in the United States under the Bracero Program.

When the war was over, American farmers said they still needed the strong backs and willing labor of Mexican workers. Mexican citizens became a permanent part of the agricultural workforce of the United States from then on. The landscape had shifted from the widespread deportations of the 1930s, when there were far more American workers than there was work to do. U.S. farmers pressured the State Department to continue the Bracero Program, and more than twenty-six thousand Mexican agricultural laborers were in American fields in 1946.

MEXICAN-AMERICANS WERE A growing presence on the streets of California's big cities. During the war, the streets of Los Angeles were teeming with workers who poured in to work in the plants supplying America's vast military, alongside soldiers and sailors on leave and reporting for duty to be shipped abroad, and with a new group of young, American-born Latinos. It turned out to be a volatile mix.

Many young first- and second-generation Mexican-Americans were below draft age, but were old enough to share in the general prosperity brought to Los Angeles by the war. There was work, and work meant money for leisure-time activities, and the public display of an evolving culture that was no longer Mexican and not quite American either.

Styles have long zipped around America from one group to another. Look at the way in recent years baseball caps first had their brims pushed to the side, then pushed to the back. Then the familiar team logos moved from their traditional position on the front of the crown, grew in size, changed color, gained metallic stitching and ever more elaborate trim, and jumped from black and Latino urban youth to the white majority. In much the same way the man's suit, an emblem of adulthood, respectability, and conformity, was revolutionized . . . reworked . . . reimagined . . . and somewhere along the way became the zoot suit.

The "drapes" of Harlem, featuring high-waisted pants with legs ballooned at the knees, narrowing to a tapered "pegged" ankle, held up by dressy suspenders, topped with a jacket that reached the knees with a cinched midsection and flamboyantly padded shoulders, were embraced by Southern Californians in the early war years.

In wartime, the production of automobiles built for civilian use was severely curtailed, gasoline and meat and much else was rationed, and the zoot suit was also banned, because it used so much fabric. The June 21, 1943, edition of *Newsweek* said that despite the War Production Board ruling, "the zoot suit has continued to thrive—mainly through the diligence of bootleg tailors." Seven decades later it may seem a little silly to take youth fashion so seriously as a possible source of rebellion in wartime. *Newsweek* concluded that the U.S. government was taking no chances. "The War Frauds Division got an injunction forbidding one shop to sell any of the 800 zoot suits in stock. Claiming that the shopkeeper had contributed to 'hoodlumism,' agents said they had found that great numbers of zoot coats and pants were being made in New York and Chicago."

What could be better for an eighteen-year-old eager to signal his membership in a distinct culture? Your parents, often Mexican-born, tried to attract as little attention to themselves as possible and wanted you to do the same. You adopted a new barrio language, Caló, mixing archaic Spanish, English, and the Spanish of Mexico. Caught out between two cultures, not quite at home in either, you could now invent yourself.

The invented self who emerged on the streets of Southwestern cities was the pachuco, a working-class kid with his own clothes, his own language, a gravity-defying, swooping marcel-style hairdo (short on the sides with long waves of hair atop the head held in place by gel), and a street posture meant to signal a cool contempt for the conformity to the mainstream that was desired by worried parents and white authority figures.

Drop into this volatile mix a state on edge from fear of foreigners, suspicion of infiltration of fifth columnists (residents in sympathy with a country's external enemies), and wild rumors circulating about the Nazi recruitment of Mexicans in California. Something was bound to happen, and it did.

In Los Angeles on the night of June 3, 1943, a sailor thought a pachuco was lunging for him, and a fistfight started. Fights between zoot-suited young men and soldiers and sailors escalated into days and nights of street battles. The newspapers, the police, and elected officials quickly took sides, and it was no surprise that public opinion landed heavily on the side of uniformed servicemen.

Once the violence began, it grew, and spread. On June 7, the *Los Angeles Times* warned of storms ahead. Instead of heading off the trouble, the newspaper helped get the word out. Men in uniform began to drive in from as far away as Las Vegas to get in on the action. Some two thousand soldiers and sailors rushed into private homes and movie theaters looking for young zoot suiters to beat up. Eventually the crowd was stopping cars on the street, dragging away drivers and passengers, and destroying the cars.

For more than a week groups of men, soldiers, sailors, and their allies set upon Mexican teens, often stripping them down to their underwear right on the streets and setting their clothes on fire. Even as the violence subsided in the city of Los Angeles, it spread to the nearby cities of Pasadena and Long Beach, and as far away as San Diego and Phoenix. This wasn't just about clothes and youthful rebellion anymore. Latinos may have been the first victims, but they were eventually joined by African-Americans, Asians, and their white friends. If you were different enough, you were fair game.

It's a small thing, but notice: In much the way massacres of American Indians ended up being called "battles" in history books, the disturbances came to be known as the Zoot Suit Riots, not "the Sailor Riots" or "the Soldier Riots." In this one small turn of a phrase, victim becomes perpetrator; the target becomes the cause.

Eventually, investigations, hearings, and inquiries would conclude that the sailors started the riots. While no sailors were arrested or charged with a crime, more than five hundred Latinos were charged with crimes such as assault, disorderly conduct, and vagrancy. The *Los Angeles Times*, after playing a role in raising the temperature on the streets of the city, went as far as to run a headline: "Zoot Suiters Learn Lesson in Fight with Servicemen." Commission findings did not matter. The *Times* verdict more likely mirrored the attitudes of many of its Anglo readers: "Those gamin dandies, the zoot suiters, [have] learned a great moral lesson from service men, mostly sailors." *Gamin* is not a word used in newspapers today. It means a raggedly dressed street child.

"All that is needed to end lawlessness is more of the same kind of actions that is [sic] being exercised by the servicemen," the *LA Times* went on. "If this continues, zooters will soon be as scarce as hen's teeth."

After years of economic depression, the sailors roaming the streets looking for Mexican teenagers probably were not all that different in socioeconomic terms from their targets. In June 1943, all a poor kid from Anywhere, USA, had to do to separate himself from working-class Latinos in southern California was put on a uniform.

Zooters were, from the outset, heavily Latinos. Yet the media accounts of the riots, and the investigations that followed, played down the ethnic identity of the boys who were beaten, stripped, and hunted in their own hometown. The *Los Angeles Times* chose to stress cultural and social differences, rather than ethnic ones, telling its readers racial prejudices were not a cause or catalyst, because zoot suits were worn by many different races.

What had the Mexican and Mexican-American young men done? Their main offense was just being who they were. Not only were they "outsiders" (a peculiar designation for residents of a city founded by a column of Spaniards, Indians, and mestizos coming up from Mexico and naming their city for a revered title of the Virgin Mary, the Queen of Angels), but they were outsiders exuberantly embracing a separate style of dress, of speech, even their own dances. They were not hiding. They were not pretending to accept mainstream Anglo norms.

In his book on the zoot suiters, University of Southern California historian Mauricio Mazón grasps the strangeness of the fights on the streets. "They are a remarkable event in that they defy simple classification. They were not about zoot-suiters rioting, and they were not, in any conventional sense of the word, 'riots.'

"No one was killed. No one sustained massive injuries. Property damage was slight. No major or minor judicial decisions stemmed from the riots. There was no pattern to arrests. Convictions were few and highly discretionary. There were no political manifestos or heroes originating from the riots, although later on the riots would assume political significance for a different generation. What the riots lack in hard incriminating evidence, they make up for in a plethora of emotions, fantasies, and symbols."

Those ten nights in Los Angeles have launched dozens of books and articles, films and theatrical works. History, and memory, can accomplish odd and useful things. Mexican-American community organizations in Los Angeles had already been jolted into action by what came to be called "the Sleepy Lagoon Murder," the killing of a Mexican-American man, José Díaz, in 1942. Though Díaz's fatal wounds were consistent with being hit by a car, almost two dozen Latino men who had been fighting were charged with involvement in Díaz's death.

Several were acquitted on all counts, but twelve of the young men were convicted of three serious charges: murder, assault with a deadly weapon, and intent to commit murder. An all-white jury sentenced three of the young men to life in prison, and three others were given five years to life. To the wider Anglo world, the murder was a sign of the delinquency and danger associated with Latino young men. To the Mexican civic leaders of Los Angeles, it was a reminder of the suspicion, contempt, and ignorance that shaped the majority view of their lives.

A group calling itself the Youth Committee for the Defense of Mexican American Youth wrote a letter to Harry Truman's vice president, Henry Wallace, one of the most liberal politicians ever to hold high public office in the United States. The strategy behind the letter was straightforward, astute, and at the same time strangely touching. The committee told Vice President Wallace, "We feel you should know about the bad situation facing us Mexican boys and girls and our whole Spanish-speaking community."

The note went on to tell of the accused in the Sleepy Lagoon Murder, conceding that some were no angels, but offering a glimpse of day-to-day life in *el barrio*. "These 24 boys come from our neighborhood. In our neighborhood there are no recreation centers and the nearest movie is about a mile away. We have no place to play so the Police are always arresting us. That's why most of the boys on trial now have a record with the Police."

Then the letter turned an important corner and got down to business. The young people, in effect, told Henry Wallace, *This is what our lives are like, Mr. Vice President. Some of us work in defense plants. Many of us have older brothers fighting in the Pacific*: "There is still a lot of discrimination in theaters and swimming pools and the Police are always arresting us and searching us by the hundreds when all we want to do is go into a dance or go swimming or just stand around and not bother anybody. They treat us like we are criminals just by being Mexicans or of Mexican descent."

The letter continued with a plea for prowar educational materials in Spanish and English, more volunteer opportunities and access to public places, and relief from the discrimination the young people saw in their daily lives. Just to reiterate, one last time, the letter closed, "We don't like Hitler or the Japanese either."

The arrests immediately following the death of José Díaz set off a wave of anti-Mexican panic. Southern California newspapers called for a crackdown, and police departments responded with hundreds of arrests of young Mexican men on a wide variety of charges.

The Sleepy Lagoon convictions were overturned on appeal in 1944. In reviewing the record of the first trial, the appellate judge found a long list of irregularities: The crowded courtroom made it impossible for the accused to sit with their own lawyers; the sarcastic and dismissive trial judge, Charles W. Fricke, consistently treated all attempts by defense lawyers to protect their clients' interests with withering contempt. The evidence presented at trial, the appeals court found, was contradictory, unsubstantiated, and insufficient to sustain guilty findings in charges as serious as murder.

Yet the judge would not concede that the Sleepy Lagoon defendants had received unfavorable treatment in court because they were "of Mexican descent." He noted that the murder victim, José Díaz, was also Latino, as were the young men injured in a group fistfight leading up to the arrests. The reversal shot down accusations of prejudice as bluntly as it shot down the convictions by concluding, ". . . there is no ground revealed by the record upon which it can be said that this prosecution was conceived in, born, or nurtured by the seeds of racial prejudice.

"It was instituted to protect Mexican people in the enjoyment of rights and privileges which are inherent in every one, whatever may be their race or creed, and regardless of whether their status in life be that of the rich and influential or the more lowly and poor."

THE ZOOT-SUIT RIOTS and their aftermath were understood very differently by Latinos. Looking back, José Ángel Gutiérrez noted the paradox of Americans fighting Americans during wartime. "This was happening as the US was fighting the Nazis. America was supposed to stand for tolerance, for equality. Yet servicemen were bashing [the] hell out of other Americans because they weren't standard-issue white Americans—at a time when Mexican Americans were making a mighty contribution to the war effort. These beatings and the humiliation colored the worldview of generations of Latinos to come. People like me."

People like me. It is a vitally important phrase to keep in mind as the Second World War moved toward its conclusion. What could Latinos have concluded in the 1940s about their fellow citizens? Did the others think we were equal? Did they think we were Americans? Did they even think we were "doing our part" to win this war? For Mexican-American civic leader Paul Coronel, speaking at a public meeting, the answer to all was clearly no. "American people have not regarded the Mexican American as an equal, racially or economically. Our American institutions, our schools, communities, [and] churches, have regarded the Mexican as a problem and not as an asset to our American society."

Beating the Japanese and Germans was going to be one thing. Defeating entrenched social norms and long-held stereotypes was going to be more complicated. A new fight began for thousands of servicemen: The freedom and liberation American soldiers, sailors, airmen, and marines had brought to people around the world now had to be secured back home.

Millions of people who helped the United States win the war were coming home hoping for their share of the victory, and a "return to normal." At the same time the old normal was not going to be good enough for men who had advanced in uniform, risen in status, and might not be willing to simply return to the life they left behind years before. A returning veteran noted, "Mexican-American soldiers shed at least a quarter of the blood spilled at Bataan [a brutal battle to recapture the Philippines]. What they want now is a decent job, a decent home, and a chance to live peacefully in the community." A Mexican-American newspaperman echoed that hope. "After this struggle, the status of the Mexican-Americans will be different."

IN SEPTEMBER 1945, just a few weeks after he was celebrated by the new president, Harry Truman, who draped the country's highest military honor around his neck, the "Fearless Mexican," Macario Garcia, came home to Texas. He spoke before the Houston Rotary Club and was celebrated at a party and dance by the League of United Latin American Citizens, LULAC, near his hometown of Sugar Land.

It was the next day, September 10, 1945, that Garcia stopped at the Oasis Café for a soda. Newly demobilized servicemen and -women were everywhere in those days, in ports and railroad stations, streaming out of bases and forts onto the streets of cities and towns. Back home, Sergeant Garcia was not a decorated hero, not the "Fearless Mexican" of newsreels and press releases. For some, he was still just a Mexican.

He was refused service. A sign in the restaurant window read, No Dogs, No Mexicans. Mac Garcia knocked over tables and broke windows. He punched the woman who owned the place in the mouth, and was attacked by her brother, holding a baseball bat. When the fight was over, the Medal of Honor recipient was arrested for aggravated assault. Extraordinary heroism on the battlefield wasn't going to be enough. The Bronze Star ribbon on your uniform that told the world you were ready to bleed for your adopted country, and the Purple Heart that showed you had, weren't going to be enough.

In the bad old days, Macario Garcia might simply have been thrown into jail, without too many questions about the circumstances of the fight, or who might have been at fault. In 1945, even in Texas, it made a big difference if a Mexican dragged out of a fight had just won the Medal of Honor.

National radio star Walter Winchell, nobody's idea of a liberal but a man who knew a good story when he saw one, took to the airwaves. "This hero . . . [who] fought for our country and won the highest award our country can give, is named Sergeant Marcio [*sic*] Garcia, a Mexican. He was refused service, though he was wearing the United States uniform at the time. The persons responsible for this dreadful assault could hardly be Texans. Texans do not fight with baseball bats."

Since Texas split from Mexico a century before, cases like this attracted little attention. A Mexican was charged with a crime. An Anglo prosecutor brought the case; a mostly Anglo or all-Anglo jury heard the case. Guilty as charged. Mac Garcia, however, was a Mexican with a Medal of Honor. Network and syndicated media had new reach and power, and could make national stories out of local ones. Garcia also had LULAC, the Hispanic civil rights organization founded in 1929 in his corner, and LULAC had friends. Garcia was defended in court by John Herrera, a descendant of historic figures in Texas history who was to become a LULAC national

"Mac" Garcia's travels in Texas were well-covered in the state press after he returned from Washington with the country's highest military honor. When he was refused service in a South Texas café, the story was eventually covered nationwide.
CREDIT: NARA

president, and later was defended by former Texas state attorney general James Allred.

National and regional press flocked to the story. In the glare of national attention, the case was repeatedly postponed and then quietly dropped. Like so many of his wartime comrades, Garcia moved on to the business of living. He became an American citizen, got married, had three kids, finished his high school diploma. As if to illustrate the duality, the twin identities of Latinos, Garcia also earned the rare distinction of receiving one of Mexico's highest military honors, the Mérito Militar.

When he died in a car crash in 1972, the Houston City Council named a street in his honor. The Macario Garcia Army Reserve Center was dedicated by Vice President George H. W. Bush, and a middle school now bears his name in his hometown of Sugar Land. Just half a century separated a decorated vet and his encounter with a No Dogs, No Mexicans sign, and a school dedicated to his memory.

Untold thousands of Latino vets went home, like other Americans, and got started in civilian life. Indignities large and small were visited on other returning Latino soldiers, sailors, and marines who had not been given the country's highest award for bravery.

Up in Chicago, the hunger for new housing for returning servicemen saw white veterans turning over cars, swinging bats, and throwing rocks to keep black vets out of newly built public housing. The GI Bill of Rights opened the doors to the middle class for millions of new civilians, but black and brown veterans found their benefits harder to use: There were too few seats in colleges and universities that admitted more than a token number of blacks and Latinos; the GI Bill provision that guaranteed mortgages for veterans also required they be used to purchase new rather than existing houses, but too few new homes were built in the ghetto and the barrio.

Returning to cities that had built hardly any new housing in the previous fifteen years, they struggled to find a place to live with new brides. Old employers had gotten along without them. Their fellow citizens were sometimes slow to learn how much expectations were raised in young Latinos by all the growing up they did while liberating other countries, and fighting side by side with men from everywhere.

Eugene Calderon went home to New York City. He earned an undergraduate degree from New York University and a master's degree from the City University of New York. The onetime gang leader became a policeman. His son said his father went back to *el barrio*, his old turf. "He literally went back to the police station where they knew him. The day he walked in they recognized who he was and they wanted to arrest him. He had to show them the badge and the whole thing."

Calderon did not just serve his time and build a career for himself. Looking around and seeing a department with only a few Latinos, in 1957 he helped found the Hispanic Society, to represent the interests of Latino officers inside the department, and help recruit more Latinos to the nation's largest police force. After a successful career at the NYPD, Calderon moved on to administrative work at New York's Board of Education.

The former gang leader rose to become first the administrator for the school district that included East Harlem, and eventually the deputy superintendent of the city's board of education. Calderon oversaw New York schools at a tumultuous time, when minority parents confronted a largely white teacher corps and administration to demand more local control and a better-quality education. He played what you might call an insider-outsider role, helping to create some of the premier educational institutions of Puerto Rican New York: Aspira, a group encouraging high school completion and college for young people, and El Museo del Barrio—the Museum of the Barrio—which showcased the work of Latino artists and taught Latino history through art.

He built a life of achievement: World War II veteran, trailblazing police officer and detective, cofounder of community pillars, a senior leader of the largest school system in the country. When he died in 2007 the *New York Times* did not run an obituary.

EQUAL RIGHTS FOLLOWING the war were demanded by men like Dr. Hector P. Garcia. He was born to schoolteacher parents in Tamaulipas, Mexico, in 1914. His family, like thousands of others, fled the violence and instability of the Mexican Revolution by coming to the United States. José and Faustina Garcia opened a dry-goods store in Mercedes, Texas.

The Garcia family grew to include ten children. After education in the University of Texas system, Garcia received his medical doctorate in 1940. Remarkably, he and five of his siblings became physicians. Garcia enlisted

Hector Garcia, MD, with his medical school classmates before the outbreak of the Second World War. Dr. Garcia (*front row, right*) often found his superior officers reluctant to believe he was not only college-educated, but a trained physician. He served as a combat infantryman and in the medical corps; he left the U.S. Army as a major. CREDIT: TEXAS A&MU-CC

in the U.S. Army as soon as his residency was completed in 1942, and volunteered for combat duty. As a trained physician and already in his late twenties, Garcia could have avoided the most dangerous-duty wartime service. Instead, he commanded an infantry company in Europe, eventually won promotion to major, and was awarded the Bronze Star and six battle stars. Those medals weren't all he got in Europe. He met and married an Italian woman, Wanda Fusillo, and brought her back to Texas, opening his first civilian practice in Corpus Christi on the Texas Gulf Coast.

Garcia was familiar with LULAC and its work, but as time went on he heard more and more stories of discrimination touching his fellow veterans. He talked with his friend Vicente Ximenes about an organization specifically for Latino veterans: "Our idea was for our people to have a place where they could come and complain about discrimination," recalled Ximenes.

"Many of his patients were veterans. As Hector knew well, under the GI Bill of 1944 they were entitled to medical benefits, low-cost loans to

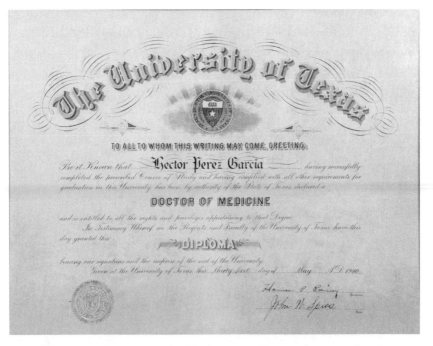

Hector Garcia's medical diploma from the University of Texas at Galveston. Born in the Mexican state of Tamaulipas, Garcia was a naturalized American citizen and the descendant of Spanish land-grant holders. Like thousands of Mexican families, the Garcias fled north to escape the tumult of the Mexican Revolution. CREDIT: TEXAS A&MU-CC

start businesses, and financial help to attend college. But only the Anglo veterans were getting those benefits. I did utilize the bill, but it was a never-ending struggle to be treated the same as Anglo vets."

Rolando Hinojosa-Smith was a teenager when the men came home to Mercedes, the town where Hector Garcia grew up. More than sixty years later he remembers what his neighbors faced when they tried to enroll in college. "You had to report to the county courthouse to submit your discharge papers, so you could enroll in college. And the men in charge of making the referrals were some bad guys.

"*Mexicanos* would come over, and they would refer them all to manual trades schools: 'Hey, there's a boatbuilding school over in Odessa.'" Hinojosa-Smith encountered the educational steering firsthand when he came home from the Korean War. "When I said I wanted to enroll in the University of Texas in Austin, I told them my brothers had both gone there and had all graduated. I don't think they believed me."

In March 1948, Hector Garcia brought seven hundred veterans together in Corpus Christi. From that meeting came the American GI

Forum, dedicated to fighting for the rights of Latino vets. The organization's motto, "Education Is Our Freedom and Freedom Should be Everybody's Business," reflected that earliest orientation toward making sure Latino vets received their full benefits as equals to other Americans.

Right around the time of the GI Forum's founding, a case of discrimination emerged that energized the new organization and began its history of activism.

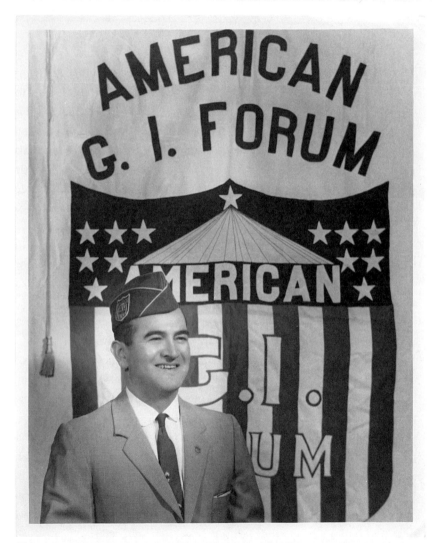

After the war was over, Garcia became a civic leader. A steady stream of stories from Mexican-American veterans denied equal housing, employment, and educational opportunity led to the founding of the American GI Forum. CREDIT: TEXAS A&MU-CC

Until a constitutional amendment swept away poll taxes, they were widely used, especially in Southern states, to exclude minority voters from the polls. Dr. Garcia wanted to turn organized vets into voters, and he urged them to pay their poll tax and increase Latino political power.
CREDIT: TEXAS A&MU-CC

The American GI Forum Says: BUY YOUR POLL TAX

Felix Longoria, a Mexican-American army private from Three Rivers, Texas, had been killed in the Philippines. It took more than three years for the remains to make their way from the Pacific islands to South Texas. The Rice Funeral Home in town refused to handle the burial. Its owner, Tom Kennedy, reportedly told the soldier's young widow that it did not make any difference that Longoria was a veteran, because "You know how the Latin people get drunk and lay around all the time. The last time we let them use the chapel, they got all drunk and we just can't control them—so the white people object to it, and we just can't let them use it."

Many Americans may not be aware of the past segregation of Latinos in daily life that existed in many places in the American Southwest.

Private Felix Longoria of Three Rivers, Texas, with his wife, Beatrice, and his daughter, Adela. Longoria, killed in the Philippines in the closing days of the Second World War, was denied burial in his local cemetery by a nearby funeral home when his body finally made its way back to Texas from the Pacific. CREDIT: ADELA LONGORIA

Schools, movie theaters, retail stores, and other institutions often had different accommodations, inferior ones, for their Mexican and Mexican-American customers. The system was not as deeply entrenched or thoroughly abusive as Jim Crow in the South of the old Confederacy. It varied from place to place, and varied in its severity, but systematic exclusion and second-class treatment were common for Latinos in the Southwest for decades before the civil rights movement.

Vicente Ximenes remembers not attending a school with Anglo children until he was a teenager, and even then the welcome mat was hardly rolled out at his feet. He was one of only five Mexican-American graduates of the local high school, and he and his friends arrived at the graduation banquet only to find they were seated not with their classmates but "at the corner. There were five seats for those five Mexican Americans that had graduated," said Ximenes. He and his friends decided to skip graduation and get their diplomas by mail. "We had to give a message to our teachers, that things had to change, that we were hurt, but we had graduated," he said.

Hinojosa-Smith said small towns in the Rio Grande Valley, where Anglos and Mexicans lived side by side for generations, were heavily segregated. "In towns like Mercedes, railroad tracks divided Texas Mexicans from Texas Anglos." Mexican residents of these small towns were always in the majority, Hinojosa-Smith said, but things started to change after World War II. "My father got two veterans to run for seats on the county council, and they won." He remembers the growing sense that it was possible for Mexicans to begin to push back. "And that never would have happened in the twenties or thirties. We just said to ourselves, 'We don't have to be like this all the time.'"

In earlier decades, in response to mistreatment, exclusion, or discrimination, "There would have been silence. There would have been resentment, naturally. As for action, no.

"Schools were also segregated for the longest time. I went to hundred percent Mexican schools, as did my brothers and sister." Rolando Hinojosa-Smith got his place at the University of Texas after the Korean War. He earned a PhD and became a professor and a celebrated writer.

In the context of 1940s Texas, neither Anglos nor Mexican-Americans would be surprised at a funeral home sending a Mexican family elsewhere for a burial. However, Ximenes and Garcia and the rest of the GI

SAN ANTONIO, TEXAS, FRIDAY, MARCH 11, 1949   44

Chapel Refused Reburial, Says Dr. Garcia

A HEARING into the reburial of Felix Longoria, a Three Rivers Latin-American truck driver who lost his life on Luzon, is under way at Three Rivers by a committee of the Texas House of Representatives. In photo above, young Longoria's father, Guadalupe Longoria, Sr., (left) is questioned by Atty. Gus Garcia of San Antonio about statement Garcia prepared for him. Longoria had trouble remembering signing it and where it was prepared. Left to right, are: Longoria, Garcia, Three Rivers Atty. Harry Schulz and M. A. Childers of San Antonio, counsel for T. W. Kennedy, Jr., owner of funeral home in Three Rivers.—**Evening News Photo.**

The refusal of a local funeral home to handle the Longoria funeral was typical of the indignities large and small suffered by Mexicans and Mexican-Americans in small Texas towns. The sensitivities of the public toward the plight of veterans helped the story make local, then national headlines. CREDIT: TEXAS A&MU-CC

Forum were convinced that Private Longoria, killed in the service of his country, would bring awareness of the daily humiliations of prejudice to a wider world.

The offense is well detailed in a poster publicizing a rally in support of the Longorias and against the funeral home:

El American GI Forum de Corpus Christi requiere su presencia para que venga a oir los datos de esta CRUEL HUMILLACIÓN a uno de nuestros HEROES Soldado de la ultima gran GUERRA. Todos los veteranos y sus familias y público en general deben asistir sin FALTA o sin EXCUSAS.

Cuando una casa Funeraria se Niega a Honrar a los RESTOS de un Ciudadano Americano solamente porque es de origen mejicano entonces es TIEMPO que no unicamente el American GI Forum sino todo el pueblo levante a protestar esta injusticia.

The American GI Forum of Corpus Christi requires your presence to come hear the details of this CRUEL HUMILIA-TION of one of our HERO soldiers of the last great WAR. All veterans and their families and the general public must assist without FAIL or without EXCUSES.

When a funeral home neglects to honor the remains of an American Citizen only because he is of Mexican origin, it is therefore TIME not only for the American GI Forum but the entire community to rise to protest this injustice.

Garcia sent telegrams to people of influence, hoping to bring attention to the Longoria family. The response to almost every note he sent was silence. *Almost* every note. One sent to an ambitious new U.S. senator from Texas, Lyndon Johnson, got a reply. Garcia's telegram read in part:

In our estimation, this action in Three Rivers is in direct con-tradiction of those same principles for which this American soldier made the supreme sacrifice in giving his life for his country, and for the same people who now deny him the last funeral rites deserving of any American hero regardless of origin.

Senator Johnson sent a return telegram to Hector Garcia:

I deeply regret to learn that the prejudice of some individuals extend even beyond this life. I have no authority over civilian funeral homes, nor does the federal government. I have today made arrangements to have Felix Longoria buried with full military honors in Arlington National Cemetery. . . . This

Texas hero [will be] laid to rest with the honor and dignity his service deserves.

Felix Longoria was buried at Arlington National Cemetery on February 16, 1949, with all the pomp and fanfare a U.S. senator could provide. There is no picture of the Texan standing at the graveside with the grieving family.

In *Master of the Senate*, part three of his biography of LBJ, Robert Caro details that once the language in the Johnson telegram was made public, Johnson launched a blizzard of denials and obfuscations to the Anglo press. After all, the Texas establishment was pretty happy with things in the state as they were and was not sympathetic to the mission of the GI Forum.

For the young civil rights organization, the Longoria affair had been an instructive and useful victory. In the years to come, the American GI Forum's concerns moved far beyond those of returning servicemen. It became a modern civil rights organization, working to end school segregation, the injustices of local court systems, and the poll taxes that served

Early in his working life, Lyndon B. Johnson taught Mexican students in the small South Texas town of Cotulla, about halfway between San Antonio and the Mexican border. His early experience as a schoolteacher shaped his views toward civil rights in his later political career. He took up the cause of the Longoria family and helped them arrange Felix's burial in Arlington National Cemetery. CREDIT: LBJ LIBRARY

Long after they first crossed paths over the Longoria affair, Dr. Hector Garcia of the American GI Forum and LBJ remained allies. Here Garcia meets the Senate majority leader and his wife, Lady Bird, during a visit to Texas. CREDIT: TEXAS A&MU-CC

to keep minorities from voting. Hector Garcia, the south Texas doctor at the helm of the GI Forum, was enraged by all the injustices he saw in the daily lives of Mexicans and Mexican-Americans, especially in the counties bordering Mexico, some of the poorest places in America.

He investigated the living conditions of migrant workers in Texas, which led first to a booklet from the GI Forum, "What Price Wetbacks?" then to testimony to the National Advisory Committee on Farm Labor. The GI Forum took aim at the Bracero Program, still delivering low-cost farm labor from Mexico long after the war was over. Garcia told the committee, "The migrant problem is not only a national emergency; it has become a national shame on the American conscience."

Vital cogs in the machine that brought fresh produce to markets and kitchen tables, migrant workers who crossed the border under the Bracero Program were extremely useful to the food business. Farmers supported continued congressional authorization for the program. Garcia saw the migrant workers, especially the children, as they were: exploited, sick, and poor.

"If he lives to be of school age, he will never average more than three years of schooling in his lifetime. His parents may be completely illiterate. If he lives to be an adult, he may average as high as $60 a month. He will live, if he is lucky, in a substandard home and die an early death from tuberculosis.

"The only piece of property he owns in this world, however, will be his grave. I feel it is our moral obligation to recognize that the migrant's world is really part of our own world. To me, it is more than that since these people are my brothers and sisters."

Once again, we are face-to-face with the duality of Latino life in America. Hector Garcia, born in Mexico to educated parents, moved to the United States during the Mexican Revolution. Through education he was able to become a prominent and respected man, an officer in the U.S. Army, and, moving in ever more powerful circles, sought after by prominent political men in the pro–civil rights wing of the Democratic Party: Hubert Humphrey, George McGovern, and Arthur Goldberg.

Garcia's "brothers and sisters" were now coming in the tens of thousands, and were a major source of Mexican immigration to the United States. Like him, these immigrants were born in Mexico, but he saw the Bracero Program built to keep them as something like American serfs. Poorly paid, poorly housed, and poor in health, they were unlikely to prosper the way the Garcia family had.

Boy Scout Troop and Cub Scout Pack 104, sponsored by the American GI Forum's Lubbock Chapter. Dr. Garcia saw his organization as a developer of future civic leaders and a spur to assimilation and acceptance in the wider community. CREDIT: TEXAS A&MU-CC

While the American GI Forum may have deplored the Bracero Program, there were no shortage of Mexican farmworkers willing to take a chance and make the crossing. A surging American economy in the postwar years raised the wage differential on the two sides of the border even higher; there was no place in the world where an international border separated workers making such vastly different wages. By the time the Bracero Program was ended in 1964, it oversaw five million crossings (many by the same workers, who returned year after year).

In the late 1940s, Antonio Nunez had the dream. He thought he would work five or six years in the United States and build a house back home in Jalisco state for his mother. He signed on as a *bracero* to work in Brawley, California, in the hot, dry, irrigated farmland east of San Diego. Nunez remembers the physicals. "We undressed; we took off all of our clothes. And later, there was a doctor.

"Here he put his fingers like so"—he motions to his genitals—"to see that we didn't have hernias." Even more intrusive inspections were made, said Nunez, "to see that it wasn't bad, that I didn't bring infections."

Like cattle, *braceros* were fumigated in clouds of DDT to make sure they didn't bring insect pests from Mexico. The workers demonstrated that they really were laborers by showing the calluses on their hands. "We were obligated to work every day. Sunday didn't exist." Nunez remembered the hard work in the cotton fields, ten hours a day: "It is tough because the sack, the bag, is long. Cotton is very light and to fill a bag to a hundred kilos [220 pounds] you need a great deal of strength."

If the searing heat of the Southern California deserts didn't get them, and if they didn't collapse under the weight of an enormous bag of cotton bolls, picking was hell on the workers' hands. "The cotton buds have like five corners. One has to grab the boll and pull it out. But when holding the cotton, the pricks cut you. You bleed from the spikes. Oh, it was terrible!"

The work was hard. The conditions were awful. The pay was lousy. For Nunez and so many other *braceros*, the work offered opportunities unavailable back home. "When we began to come to America, it changed our lives. We completely changed, because I could buy things, like corn. I would go and buy a money order to send money to Mexico to my mother. I sent almost all of it."

Multiply Nunez's story and the effect his remittances had on his family by tens of thousands. In the early 1950s, two hundred thousand *braceros* came to the United States each year. More and more Mexican families knew firsthand, or from a close relative, that crossing the border changed lives. At the same time Latinos already in the United States wondered about the changes so many new arrivals would bring to the fields.

That GI Forum publication, "What Price Wetbacks?" is a clue. *Wetback* was, and still is, a derisive term for undocumented border crossers, with the implication being that they had waded or swum across the Rio Grande. Published by a group of World War II veterans, led by a Mexican immigrant, "What Price Wetbacks?" threatened a future America inundated with illiterate, desperate, even criminal foreigners.

Faced with a choice, as Garcia saw it, between the quality of life and economic well-being of Mexicans in Texas and those back in Mexico, he chose Mexican-Americans. The Bracero Program would continue for another decade, to the relief of Antonio Nunez. "The Bracero Program was initiated for the sake of America and for the good of Mexico—because it was very good for Mexico. If I had never had it, I could not buy pants down in Mexico!"

Through the wartime labor shortages and into the postwar boom, agricultural workers came north from Mexico under the Bracero Program. Dr. Garcia and the American GI Forum came to oppose the widespread use of imported labor, even publishing a book called, "What Price Wetbacks?" to oppose the extension of the Bracero Program. CREDIT: LIBRARY OF CONGRESS

Mexican workers arrive by train in Stockton, California. What began as a stopgap program to supply the U.S. war effort with both draftees and low-cost food, the Bracero Program did not stop when the soldiers came home. Reliance on Mexican labor only deepened on American farms in the postwar years. CREDIT: LIBRARY OF CONGRESS

Nunez's employers sponsored his permanent residency—one of the estimated 350,000 people who eventually shifted from *bracero* to immigrant. Nunez eventually became a citizen as well, not an outcome publicly contemplated when the first workers came in 1942. All in all, Nunez sounds like a guy who thinks he's done all right by America, and is sure America has done well by him. "There are many people who feel bad to say they were a *bracero*. No! That is something to be proud of, and I am very proud. Just as I am proud to have been able to become a citizen.

"Yes, I love this country very much. Right now I tell myself, 'I begin to live when I came to America.' "

Imagine a country in frantic motion. Millions of servicemen and -women had come home. Hundreds of thousands of couples forced to postpone weddings and childbirths got busy setting up households. Servicemen leaving active duty far from their hometowns decided to stay where they were released from active duty—in San Francisco or New York, for instance—rather than heading home to a small town in the South or the Great Plains. Populations of new people in new places swelled.

The Census Bureau captured this movement beautifully with a population snapshot in 1949. The bureau found twenty-eight million people, or about one out of every five residents of the United States, were living in a different house from the one they had lived in a year earlier. Of the twenty-eight million, nineteen million had moved within a county, four million had changed county residence within a state, another four million had moved from one state to another, and half a million had been living abroad a year earlier. Even with this striking evidence of mobility, census tabulators found the country was slowing down! Even more movement had been observed in the years just after the victory over Japan in 1945.

During the postwar years ever larger numbers of Mexicans crossed the border and went to work without the oversight of the Bracero Program. Estimates by the U.S. Justice Department and the Immigration and Naturalization Service ran as high as three million. Walt Edwards, who worked as a Border Patrol agent starting in 1951, told the *Christian Science Monitor* that if he and other agents made arrests, farmers would call the agency's regional office in El Paso to complain. "And depending on how politically connected they were, there would be political intervention," said Edwards. "That is how we got into this mess we are in now."

Farming families came from rural Mexico and followed the crops and the seasons as migrants in the United States. While urbanizing Mexican-American descendants of earlier migrations struggled to enter the American mainstream, the new arrivals filled shanty towns, got scant education, and often worked themselves into early graves. CREDIT: THE DOLPH BRISCOE CENTER FOR AMERICAN HISTORY, THE UNIVERSITY OF TEXAS AT AUSTIN

Joseph White, a retired twenty-one-year veteran of the Border Patrol, told the *Monitor* that in the early 1950s, some senior U.S. officials overseeing immigration enforcement "had friends among the ranchers," and agents "did not dare" arrest their illegal workers.

The Eisenhower administration, struggling to deal with a recession, decided to break up the cozy arrangements that saw increasing numbers of border crossers head to work in the United States. In the summer of 1954, Attorney General Herbert Brownell and INS commissioner Joseph Swing launched "Operation Wetback." More than a thousand Border Patrol agents, working with state and local police departments, conducted sweeps, raids, and house-to-house searches through factories, farms, and neighborhoods in California and Arizona. In those two states, more than fifty thousand undocumented workers were arrested, and almost half a million more were estimated to have left on their own.

When the operation spread to Texas, more than eighty thousand were arrested, and five to seven hundred thousand were estimated to have headed back to Mexico on their own. To make return to the United States more difficult, trains and buses took deportees deep into Mexico before setting them free. Thousands more were deported on two ships that sailed from the Texas Gulf Coast to Veracruz, five hundred miles to the south.

The last time problems in the labor market and suspicion of foreigners had taken hold this way, the United States deported almost half a million Mexicans and Mexican-Americans back to Mexico. American citizens who had never laid eyes on Mexico were rounded up and suddenly deported, without so much as a hearing. Twenty years later there were employment problems again, and again Mexicans became the scapegoats. Operation Wetback deported more than a million people, among them many American citizens. And this time police and courts ignored the civil liberties of Mexican nationals and U.S. citizens alike.

But the Latinos themselves had changed. This time they had help. This time there were community-based organizations to push back, and a growing sense that the war had earned a voice for the community. And maybe . . . the country had changed a bit too.

In 1957, Guy Gabaldon, the Pied Piper of Saipan, was profiled on the popular network TV show *This Is Your Life*. The announcer got the studio audience ready with a breathless and provocative opening. "In a few moments our principal subject will walk through that door and into a *This*

Living in the same states, often in the same towns as the newest arrivals, aspiring, Americanizing veterans, like those at the American GI Forum Annual Convention in 1959, exposed a tension that runs through Latino history in the United States. More than any other immigrant group, Latinos have had the experience of long-settled families living in community with brand-new immigrants. CREDIT: TEXAS A&MU-CC

Is Your Life story of violence, of strange gentleness, of killing and compassion, of material poverty and spiritual growth. A story of heroism with such impact you'll never forget it. Now we've arranged for our principal subject to take a unique tour of our NBC studios and he should be coming through that door right now."

The program host, Ralph Edwards, intercepted the "touring" audience members: "Welcome to the tour. Here's the tour right here. You are? An ex-marine? And you? And you?

"And what is your name?"

"Guy Gabaldon."

"Well, Mr. Gabaldon . . . *this is your life.*"

"Shucks . . ."

Then followed Gabaldon's story, delivered with the mixture of sentimental schmaltz and patriotic uplift that made *This Is Your Life* a hit. In detail, wartime comrades described Gabaldon's capture of fifteen hundred Japanese prisoners. After the ho-hum reaction from the Marine Corps and the Department of the Navy in the hectic final months of the war, Guy Gabaldon was now a national hero.

Yet, in Hollywood's eyes, not a hero who would be embraced by all Americans. In 1960, Warner Brothers made a movie about Gabaldon,

Hell to Eternity. Short and wiry five-foot-four Gabaldon was played by six-foot-one all-American boy Jeffrey Hunter (who would go on to play Jesus in *King of Kings*). Producers wanted Gabaldon's heroism. They just weren't sure they wanted the Mexican-American hero. For that matter, they didn't want a single Mexican-American actor in the cast, either.

AFTER A HALF century of massive immigration from Europe from 1870 to 1920, the United States slammed the door shut on immigrants with a rewrite of the immigration laws. Just a few years later came the Great Depression, followed by ten years of devastating worldwide war. By the 1950s, the percentage of Americans born in a foreign country was on the decline. The country had shifted during years of low immigration from a place where immigrants had a big role in the culture—Al Jolson, Irving Berlin, Enrico Caruso—to 1950s America, where the children and grandchildren of immigrants flavored and defined American life—Joe DiMaggio, the actors John Garfield, Kirk Douglas, entertainers like Jimmy Durante, politicians like New York governor Herbert Lehman and Rhode Island's John Pastore.

As the percentage of foreign-born Americans began to decline, so did many Americans' intimate, close-in memory of the challenges and struggles in the lives of immigrant people. That only made it easier to look at newcomers from Latin America with no glimmer of familiarity. Threadbare clothing, callused hands, and nutritional diseases provoked no memory of deprivation and hard labor. Latino immigrants, as the mania for assimilation and "Americanism" rose through the 1950s, would get precious little sympathy from people whose own parents and grandparents faced many of the same challenges just a short time ago.

As the Ellis Island generations and their descendants set aside the daily use of German, Italian, Yiddish, and Polish, Spanish speakers came to the United States in greater and greater numbers. As we have seen, since the days before a United States even existed, most Spanish speakers came from Mexico.

The late 1940s saw an enormous number of Latinos arrive from another place. The late 1950s would bring newcomers from yet another place. In the 1960s, they came from a third. The three homelands were Puerto Rico, Cuba, and the Dominican Republic. Each in their own ways would shape

Hispanic-American identity and American culture. For this rapidly growing population the term "Mexican" just wouldn't work. The coming years would create a New World people on American soil that could not have been made back in other hemispheric homelands: Latinos.

Viva Kennedy Clubs represented a convergence of interest perfectly suited to the times. Senator John Kennedy's (D-MA) campaign saw great possibilities for votes among a heavily immigrant and Roman Catholic ethnic group, and young Latino politicians saw it as a way to begin playing on a national stage. CREDIT: TEXAS A&MU-CC

If standing with a sign was not your style, you could show your support for the Massachusetts senator on your car's bumper. CREDIT: TEXAS A&MU-CC

West Side Story. On the streets of Manhattan, the recently arrived Puerto Ricans and their street gang, the Sharks, confront the white ethnic, native-born Jets. Shakespeare's Verona moved to the tenements, with Puerto Ricans and the sons of earlier immigrants the twentieth–century Montagues and Capulets. CREDIT: GETTY IMAGES

I LIKE TO BE
IN AMERICA

4

BY 1950, Americans were going ahead and doing all the things they had put off for a long time, through Depression and world war:

They got married.

They had kids.

They bought houses.

They moved from center cities, places where many of their families had begun their lives in America, out to just-built places they could now reach easily on the new highways rolling out in every direction.

Latinos were on the move too. They were coming to America in larger numbers, and were moving within the country too, and far beyond the places they had long lived since the Southwest and Florida were parts of the Spanish Empire.

It was a good time to come to America, if you were looking at the country from a cruising altitude of thirty thousand feet. There was strong economic growth and a lot of places hungry for workers. Down on the ground, in Boyle Heights in Los Angeles, in the South Bronx, in Miami, things were a lot more complicated.

In the perennial debates about immigration, legal and illegal, you rarely hear about how hard it is to leave everything you know—family, language, way of life—and jump into a place with almost nothing that is familiar and start to make a new life. Talk to immigrants later on in their lives and you hear the stories they were less anxious to tell, when every day was dominated by the act of getting over, of adapting, of running just to keep up.

Since we revere our immigrant past in ways large and small (our immigrant present is a different matter), we have celebrated the triumphs of immigrant life in our common culture, but only in particular ways. Story after story is canned in a heavy syrup of sweet sentimentality, and built on the foundation of America's transformative power.

In *The Goldbergs*, on radio from 1929, and from 1949 to 1956 on television, a Jewish family climbs the American ladder from an apartment building in the Bronx.

In George M. Cohan's 1922 Broadway hit *Little Nellie Kelly*, the heroine of the title is pursued by both an Irish laborer and an American millionaire. True love triumphs over the cash, and Nellie, daughter of an Irish-American policeman, stays true to her Irish boyfriend, Jerry Conroy.

In *I Remember Mama* (1944), the joys and sorrows of the Hanson family from Norway are played out on a street of row houses in San Francisco. The stage play was written by an immigrant from London, John Van Druten, based on a novel by the Norwegian-American Kathryn Forbes.

In *Abie's Irish Rose*, Anne Nichols's play that opened on Broadway in 1922, which ran for more than five years and spawned two movies and a radio series, tension gives way to harmony as a family of Irish Catholics learns to live with their daughter's love and marriage to a Jewish boy, and vice versa.

The Jazz Singer (1927) presents the pain and possibility of assimilation, as Al Jolson's Jakie Rabinowitz, descendant of a long line of Orthodox Jewish cantors, turns away from his father's insistence that he continue the family tradition and instead "becomes" Jack Robin, vaudeville entertainer.

For more than a half century, wave upon wave of European immigration broke on American shores, and started families up the ladder to assimilation and success in politics, business, and popular culture. The Goldbergs, the Hansons, the Murphys, the Levys, and the Rabinowitzes are all Europeans, or of European stock. Any troubles they might have had after arriving in America were receding in memory. Now they were secure enough in their status as Americans that they could mine it for drama and comedy.

Desiderio Alberto Arnaz y de Acha III gave America something new to think about.

Desi Arnaz was handsome, talented, and, as time would tell, a smart businessman too. He married the ingenue turned comedienne Lucille Ball, every bit his equal as a performer and businesswoman. The two made television history, and American cultural history as well.

A member of a wealthy and well-connected family, Arnaz grew up in privilege in Cuba, until his family ended up on the wrong side of coup leader Fulgencio Batista and lost everything. Anticipating the loss and turmoil that would come to Cuba's wealthy in later decades, Arnaz ended up in south Florida. He met Lucille Ball in Southern California during World War II, and the two first became man and wife, then collaborators. Originally, their television show was to feature the couple as the Lopezes, two successful performers who try to balance marriage and career. Later, the premise was rewritten, putting Lucy Ricardo in the home and changing Desi's Lopez to Enrique "Ricky" Ricardo, bandleader and nightclub owner. The result, in 1951, was *I Love Lucy*.

The story—native-born spouse marries immigrant spouse, hilarity ensues—was an old one. What was new this time was where the immigrant came from—Latin America—and how he lived. Unlike the Latinos of decades of movies and other television shows, Ricky Ricardo was not a criminal, a cowboy, a peasant, a lounge lizard, or a victim. He was a bon vivant: sophisticated, good-looking, and able to take advantage of the good life in America. While it was never clear why a musician and nightclub owner, possibly one of the most urbane characters on television, would do it, he and Lucy even moved to the suburbs, like millions of other Americans were doing at the time.

While people across the country who had never met a Cuban or heard someone speaking Spanish laughed it up over Ricky's explosions in his mother tongue when another of Lucy's harebrained schemes went wrong, musician Bobby Sanabria saw something else entirely. "I think for Latinos in the fifties, he was a great source of pride. That we had somebody. That you could turn on the TV and say, 'Hey, he's one of us.' Every community wants to feel that they're represented, and he represented us. Here's a successful bandleader, he has a beautiful wife, and he's living the American dream."

The comic plot twists depended heavily on making Ricky more foreign, and heightening the contrasts by making him more American at the same time. Lucy Ricardo never seemed to learn a word of Spanish, or purposely mangled what she did say for comic effect, even though her husband moved easily between the two worlds of English-speaking domesticity and his Latin bandmates. While the women at the club moved with instinctive grace to the rhumbas and cha-chas gaining great popularity in American clubs, Lucy the comedienne could only make a broad pantomime, sometimes "going native" in a black wig.

Cuban-born author Gustavo Pérez Firmat remembers the moments his wife would provoke an outburst of "Latin" temper: "Ricky used to swear in Spanish. He used to get mad at Lucy—*esta mujer, carajo* . . . 'I'm gonna kill this woman' . . . he would never say this in English. But it was assumed that no one in the audience could understand Spanish. It was supposed to sound like gibberish. He said things you weren't allowed to say in English. Ricky Ricardo lived the dilemma and delights of biculturalism right on that television screen."

The "fish out of water" plotlines were milked for laughs, but also made it possible for Ricky to stay who he was: a Cuban. Sanabria remembers a recurring song that might have seemed a little silly to American audiences. "When you hear the song, 'Babalu Aye,' mainstream America was probably laughing it up, going, 'Babalu'! Little did they realize they were being exposed to this incredibly deep West African culture we inherited in the Caribbean."

The song "Babalu Aye" is a reminder that *I Love Lucy* was a mainstream 1950s situation comedy and not a National Geographic documentary. People who hardly remember a note Ricky Ricardo sang even after decades of reruns, when trying to imitate him, will swing an imaginary conga drum, pound it, and sing, "Babalu"! Even Lucy did.

As Sanabria says, it is a moment of exposure, however accidental, to a deep and complex part of Caribbean culture.

As long as he's singing in Spanish!

The lyric tells of a man preparing a ceremony that is part of the devotion to Babalu, a West African *orisha*, or spirit deity, that came to the West Indies with captives headed for enslavement on the plantations. While outwardly converting to Catholicism, the slaves continued to practice their old religion, using Christian saints to represent their African deities.

You may see in a Caribbean grocery store or a shop window a statue or portrait of San Lazaro, Saint Lazarus, from a parable of Jesus in the Gospel of Luke. Lazarus is a poor servant, shown in rags, on crutches, with a dog walking alongside him that licks the sores on his legs. A rich man, called Dives, lives it up on earth, but when he dies he is punished in hell, while Lazarus is freed from his sufferings on earth by the comforts of heaven. For deeply faithful Christian believers there are few more powerful ideas than a promised respite in the afterlife from all the sorrows of earth. Lazarus is also, in the Afro-Caribbean mix of West African and European religion, Babalu Aye, the *orisha* in charge of health.

In the Spanish-language song the candles are readied, to be set in the shape of a cross. The tobacco and brandy that are also part of the wake for Babalu are invoked. The singer needs money, is unlucky in love, and sings his song to Babalu.

In English, the original sense of the song is sadly lost to the lust for the exotic, and an impatience with themes that run to ancient, and definitely non-Christian, rites being celebrated to the beat of drums in the jungle that might not successfully cross over for those whose knowledge of Cubans runs as far as . . . let's say, Desi Arnaz.

Oh, well.

If Americans had any problem with a show that featured a black-haired Cuban married to a redhead from Jamestown, New York, it was hard to tell from the ratings. When the fictional Lucy Ricardo gave birth to the actual baby Desi Arnaz IV, it became one of the most-watched television programs in history. In 1953, television was still fairly new, but on January 19, forty-four million Americans watched, fully two-thirds of all the sets in America, as *I Love Lucy* welcomed "Little Ricky." Lucy and Desi's real-life child was the cover illustration of the first nationally distributed issue of a new magazine, *TV Guide*. That is crossover appeal.

Even as Cuban-American "Little Ricky" was becoming America's favorite baby, in most places in the country Latinos were still strangers. Outside the Southwest, where Spanish speakers had lived for 350 years, Latinos were still rare. The 1950s would become the decade when Cubans, Puerto Ricans, and Dominicans would begin to arrive and settle in large numbers, mostly in the Northeast and Florida. They would accept, and challenge, cherished American ideas about assimilation and the melting pot. With their homelands a daylong drive from the United States or a few hours away by plane, the interplay between the old country and new was different than it had been for many Americans' ancestors who boarded steamships thousands of miles away, assuming they would never see their homes again. Modern communication brought Spanish-language radio and television into the home. To some Americans new and growing barrios represented their desire to remain tethered to the countries they left behind instead of fully embracing the task of becoming an American.

IN 1957, PLAYWRIGHT Arthur Laurents and composer Leonard Bernstein dusted off the old love-across-ethnic-barriers idea for a new Broadway musical. This one would not have a "we're all human after all" comedic kumbaya at the end, like *Abie's Irish Rose*. It was to be a retelling of Shakespeare's *Romeo and Juliet* with warring clans and young death. The original title was *East Side Story*, with a Jewish Juliet falling for an Italian-American Romeo. The newspapers of the day were full of gang wars, but by the late 1950s increasingly middle-class and suburbanizing New York Jews were a tougher fit for the Montagues or the Capulets reimagined as street toughs.

One gang, the Jets, became a motley collection of working-class whites. The other, the Sharks, was composed of the new kids on the block, Puerto Ricans. Now *West Side Story*, the show opened on Broadway to wide acclaim, with two of the leading Puerto Rican roles played by Carol Lawrence as Maria and Ken LeRoy as Bernardo. Chita Rivera, the daughter of a Puerto Rican–born musician and a U.S.-born mother, played Bernardo's sister, Anita.

While *West Side Story* continued its Broadway run, the low-intensity conflict on the streets of tough New York neighborhoods left the realm of Leonard Bernstein and Stephen Sondheim's Tony Award–winning ballads and splashed onto the front pages of the New York tabloids.

Though the Irish, Italians, and Jews of earlier generations had all been through it, Puerto Rican gang membership was portrayed as a new and different kind of menace. While white boys of many ethnic backgrounds still joined gangs, it was black and Puerto Rican gang membership that was most widely discussed in the press, studied by commissions, and worried over by the grandchildren of ancestors who lived in neighborhoods that were rife with gang enterprises and gang violence.

Edwin Torres, jurist, author, and son of Spanish Harlem, watched it all unfold in the late 1940s and early 1950s. "There were gang wars going on. There was a pool hall at 106th and Madison—and I was hanging out there with my pals from the 'hood. My father happened to walk by and saw me. He rapped on the window—to come out. He told me, 'Go back in there, finish your game—but this is the last time you set foot in there.' He always said there is only one way out of here: *los libros*, the books."

Torres did as he was told. He was the only Puerto Rican student at the elite public Stuyvesant High School, and then attended the City University of New York. After service in the Korean War, Torres went to Brooklyn Law School on the GI Bill, and was a celebrated symbol of "making it" when he became the first Puerto Rican assistant district attorney in New York. The boy whose success at school sent him to college instead of the gangs was assigned to the Capeman case, forever intertwining his life with that of a young killer who illustrated a different side of Puerto Rican life in New York.

Salvador Agron was a teenager from Mayagüez, Puerto Rico, a city on the island's west coast. His mother brought Salvador and his sister from Puerto Rico to New York in the early 1950s. On August 29, 1959, his gang, the Vampires, was set to meet an Irish gang on Manhattan's West Side for a fight. When the other group failed to show, Agron and his boys just fought who they found, killing two teenagers. Agron wore a black cape with red lining, and came to be known by the cops looking for him, and eventually by the newspapers, then the world, as the Capeman.

The Capeman murders riveted New Yorkers with lurid details, the frightening lack of regret demonstrated by Agron when he was detained, and his seeming willingness to die for the crime: "I don't care if they burn me. My mother can watch."

At Agron's arraignment, magistrate David Malbin sounded like he had already heard the evidence and judged the case. He said it was getting "very monotonous when you see these young punks coming before us."

Though juvenile defendants, Agron and his accomplice, Antonio Hernandez, were allowed to talk to reporters during a break in the proceedings, the kind of encounter that would never happen today. A reporter asked, "How do you feel about killing those boys?" With a shrug Agron replied, "Like I always feel, like this." Another reporter asked, "Was it worth killing a kid to be here today talking on a mike?" Agron answered, "I feel like killing you. That's what I feel like."

Professor Lorrin Thomas of Rutgers University maintains that the reason the Capeman trial got the kind of attention it did when violent street gangs had been a feature of New York life for more than a century was in part the postwar narrative of a society in decline. Agron himself was also a factor. "He showed no remorse. That's what got to people. They saw the Capeman as a symbol of evil—a symbol of a society falling apart. He infuriated people. He confirmed white New Yorkers' worst fears about Puerto Rican youth and exposed the ethnic and class tensions that had been building in New York since the previous decade."

Agron also divided Puerto Ricans. When Edwin Torres looks back, he says, "I almost had a fistfight with the guy in the courtroom—as we walked past each other, he called me *alcahuete* . . . I almost punched him." *Alcahuete*, a pimp. The implication was that as a prosecutor Torres had taken the government's side against his own people.

"Killed Because 'I Felt Like It.'"
New York's tabloids reinforced the already rampant stereotype of an amoral, violent Puerto Rican underclass. Salvador Agron, "the Capeman" or "Dracula," was sentenced to death for killing two teenagers with an accomplice, Antonio Hernandez, "the Umbrella Man." Agron was sentenced to death, and the sentence was later commuted.
CREDIT: NY DAILY NEWS VIA GETTY IMAGES

After the guilty verdicts were handed down for Agron, Hernandez, and the five Vampires who were their codefendants, the *New York Times* ran a set of profiles of the seven. It is depressing reading, briefly detailing lives of poverty, instability, and failure. Touching, and perhaps unintentionally revealing, is the sketch for Rafael Colon, who pled guilty to first-degree manslaughter. "Oldest of the seven at 27 . . . Immature mentally and physically . . . Emaciated . . . Said he has always been hungry. Stands five feet five inches, weighs barely 100 pounds . . . Arrived here alone from Puerto Rico four years ago . . . Has no home, slept at homes of fellow gang members, in halls, on roofs . . . Worked for short time as dishwasher in Newark restaurant. Was discharged for habitual lateness . . . At ease only with boys many years his junior . . . When told of penalty he faced, he replied, 'What difference does it make? I haven't lived anyway.'"

Agron was sentenced to death for the murders, becoming the youngest person sent to death row in New York history. After time on death row, and time as a cause célèbre, Agron had his sentence reduced, and his accomplice, Hernandez, though older at the time of the murders, was also spared the electric chair.

The Capeman's story was not read as that of a perhaps sociopathic boy, but as representative of a community of violent, immoral people whom no one wanted in New York in the first place. While white actors like Carol Lawrence and Ken LeRoy did modern dance and acted like Puerto Ricans on a Broadway stage, real Puerto Ricans acted like vicious animals, or so you would assume from the newspapers.

When *West Side Story* moved to the silver screen, Carol Lawrence's voice moved to Hollywood, but her face didn't: Natalie Wood, the daughter of Russian immigrants, became Maria in brownface, lip-synching to Lawrence's beautiful voice. George Chakiris, son of Greek immigrants, became her brother, Bernardo, the leader of the Sharks. In the footsteps of Chita Rivera, a Latina was cast as Anita, this time Puerto Rican–born Hollywood veteran Rita Moreno. "I understood this girl, Anita, very, very well," Moreno recalls. "I understood prejudice very well. New York was not a friendly place for Puerto Ricans. I found out early on that it was not good to be from another country."

Moreno, the only Puerto Rican lead player, remembered the transformation of the actors into gangsters, girlfriends, and seamstresses. "All the actors playing Puerto Rican characters wore an identical shade of brown

Teenage Rita Moreno. She came to New York at five and by her teen years was already working as an actress on Broadway. She moved on to Hollywood, where, in her own words, she played "a lot of Señorita, Conchita, Lolita spitfire roles." CREDIT: COURTESY OF RITA MORENO

makeup. Boy, oh, boy, did I hate that; I kept trying to tell them that Puerto Ricans were all colors, from pitch-black to beige. But Jerome Robbins kept saying, 'I want more contrast.' I was so offended by that.

"I was very torn. There was always that niggling, terrible feeling that you weren't representing your people. But Anita was a wonderful role, with this astonishing music."

Moreno came from Puerto Rico to New York in 1936, a time of terrible economic suffering in the big city. Back on the island, it was even worse. Early on, she became a performer to help support herself and her mother. At the tender age of thirteen, she got her first role on Broadway, left school, and began to build a career. She became one of Hollywood's go-to exotics, appearing in such movies as *The Fabulous Senorita*, *Latin Lovers*, and *The Yellow Tomahawk*. She played American Indians, Asians, and Mexicans.

"I played a lot of señorita, conchita, Lolita spitfire roles. Everything but an American girl," Moreno recalled in her eighties. "I was always the utilitarian ethnic. I hated it."

Rita Moreno with her Oscar. CREDIT: ©
BETTMANN/CORBIS

The movie made an even bigger splash than the Broadway play, winning ten Academy Awards, including Oscars for Chakiris and Moreno, for Best Musical Score, and for Jerome Robbins and Robert Wise for Best Director.

Moreno was the first Puerto Rican actress to win an Oscar, the first Puerto Rican since José Ferrer for *Cyrano de Bergerac* in 1950, and the first woman born on the island to win. In the following years she would make show business history by adding an Emmy, a Grammy, and a Tony Award.

The writer Stanley Crouch once observed that *West Side Story* was the result of three gay Jews imagining what it was like to be Puerto Rican, but the musical has undeniable strengths: the score that has contributed such standards to the American Songbook as "Maria," "Somewhere," "Tonight," and "I Feel Pretty"; the doomed lovers; the groundbreaking modern dance. While it is no fault of the stage musical or the movie that followed, it became all many Americans knew about Puerto Ricans for decades.

"It's an image that's had enormous staying power," insists Juan González, who more than a decade after the Broadway run and the movie was working on a small newspaper in eastern Pennsylvania. "Virtually everyone I met for the first time would say to me, 'Oh, you're Puerto Rican. Do you carry a knife?' It was instantaneous. They must have seen *West Side Story* and that's how ingrained the stereotypes were. They were disseminated through the heartland of America. It was such a well-done musical. The songs stay with you for life. And the images stay with you for life.

"There are millions of Americans who have never met a Puerto Rican in their lives, and the image they carry of Puerto Ricans is the image they saw in *West Side Story*."

One memorable set of lyrics comes from "America," when the Puerto Ricans are hanging out and playfully arguing about whether it had been a good idea to leave the island in the first place, and whether New York really is a promised land for them. First, Rosalia sings a tribute to her homeland, the lovely island. Anita's reply speaks not of tropical fruits and flowers but of bugs, crime and intemperate weather, not like her beloved Manhattan. The tempo picks up; the music swells. The young men and women sing of the joys and deprivations of both Puerto Rico and New York, the only America most of them have ever seen. On Broadway, Stephen Sondheim's lyrics hit the nail on the head. The immigrant has brought Puerto Rico with her to America! Rosalia, dreaming of the day she returns home, sings, "Everyone there will give big cheer!" and gets Anita's deadpan response: "Everyone there will have moved here."

IN 1948, PUERTO Ricans did something they had hoped to do half a century earlier: They elected their own chief executive, a governor. Puerto Rico had governors since 1509, since Ponce de León, of Florida exploration and Fountain of Youth fame. He held the job for most of the next decade.

For the next four hundred years, most of the governors were generals, military men sent from Madrid or Washington to run the affairs of a colony or possession. Ponce de León's grandson had the job in the sixteenth century; President Roosevelt's son Theodore Junior held it in the twentieth century, after his father helped win Puerto Rico by beating Spain. When Americans started to arrive in San Juan to serve as governor, many of them did not even speak Spanish.

What paved the way for Puerto Ricans to get their own governor was the Elective Governor Act of 1947, approved in Washington. The first elected governor was Luis Muñoz Marín, son of the famed anticolonial leader Luis Muñoz Rivera. In 1950, at the end of Muñoz Marín's first term in office, the constitution of the Commonwealth of Puerto Rico came fully into effect, and the island was running its own affairs in a way unseen since the American invasion. The constitution set out the number and responsibilities of Puerto Rican senators and representatives, and called the "coexistence in Puerto Rico of the two great cultures of the American Hemisphere" one of the "determining factors" of Puerto Rican life and democracy.

Also arriving with a Puerto Rican governor was a new approach to the Puerto Rican economy and its development, called Operation Bootstrap in Washington, and *Manos a la Obra*, "Hands to the Job," in San Juan. The new government borrowed heavily, and built long-needed infrastructure: sewers, roads, electrical distribution systems. In a presentation before a group of prospective investors in New York, the governor dismissed stereotypes about Puerto Ricans that likened them to a lazy man lying on a mattress, asking for a cup of coffee. "That is all changed. The attitude now and for some years has been for the people of Puerto Rico to help themselves to the best of their ability, to face their democratic responsibilities, and to solve their own problems.

"Today the people of Puerto Rico are not lying on a mattress, but are standing on their feet helping themselves to the best of their ability, yet still in need of a helping hand. . . . I feel that Puerto Rico deserves the understanding and help of all of the citizens of the United States."

Earlier in the century, as explained in chapter two, the U.S. Congress had defined products from Puerto Rico, agricultural and manufactured, as imports, as if they were being brought into the United States from a foreign country. Over time, this had the effect of destroying the Puerto Rican–owned agricultural export sector, leaving more and more land to be snapped up by American-based multinational sugar producers.

The Great Depression and a series of unusually destructive storms applied the final blows: By the late 1930s and early 1940s, Puerto Ricans were underemployed, undernourished, and increasingly desperate. As early as 1933, unemployment reached a staggering 33 percent, significantly higher than that of the mainland United States. In 1937, agricultural economist Esteban Bird calculated that in the 1930s the Puerto Rican rural worker had an income of twelve cents a day for each family member, by Bird's reckoning only four cents a day more than the cost of feeding a hog in the United States.

This was in Puerto Rico as it was on the United States mainland a recipe for conflict and radicalization. There was increasing opposition

Hundreds of thousands of Puerto Ricans, despite rising levels of aid from the U.S. mainland, still lived in desperate poverty as the island became a commonwealth and elected a Puerto Rican governor. For many, life was little better once they arrived in New York. CREDIT: © BETTMANN/CORBIS

to American rule and bloody armed clashes between workers and militias. Muñoz Marín's Popular Democratic Party, the PDP, or *populares*, grew from this hostility to the U.S.-based sugar interests that had brought so much misery to the common worker during the wild swings in the price of sugar during the Depression.

The production needs of World War II brought some industrialization to Puerto Rico, with factories on the island producing goods for the war economy as a hedge against a German naval blockade. Factories, military bases, and roads to connect the bases were all built in the war years. When the war was over, tax incentives lured investment in a new, industrialized island.

Sugar production continued to decline, which meant less and less employment for rural Puerto Ricans. Encouraged by Operation Bootstrap, the island urbanized, and agriculture became a smaller share of the overall economy. This process left many Puerto Ricans between two stools. The world their families knew, of grinding rural poverty and low-wage agricultural work, was disappearing. In the new world of urban and suburban skilled and semiskilled labor, they saw no place for themselves.

They headed to New York by the thousands. "If not the panacea, migration became a crucial component for solving Puerto Rico's economic problems. So migration became a cornerstone of the government's modernization plan," according to Lorrin Thomas, professor of history at Rutgers University, who specializes in Puerto Rican migration and identity. Muñoz Marín's projections of a future Puerto Rico after Operation Bootstrap factored in high levels of migration to the U.S. mainland. The Department of Labor's Migration Division office in San Juan encouraged people to move north.

Juanita Sanabria had been hearing about Nueva York for years in her hometown of Yabucoa on the island's far southwest corner. "I was excited by the idea of New York—I imagined myself in this glamorous place with glamorous people. But it was really hard, too. I had never been separated from my family. We were always together. I was in the middle of thirteen kids. No one in my family had gone to New York yet—but many in the town had already left."

As hard as life could be in mainland cities, with each passing year more islanders found it harder to stay home. Even with significant aid from the government in Washington, Puerto Ricans were hungry, and much smaller in stature than their fellow Americans on the mainland.

As more Puerto Ricans headed to New York, Juanita Sanabria finally made up her mind to go. The girl from Yabucoa became a wife, a mother, and a New Yorker. CREDIT: SANABRIA FAMILY

Just as the colony became an Estado Libre Asociado, an Associated Free State with its own constitution, Juanita Sanabria decided it was time to go. "There was never enough food on the table. My father was a farmer—even though his farm had grown to almost a hundred acres, a farmer could not make a living in Puerto Rico. Even for farmers, it seemed like there was much more work in the United States."

The tightening relationship with the federal government and the injections of federal aid seemed to make the dream of an independent country even more distant than in the years after the Spanish-American War. It is a strange status, this Estado Libre Asociado, making Puerto Rico not quite part of the United States, but not quite its own country either.

Arcadio Díaz-Quiñones of Princeton University explains it this way: "This notion of nationhood—or lack thereof—makes a deep impression on the Puerto Rican psyche and identity. It is the first reminder that Puerto Ricans do not have the same say in their destiny as others. It is under the skin—never explicit—but it is more than a romantic notion; it is the lens through which Puerto Ricans view their reality, especially in New York. And it comes out through nostalgia, through music, through poetry—for generations to come." Whatever the political situation for

Puerto Ricans on the island or New York, as numbers grew so did a strong sense of nationhood increasingly unbound by geography. Whether an auto mechanic in Orlando, a garment worker in Manhattan, a public school teacher in Connecticut, or a cop in Chicago, Americans of Puerto Rican descent carried a sense of shared identity, even if they had never lived on or visited the island of Puerto Rico.

New arrivals like Juanita Sanabria found a well-established community life in New York. By 1955 some seven hundred thousand Puerto Ricans had moved to the continental United States, and most of them went to New York. More and more New Yorkers who called themselves Puerto Rican had been born there, like Edwin Torres. "My parents had come in the twenties—my father had been in the service and came to New York during the Depression to visit—when East Harlem was still very Jewish. It was a terrible time, but he stayed—it was much worse in Puerto Rico."

It would be years before the full extent of the problems were fully realized, but New York was already a city in decline. A desperate people hitched their futures in America to a city on the verge of a thirty-year slide. It was a choice that would end up for many to be calamitous, but at first the newcomers adjusted, and struggled. Juanita Sanabria saw it firsthand. "It turned out to be really hard to find a job, despite what I had been told. Eventually I found a job for a penny a dress—piecework, it was called."

Puerto Ricans moved into hotels, into building maintenance, into the Garment District. The specialized manufacturing jobs that had been a New York mainstay, offering union protection and a decent middle-class salary, were becoming scarce, according to Professor Thomas. "The jobs that had always been there for immigrants were starting to move out of the city, to the South, to the Midwest. Those who can, leave with them. But what's available to the majority are jobs as elevator operators, janitors, doormen—service jobs."

Those who can, leave with them. Puerto Ricans did not have the same mobility taken for granted by their neighbors with longer tenures in the United States. Language barriers, poverty, and persistent belief that they would not be welcome elsewhere, especially for those with darker skin, kept many Puerto Ricans concentrated in their long-term homes, even as other Americans moved south and west in search of new opportunities during a time of economic change. Puerto Ricans would stick to New York, and the Northeast, through a generation of terrible decline. A few pioneers who headed to small cities in New Jersey, western Connecticut, and eastern Pennsylvania sometimes found that in the years after they arrived, a new barrio filled in around them.

BACK IN PUERTO Rico, during the first fifteen years of Operation Bootstrap, from 1950 to 1965, more than half a million workers left Puerto Rico, and the unemployment rate declined a little over 1 percent, although it was a still pretty horrifying 11.7 percent. The number of jobs on the island wouldn't reach its 1951 levels again until 1965.

The Puerto Rican authorities had based their plans for future prosperity on having fewer people around. But the arrivals' new home in Nueva York was not so sure it wanted them around either. Or at least it found them an inconvenience. The buildings Puerto Ricans had moved into in Manhattan, the Bronx, and Brooklyn were already old when they got there. The plaster was shot, the plumbing was worse, and the heat was sporadic. Only the roaches seemed to find the buildings acceptable.

Postwar New York City was in the full throes of urban renewal. The city built expressways and parks, middle-income housing projects, and a gleaming new center for the performing arts, in part by knocking down the places Puerto Ricans lived. This was the real West Side story, says Professor Thomas. "The real drama was unfolding as urban renewal became the order of the day. Entire neighborhoods were vanishing to make way for office buildings and expressways. Thousands of tenement buildings were bulldozed, displacing thousands of families, mostly Puerto Rican and black."

The creation of Lincoln Center "displaced thousands of families" and demolished an area known as San Juan Hill. The Sharks and Jets of the movie version of *West Side Story* danced, sang, and rumbled in a set of blocks emptied of people just before the wrecking ball and bulldozer went to work. Moving powerless people created an authentic urban set for shooting a movie about powerless people.

MEANWHILE, JUST A few hundred miles to the west, Cuba had overthrown an old-style Latin American strongman only to find itself in a new predicament. Fulgencio Batista had been in and out of power since 1933. Like large numbers of Cubans, the soldier, coup leader, and onetime president spent years in the United States, though he did it in greater comfort than most of his countrymen. After his American sojourn, Batista went back to Havana in 1952, finished third in presidential elections, and led another coup, backed by the army. The U.S. government recognized the new Batista government a short time later.

Americans sent on fact-finding missions came back with dreary reports of political and economic conditions in Cuba. In Africa, Asia, and elsewhere in Latin America, armed groups were making war on the established order. With the Cold War under way, many of these wars fell into the East-West tug-of-war between Moscow and Washington.

As the Castro brothers—Fidel and Raúl—gathered support from more people across the political spectrum, the Cuban president cracked down on dissent, and tried to snuff out the resistance. (Like dictators around the world who come to believe they can save themselves from being overthrown by doubling down, Batista expanded the secret police, and jailed and executed his opponents. Fidel Castro led an anti-Batista coalition known simply as "the Movement." He downplayed his own leftist ideology and avoided alliance with the communist Partido Socialista Popular to maintain the wider alliance.)

The armed revolt that began shortly after Batista's 1952 coup gathered energy and outside support. The Cuban dictator had made enough enemies in the previous decades that money began to pour into Castro's coffers from exile communities in Mexico and the United States. Even a *New York Times* interview with Castro conducted in the hills in 1957 brought more money from outside Cuba. Support for the anti-Batista revolution widened, and began to include the middle class. By New Year's Day, 1959, Fulgencio Batista was on his way into exile with all the loot he could carry.

Bookshelves across the world groan under the weight of histories of the Cuban Revolution and its aftermath. Trying to distill the highly conflicted perspectives of history while the Castro brothers remain in power will be done by others, and likely for decades to come; for the purposes of our story, we will move away from the presidential palaces and ministries to the barbershops and fields and streets of provincial towns.

Individual Cubans had to make decisions in the heat of rapid social change. They asked themselves very basic questions: "How will I fare in the new Cuba?" "What future is there for my children in this country?"

Cubans had been coming to the United States for more than a century. There were already sizable, well-established Cuban communities in Florida and New York. Vicente Martinez-Ybor moved his cigar-making operations to Tampa from an increasingly unstable Cuba in the 1860s, and many Cubans joined him there. The 1910 U.S. census counted fifteen thousand Cubans in the country, a number that grew to more than 125,000 on the eve of the revolution's victory.

In the 1950s a family here, a single guy there, came to Manhattan, Chicago, Miami, and looked for people like themselves. The revolution changed everything. As in any convulsive change in politics there were winners and losers, and Cuba was no exception: People locked out of access to schooling and influence in society suddenly found they had it. Small businesspeople, educated professionals, and land and factory owners gradually found their home was going to be a harder place to live, and with the almost complete elimination of private property and political freedom, it was going to be harder for good.

In the beginning, it was unclear whether the Cuban revolutionary government would survive; it was also less clear for ordinary Cubans what to do about it. Some families sent their children out, while they stayed in Cuba to see what happened next. Other families began to believe there was no future for them all, at least for now. Fears were stoked of rumored Communist plans to seize and indoctrinate children on the island. Beginning in 1960, an enormous ad hoc airlift of children out of Cuba was conducted. Over the course of two years, fourteen thousand unaccompanied children were sent to the United States in a program called Operation Peter Pan. The idea was that the children, from little more than toddlers to adolescents, would make the trip and wait for their parents in the United States.

In the summer of 1961, six-year-old María de Los Angeles Torres was prepared for her trip. "They dressed me in the aqua-blue-and-white checkered dress my grandmother had made me. On it they pinned a piece of paper bearing my name."

When you are six, and becoming an unwitting cast member in a gathering geopolitical drama, the details are not always clear. "All I knew was that we stopped collecting the trading cards with the heroes of the revolution on them. But my parents had other things on their mind. Fidel had promised elections, but he didn't hold them. He jailed or executed people who opposed him. Then the regime took over private schools. That's when my parents decided to go into exile."

María, called Nena, "baby girl," by her family, took her doll Isabelita, and a suitcase packed with clothes, towels, handkerchiefs. "I remember the airport, my mother hugging me, her last words: "Take a bath every day; Americans do not have that habit." Then, as we took off, I heard some of the other kids starting to cry."

Many of the Peter Pans already had family living in the United States. Others were placed with sponsoring families located through the Catholic Church, one of the spearhead organizations for the program. Others headed to group homes set up as a temporary way station to live in America with family. Nena Torres went to live with her aunt, Nenita. "She gave me a box of chocolates. I decided to save it for my parents, and hid it under my bed. Eventually the ants got it. . . . I learned to blow bubble gum and practiced English words. At night I would cry softly, so no one would hear me."

The Peter Pans were no longer simply children; they were also symbols of the Cold War conflict between Cuba and the United States. Father Salvador De Cistierna, a Roman Catholic priest who ran the largest shelter, was featured in a film made by the U.S. government, talking to the Peter Pan children in south Florida. His talk makes it clear that the children were understood as more than just kids who needed a place to live. "You are a constant reminder that there is something very wrong in the world. I would like you to be boys and girls with a great sense of responsibility, because the new society, a new world, is waiting for you to rebuild your homeland. Cuba is waiting for you."

The generous hosts. The crusading middlemen. The precious children rescued. The accumulated weight of the triumphal narrative made it harder for children, even when grown, to talk openly and honestly about what was hard and painful for thousands of kids who left everything and everyone they knew to head for America. Calling Operation Peter Pan anything less than a success smacked of ingratitude. Nena Torres went on to become a history professor, and wrote a book about the Peter Pans. "The stories tell of a heroic flight from repression to freedom, a pain-free rescue mission sponsored by brave humanitarians. But there was a wrenching trauma of separation."

The unique forces that spurred Cuban emigration, and the peculiar hothouse of Cold War politics created a very different impression of these Latino migrants. The very fact that so many Cubans were *not* poor people seeking a better life made them more sympathetic. Gustavo Pérez

Firmat's family operated a warehouse in Cuba. "My father was a food wholesaler. In October of 1960, the warehouse was confiscated by Fidel Castro and ten days later, my parents decided we were leaving. By then almost a hundred thousand Cubans had come—mostly professionals, entrepreneurs, and white-collar workers who had lost their jobs or possessions."

During the early days of the revolution, Cuban refugees in the United States and their American supporters thought that the state of affairs could not continue. Pérez Firmat remembers, "We believed that the Americans would never let a communist regime go on, so we were counting on them to get rid of Castro. We figured it would be any day now. And in fact, they did recruit Cubans to go in and fight—everybody in Miami knew the end was near and soon we would go home."

Fidel was in power less than two years when an invasion force of fourteen hundred Cuban exiles, trained by the United States, attempted to land in the Bay of Pigs on the island's south coast. In a stunning blow to American prestige, and a practical and propaganda victory for the Castro regime, the invasion was a disaster. The hope of heading home for thousands of Cubans in America burned for forty-eight hours and was dashed.

As sociologist Alejandro Portes notes, many of the exiles now understood they would be in the United States for a long time, but they had a lot of support as they made their transition. "Because of the Cold War, Cuban immigration was not just an event; it was a cause. Magazines like *Time, Life, Newsweek,* and *Fortune* celebrated the refugees' courage, their love of freedom, their entrepreneurial spirit.

"Soon laws were bent to facilitate their entrance into the country, and once here they got a series of benefits that other immigrants didn't get . . . with food stamps, free English courses, scholarships, cash—whatever they needed to get a head start."

The door to the United States was now slammed shut for many divided families waiting in Florida for relatives to join them from Cuba. As sad as that was for adults, it was potentially devastating for the young Peter Pans. "What this meant was that a lot of the children who had come to Florida in Operation Pedro Pan would not reunite with their parents anytime soon," Nena Torres remembers. "I was one of the lucky ones; first my mother and then my father had already managed to get to Florida. For them Florida became Neverland."

Many people made up their minds to leave. It was not as simple as strolling over to a ticket office and getting on a plane. Luis Capo remembered the day he climbed into a boat with his brother Carlos and his father, Manuel, in 1966. "We sailed from Pinar del Río in western Cuba, escaped the island, literally, because leaving then was illegal. You could get shot. Your boat could be sunk. You could go to prison if they caught you.

"It was my father, and myself and another brother. Another one of my brothers was a political prisoner at the time. My mother and four of the younger siblings stayed behind as well. We arrived in Cozumel, then Mérida, then Mexico City; we were headed to the United States."

By 1966, the United States and the Soviet Union squared off in the Cuban Missile Crisis, Fidel Castro had proclaimed Cuba a communist state, and the United States had been implementing an economic embargo for four years. Cuban society bumped along, bolstered by subsidies from the Soviet Union. When his boat made landfall in Texas, Capo learned Cubans were very different from other immigrants. "We jumped an eight-foot-tall fence. We got on a bus that took us to Louisiana, and there we were stopped by the authorities. They grilled us so hard, at one point my father nearly cried. But once they figured out that we were Cuban and not Mexican, they said to us, 'Welcome to America.'"

The Capos were not thrown out because a very different legal structure had grown up around Cubans trying to get to the United States. It removed people escaping from the island from the maze of limits, restrictions, waiting periods, and visa requirements faced by others. Cubans did not have to use a regular port of entry. The possibility of becoming a public charge was not an impediment to entering the United States. Once in the country, Cubans could get legal residency and U.S. citizenship faster than citizens of other countries.

AS THE 1960S wore on, some of the bloom came off the "heroic Cuban refugees" narrative that accompanied the first wave to south Florida. Frustration was well distributed. Men and women who had been doctors, accountants, and dentists back home could not get their Cuban or European credentials past state licensing boards in the United States and practice in their new hometowns. They did whatever jobs they could find, and their reduced status translated into reduced standards of living for their families. They worked as waiters, cabdrivers, stock clerks, and laborers.

By the end of the 1960s there were three hundred thousand Cubans living in Miami. In October 1965, Jack Kofoed, a columnist for the *Miami Herald*, wrote a column headlined "Miami Already Has Too Many Refugees." "We're up to our armpits with Cuban refugees," he wrote. "Many have become good, solid members of the community, but others have become a drag, and a number have added to the criminal problem. As a whole, they impose burdens, financial and otherwise." And it was about to get worse, Kofoed said. Castro had announced that anyone dissatisfied with the revolution could leave, and Kofoed wrote that that meant Castro was about to unload the old and infirm, and thousands of political prisoners, with the door to the United States held open by President Lyndon Johnson. Kofoed asked, "What's to be done with them? How can they be absorbed? They will add to the unemployment and welfare problems."

In a column a month later, Kofoed's complaints went beyond the economic and political, echoing observations made by old-timers about generations of immigrants to the United States: "The average Miamian is not really concerned with the amount of tax money spent on refugees. He is about actions which seem quite normal to Cubans. These include playing TVs and radios at the highest possible pitch at all hours of the night, the tendency to gather in groups in the middle of sidewalks, talking loudly and refusing to move for passersby . . . bad driving and disregard of traffic signs and signals . . . crowding of three and four families in a one-family house, which in the long run is certain to turn any neighborhood into a slum."

Kofoed reminds Cubans they came as guests of the American people, and were given money, food, and jobs. "As guests, you should try to adapt yourself to our way, not expect us to change to yours." If Kofoed's views were too far out of step with white Miami, there was little evidence of it in the *Herald*, which ran his column for thirty-five years.

The expanding Cuban population was also upsetting the binary, black-white notions of race that had long prevailed in Florida, once a breakaway Confederate state with racially segregated public space. African-American residents seethed as dark-skinned Cubans attended white schools traditionally closed to them. One minister concluded, "The American Negro could solve the school integration problem by teaching his children to speak only Spanish."

Pérez Firmat recalled that many Miami Cubans were unaware of the resentments swirling around them, or behaved as if they were. "We were in our own world. We didn't really see how others think of us. We were too preoccupied with being Cuban and building in Miami our replica of the Havana we'd left behind.

"So much seemed unchanged—we ate the same foods; the same people that visited us in Cuba came to visit our house in Miami. But things were different—I didn't have my own room; there were five of us in the Florida room."

Anti-Castro organizing and plots did not end with the failure of the Bay of Pigs invasion. Miami remained awash in intrigue, in rumors of plots and dreams of plots to overthrow Castro so that the exiles could go home. The anti-Castro militant organization Alpha 66 was founded in Puerto Rico in 1961 for the express purpose of overthrowing the Castro regime. It was widely believed in exile circles that the Cuban government would not last.

When Carlos Capo arrived in Florida, his "welcome" from earlier refugees consisted of confident assurances that his boat journey to Texas had been a wasted effort. "They told us we should have stayed in Cuba—didn't we know? Castro's days were numbered; everyone 'knew' that Alpha 66 was about to overthrow Castro—and Cuban exiles would go home. So why bother coming here now? But we had made this journey and arrived safely and now we had to just go for it."

The Capos made furniture before the Cuban Revolution. First, they went to work in a furniture factory. Then, says Luis Capo, they opened one of their own when they came to the United States. "We worked eight hours a day at the factory and then worked another eight- to ten-hour shift at our small furniture shop. Sometimes we slept no more than two or four hours a day. And everything in English, because that was 1966. Miami was not then what it is today."

The Capos opened their first place with a small loan solicited through contacts. Carlos Capo noted that government help was a big turning point, in the form of a ten-thousand-dollar loan from the U.S. Small Business Administration. They named their store El Dorado, after the sailboat that carried them out of Cuba.

With the dreams of quickly overthrowing Castro fading, many professionals took the long road to American qualifications and got their licenses, often a lengthy process that involved not only English-language classes but heading back to colleges and grad schools to bridge Cuban credentials to American requirements.

In the national economic growth of the 1960s, and even during the

Manuel Capo stands next to the delivery truck for the family furniture business in Havana. He would later sail to Mexico and make his way to the United States to start all over again. CREDIT: CAPO FAMILY

The Capo brothers named their Miami furniture store after *El Dorado*, the boat that brought them out of Cuba. CREDIT: CAPO FAMILY

slowdown and recessions of the 1970s, Cuban economic and political power in Florida grew. Like the Capos, other Cubans built their own enterprises, and rose in the corporate world to run enormous publicly traded enterprises, like Roberto Goizueta, who became chairman and

CEO of the Coca-Cola Corporation in 1980, and Carlos Gutierrez, appointed CEO of the Kellogg Company in 1999 and later George W. Bush's secretary of commerce.

Historian María Cristina García says the United States had never seen anything like it. "No immigrant community in U.S. history had gained so much economic and political power in the short time Cubans had. And all these gains were attained by *not* assimilating into the existing culture. In fact it is arguable that by remaining Cubans, and remaining focused on maintaining their heritage in the expectation of returning home, Cubans were able to succeed as they did."

Pérez Firmat echoes that idea: "Cuban children, like me, grew up immensely proud of who we were, believing that our experience was special. Discrimination against us never changed that feeling." Once the chance to return to Cuba was taken off the table, it can be argued that Cubans began to act less like refugees, and more like immigrants.

However, during these decades of success, a strong narrative of loss ran like an undercurrent to the Cuban story. It may be one of the most important differences between Cubans and other Latinos who came to the United States in the twentieth century. While family lore about coming to America from Puerto Rico or Mexico might begin with privation and the chance of something better in America, the Cuban family story begins with comfort, followed by privation in the new home. Significantly featured, especially in the stories told by older people, is a place that was better for them, one that was taken away.

The United States was impotent in getting it back for them, Pérez Firmat pointed out. "Each new president promised and didn't deliver." Over the years, the aging of the exile generation could be seen in Miami. "At some point, it became a very sad city. People kept dying—before going home. My father died in Miami, with his dream unfulfilled. Miami is not the city it is because of the people who live here—but because of the people who died here—because of the dreams that came to rest here."

The disappointment could take the form of dark humor. An old joke featured in Ana Menéndez's collection of stories is rooted in Cuban south Florida. A mutt on a Miami street ogles an elegant white poodle as she comes past. He tells her how beautiful she is, and tells her of the fancy dinners he would like to buy her, and the puppies he would like to have with her.

The poodle responds sniffily, "Do you have any idea who you're talking to? I am a refined breed of considerable class and you are nothing but a short, insignificant mutt."

"Pardon me, Your Highness," Juanito the mangy dog says. "Here in America, I may be a short, insignificant mutt, but in Cuba I was a German shepherd."

Looking at the Cuban experience, Alejandro Portes concludes that the accident of geography also played a role in Cuban success. "The Cuban experience in Miami is singular—unique among the immigrant experience of the twentieth century. Had Cubans gone to New York City, it would have been a very different story. New York was a much harsher environment. While it is considered the epitome of the melting pot—it is the toughest place for newcomers to survive, not to mention thrive."

AS CUBANS MADE fateful decisions to stay or go as the Castro regime hardened its grip on their island home, another Caribbean nation was in turmoil. The Dominican Republic, once dreamed of as a part of a Caribbean confederation with Cuba and Puerto Rico, had taken a very different path from its Spanish-speaking regional peers.

The Dominican Republic grew out of the first and oldest Spanish colony in the New World. Christopher Columbus established Spanish government on the island of Hispaniola in 1493, during his second voyage to the Caribbean.

Unlike other colonies in the region, with single administrations and a single national identity, Hispaniola was marked by the odd hybrid history created on the island. Spain and France fought for dominance as a profitable sugar plantation system was established, worked by slave labor. By the end of the eighteenth century, France established its hold on the western third of the island, and Spain on the eastern two-thirds.

What followed was a century of near-constant conflict pitting two empires and two colonies against each other on one small island. The Haitian Revolution created the first black republic in the world in the former French sector, and eventually Haiti made war on the Spanish-speaking sector, creating a country that briefly called itself the Republic of Spanish Haiti, uniting the island under a French-speaking government. Under Haitian law, whites could not own land, and Spanish plantation families sought refuge in Cuba and Puerto Rico.

Spanish secessionists helped overthrow the Haitian dictator Jean-

Pierre Boyer, then wrested back the eastern sector of the island and in 1844 created a Spanish-speaking republic. Haiti did not concede without more fighting, mounting repeated invasions of the new Dominican Republic. The Haitians were rebuffed, but rivalries within the Spanish-speaking political and military elite destabilized the country so much that it began shopping itself around to other powers for annexation. The United States was distracted by its own nervous breakdown, the American Civil War, the French were not interested, but in 1861 Spain returned for a third shot at colonial administration, only to be fought off once more. Rebels pushed Spain out again, and the modern Dominican Republic was established for good, in its final form, by 1865.

This unusual history set the table for some of the motifs of Dominican life for the next century and a half: a series of fragile and corrupt governments, a high degree of racial mixing, a high degree of racial consciousness, and a resentment of Haitians that bordered on paranoia.

The Dominican Republic of the mid-twentieth century saw the full realization of these traits. From 1930 to 1961, one man's will shaped Dominican life, that of Rafael Leónidas Trujillo, who as a military man, politician, and unelected strongman typified the worst excesses of Latin American misrule.

Trujillo's tentacles extended into every part of Dominican life. Secret police surveilled and suppressed all potential dissent. The dictator took a personal stake in the country's economy and made himself and his family

Generalissimo Rafael Trujillo, the Dominican dictator, was a reliable U.S. ally and seen as a counterweight to growing leftist influence in Latin America. CREDIT: © HULTON-DEUTSCH COLLECTION/CORBIS

fabulously wealthy. There was only one legal political movement in the country. The Dominican Party had as one of its main functions, as set out in its manifesto, "to sustain, propagate, and put into effect the patriotic and political credo of its founder, Dr. Rafael Leónidas Trujillo Molina." After centuries as Santo Domingo, the capital became Ciudad Trujillo (Trujillo City), and the highest mountain in the little country became Pico Trujillo.

El Jefe, the Chief, made his eleven-year-old son, Ramfis, a colonel in the army, and owned as much as 20 percent of the country's sugar manufacturing capacity, dairies, factories, and the national arms factory. A 1953 profile celebrated the stability, strides in education, and access to health care that set the Dominican Republic apart from other Caribbean island nations: "In judging the Dominican Republic and the extraordinary man who is its dictator it is vital, first, to pay tribute to the remarkable accomplishments of the regime since Generalissimo Trujillo took over in 1930." The article also reminded readers of one of the darkest episodes in the country's long rivalry with Haiti.

What Dominicans came to call "the Cutting" was a massacre ordered by Trujillo in 1937 to rid his country of Haitians who had come to work, and settled on farms and in small towns. The generalissimo was the proponent of a political idea called simply *antihaitianismo*, anti-Haitianism, that ended up taking the lives of an estimated thirty to fifty thousand Haitians through wholesale murder, later compensated by a payment to a Haitian puppet regime at about thirty dollars per corpse.

A killer and a thief as much as a statesman, Trujillo was a loyal ally of the United States. A statement, perhaps apocryphal, attributed to President Franklin Roosevelt's secretary of state Cordell Hull sums up the feelings Americans probably harbored about heads of state up and down the hemisphere: "He may be a son of a bitch, but he's our son of a bitch." Trujillo ran a tight ship, balanced his books, was a good customer, and did not tolerate any leftist nonsense. Since the U.S. Marines trained him as a policeman during World War I, Trujillo had been a reliable player. He was even seen as a counterweight to the growing influence of the new Castro government after the fall of Batista.

Starting in 1949 and continuing through the 1950s, the opposition to Trujillo began to rise in and outside the Dominican Republic. Brutal political killings, harsh repression of the press, and the estrangement of the powerful Roman Catholic Church began to drain away American support for *El Jefe*. Even as the Cold War rivalries around the world heightened, some leaders were so irredeemable even outspoken anti-communism was not going to be enough to keep them in the good graces of the West.

The novelist Julia Alvarez could date her life in America to a summer day in 1960 back in the Dominican Republic. Her father was part of the growing underground resistance to Trujillo. A black car started showing up in their driveway. "That car could only mean one thing: We were under surveillance. In our country this was deep, deep trouble."

As historian of Latin America and Cornell University professor María Cristina García affirmed, Alvarez's family's fears of Trujillo were well-founded. "He was a psychotic, pure and simple. He kidnapped and raped women, jailed, tortured, and killed political prisoners by the thousands. Informers were everywhere. Everyone feared him."

A friend at the U.S. embassy confirmed Alvarez's father's suspicions, and helped the family leave the country. In short order, the whole family was on a plane to the United States, a country that had long fueled Alvarez's girlhood imagination. "All my childhood I had dressed like an American, eaten American foods, and befriended American children. I spent most of the day speaking and reading English. At night, my prayers were full of blond hair and blue eyes and snow. I had dreamed of just

Young Julia Alvarez (*second from left*) with her sisters before the family fled the Trujillo regime and headed to the United States. CREDIT: JULIA ALVAREZ

such a plane ride as this one. All my childhood I longed for this moment of arrival. Here I was, an American girl, coming home at last."

She was not the first immigrant, and she would be far from the last, to get a sharp surprise when the country they had dreamed of and prepared for turned out to be very different from what they expected. "My Dominican classroom English, heavily laced with Spanish, did not prepare me for New York City English. I couldn't tell where one word ended and another began.

"Boys would taunt us, would yell at us: 'Spic!' Of course my good mother insisted that the kids were saying: 'Speak!' But I knew enough English to understand that she was wrong. If that wasn't clear enough, sometimes those boys threw stones at us."

Worse times were coming for the Dominican Republic. The Alvarez family would watch events unfold from a middle-class neighborhood in Queens, New York.

In May 1961, Trujillo's car was ambushed and the dictator was assassinated. Several men were killed in an ensuing gun battle, and as Trujillo's son tried to retain the family's hold of the country, all of the attackers but one were arrested and executed among a general crackdown. The surviving attacker, Antonio Imbert Barrera, was later declared a national

Rafael Trujillo's bullet-riddled automobile. The dictator's assassination led to instability in the Dominican Republic that culminated in a lightning invasion by the United States in 1965. CREDIT: © BETTMANN/CORBIS

hero, made a general, and given a state pension. Imbert denies the connection, but rumors that the Central Intelligence Agency played a role in the Trujillo assassination have swirled around it for the last half century. CIA-connected or not, the death of Trujillo did not bring an end to his era; the rival factions inside Dominican politics would continue to fight it out for years.

Despite the Cold War standoff with the Soviet Union in Europe, and the escalation of involvement in Vietnam, problems in Santo Domingo did not escape Oval Office attention.

Four years after the death of Trujillo, twenty-six thousand U.S. Marines splashed ashore in Santo Domingo. President Lyndon Johnson explained to the nation that the lightning invasion was necessary to keep Communism from making further inroads in the Western Hemisphere: "It becomes a matter calling for hemispheric action only—repeat—only when the object is the establishment of a communistic dictatorship."

In the great power logic that prevailed through decades of the Cold War, even the slightest implication of Communist influence was all that was needed to justify a military incursion. Politicians from barely center-left all the way to the hardest-core Marxist-Leninists were often spoken of in nearly identical terms. The U.S. invasion blocked a left-leaning social democrat from the Dominican presidency, and cleared the way for Joaquín Balaguer, a member of previous Trujillo governments. LBJ told Americans, "Communist leaders, many of them trained in Cuba, seeing a chance to increase disorder, to gain a foothold, joined the revolution. They took increasing control. And what began as a popular democratic revolution, committed to democracy and social justice, very shortly moved and was taken over and really seized and placed into the hands of a band of Communist conspirators."

Johnson reassured the country of the American interest in avoiding casualties on the Dominican or U.S. sides, and of the lack of interest in Washington choosing the eventual leader of the Dominican Republic. During the American occupation a conservative, nonmilitary organization was established in Santo Domingo, and the U.S. Marines came home.

THE POSTWAR IMMIGRATION laws had limited the number of people who could come to the United States from Asia, Africa, and Latin America.

Since 1924, Congress set immigration quotas based on the number of foreign-born residents of each nationality already counted in the country in the 1910 census. In other words, American immigration law for much of the twentieth century was rigged to reproduce the patterns of immigration that prevailed at the beginning of the century. This formula excluded immigrants from much of the world, favoring arrivals from Europe over anywhere else, and northern and western Europeans over southern and eastern immigrants.

No more. With passage of the Immigration and Nationality Act of 1965, American law would no longer automatically block the Dominicans who wanted out of an unstable and sometimes dangerous country and others trying to leave other non-European countries. Thousands headed for New York. "We didn't think of any other place to go. To us, New York was the United States. That's all we knew anyone we knew was in New York," recalls Eligio Peña, looking back to his teenage years, when he first began thinking about leaving the Dominican Republic. "I was in boarding school in Santo Domingo. You could hear the confrontations almost every night—it was unsafe. As far as a future—it didn't look good." Peña finished school, and left the country in 1968.

In his years as a journalist, Juan González has closely covered Dominican politics, and the settling of a major new ethnic group in New York. "The new arrivals were generally better educated than either Puerto Rican migrants or Dominicans back home. They were also more politically aware than the average Puerto Rican or Mexican. But they arrived to occupy the lowest jobs—as immigrants tend to do."

Eligio Peña headed to the Bronx. "I went to Baruch College at night—and worked in a factory until I got a job at a bodega. I went to the Empire Institute for computer training. I still don't know computers. But I know bodegas—and I know supermarkets." Bodegas are the small Latino convenience stores that dot neighborhoods everywhere there are large numbers of Spanish-speakers. They open for long hours, carry Caribbean foods many supermarkets will not, and importantly, offer small amounts of credit to working-class Latino New Yorkers.

Dominicans moved into the South Bronx and Manhattan's far-northwest neighborhoods, as Puerto Ricans left the center city for New Jersey, Connecticut, and suburban New York counties.

During the 1960s and 1970s, Puerto Ricans set the Latino cultural tempo of New York. If you heard someone speaking Spanish on the street, it was with a Puerto Rican accent. If a Latino was vying for a city council seat in Brooklyn, or a state senate seat in the Bronx, you knew that person almost certainly was Puerto Rican.

On a Sunday in mid-June, Manhattan would suddenly become Boricua Central, as the National Puerto Rican Day Parade brought hundreds of thousands of marchers, bands, beauty queens, and Puerto Rican celebrities from the island and the mainland. Puerto Rican New York was the soil that nurtured Tito Puente and Cuban Pete and Piri Thomas and Rosie Pérez and Marc Anthony and Jennifer Lopez.

Juan González watched as Dominicans inhabited Puerto Rican spaces, and economic niches as well. "There's a rivalry between the Puerto Ricans and Dominicans—which has moved from one barrio industry to the other. Virtually every bodega used to be Puerto Rican–owned. Today it is rare to find one not owned by a Dominican. The same is true of the livery cab service."

Eligio Peña is grateful for the pioneering generations of Puerto Rican migrants. "The Puerto Ricans really laid down the foundation for us. If it had not been for the Puerto Ricans, the Dominicans—we wouldn't know where to go. Dominicans started to buy up the bodegas—and then we saw that there was a real need for supermarkets—the big chains had left because they didn't want to be in poor areas."

When Peña left the Dominican Republic and headed to New York, he left behind an enormous family. One by one, his fourteen siblings took advantage of the progress made by their big brother Eligio, and helped expand a growing family business. "Each year, as they graduated high school, I brought my siblings. All of them came—fifteen of us plus my mother. We all worked in the supermarket business—and we were able to expand to fourteen stores, in Manhattan, Long Island, New Jersey and North Carolina." Today the name Compare Foods is well known to Spanish-speaking customers up and down the East Coast.

TODAY AMERICA'S LARGEST city speaks Spanish in a stunning array of accents. Roughly one out of three New Yorkers is Latino, a shocking number for *los viejitos* who remember the hard times, the cracked plaster and cold pipes in East New York, the Lower East Side, and Sunset Park, when Latinos were seen as intruders bringing chaos and criminality. Their grandchildren are not unwelcome intruders. They have spread throughout the Northeast. Many have educations, homes, and a secure perch in the middle class. At the same time, many others still struggle in aging cities, plagued by the same poor housing, schools, and jobs faced by earlier arrivals.

The 2010 census confirmed the continuation of a gradual change in Latino New York. Puerto Ricans are still the largest group, at 738,000, while Dominicans have zoomed in population from those first arrivals in the tumult of coups and invasions in the 1960s to number more than 600,000. Mexicans have come to New York in enormous numbers in just the past few decades. From a little more than 50,000 in 1990, there are now some 350,000 Mexicans in New York . . . an entire Minneapolis . . . an entire Wichita . . . now making their way in the vast city. Countless others work hard to avoid the census enumerators, because they live and work in the United States illegally. Along with middle-class homeowners, college students, politicians, entertainers, and office workers, there are new thousands clinging to the bottom rungs of New York's opportunity ladder, occupying the worst housing and sending their kids daily to the worst schools.

As Peña noted, it was the Puerto Ricans of the postwar migrations who paved the way. Along with the ballplayers, boxers, actresses, and musicians, community leaders carry their people's aspirations forward in their new home. Today they are U.S. senators and representatives, mayors and county executives from all Latino groups. For Caribbeans making a political career, their godfather is a Puerto Rican who stepped off a cargo ship a near-penniless twelve-year-old orphan in 1941.

Young Herman Badillo was sent to Haaren High School in Manhattan and put in vocational training. "I was studying aeromechanics; we all were. Well, this aeromechanics thing was a disaster, because there were no engines for us to repair—but that's just how it was. Because I was Puerto Rican, they had decided I would have no higher aspirations.

"But then I began writing for the school paper. The student in charge of the paper says to me, 'Why are you taking aeromechanics? That's for blacks and Puerto Ricans.' I said, 'I am Puerto Rican.' 'But you're actually bright,' he says, 'even with the accent.'"

Badillo graduated first in his class at the City College of New York and Brooklyn Law School. A very close presidential election loomed in 1960. It was just the opening for an ambitious young lawyer from a community that arrived in the United States already naturalized and able to vote. "JFK was looking for someone to run his campaign in east Harlem. Kennedy wanted to register blacks and Puerto Ricans. So they put me on. Eleanor Roosevelt came; so did JFK. But Jackie [Kennedy] was the hit, because she spoke Spanish."

Getting Puerto Rican voters to the polls, it turned out, was not just a matter of getting them registered and interested in voting. It was also a matter of pushing past entrenched powers with no interest in having a new constituency to whom they had to answer. So Badillo played a double game. "The Italians were a real obstacle. I was running a voter registration drive. The polling places were open until ten p.m. Some guy, not knowing who I was, thinking I was Italian, said, 'You know what we're going to do with those Puerto Ricans? We're gonna close that polling spot at nine.' And I said, 'Wow, great idea.'

"They closed that polling place at nine. But I went there, and I took down everybody's name who showed up on time to a closed polling location. There were fourteen people. And with that I filed a complaint—which was the first official case of discrimination against Puerto Ricans in New York."

Herman Badillo cuts his teeth in politics. Flanked by former First Lady Eleanor Roosevelt, Badillo campaigns for John F. Kennedy during the 1960 campaign. CREDIT: HERMAN BADILLO

Badillo won the voters' rights case.

John F. Kennedy won the election.

The Puerto Rican lawyer had registered Puerto Rican and Spanish-speaking voters in record numbers, adding almost a quarter million to the rolls. Kennedy carried that population and won the election by one of the slimmest margins in history. Badillo was on his way.

Badillo was the first voting member of Congress born in Puerto Rico and a cofounder of the Congressional Hispanic Caucus. CREDIT: HERMAN BADILLO

"JFK could not have won without the Puerto Rican vote. The political establishment needed to know that—but Puerto Ricans did too. This was the first time we could feel that we made a difference."

Badillo was elected Bronx borough president in 1965, the first Puerto Rican elected a county executive on the U.S. mainland. He was elected to the U.S. House of Representatives in 1970. His unsuccessful run for mayor of New York marked him as the first Puerto Rican to run for mayor of an American city. (It was Maurice Ferre, mayor of Miami from 1973 to 1985, who was the first Puerto Rican to become chief executive of a mainland city.) During his three terms in Congress, Badillo became one of the founders of the Congressional Hispanic Caucus.

Latinos from many countries, and from more and more places in the United States, were making it in America. At the same time the most durable commodity of all, memory, was carried in many heads like a diamond: memory of a town, a home, a culture. Latinos kept theirs alive in the United States, even earning the resentment of other Americans for doing so.

The successful writer Julia Alvarez. CREDIT: JULIA ALVAREZ

One of Julia Alvarez's best-known works, *How The García Girls Lost Their Accents,* a novel that follows the daughters of a Dominican physician making new lives for themselves in New York.
CREDIT: ALGONQUIN BOOKS

Even today, not far from the Canadian border, and a long way from her Caribbean roots in the Dominican Republic, Julia Alvarez, author of the celebrated novels *In the Time of the Butterflies* and *How the García Girls Lost Their Accents,* carries home in her head. "As the leaves fell and the air turned gray and the cold set in, I would remember the big house in Boca Chica, the waves telling me their secrets, the cousins sleeping side by side in their cots, and I would wonder if the words by which I'd entered this country had set me free from everything I loved."

For Juan González, that memory, like a pearl sewn into the lining of a coat, is part of what keeps Latinos who they are in the twenty-first century. "That sense of giving up all that you love, your island—your home— which was always remembered better than maybe it really was. It fed a nostalgia that insisted on the preservation of culture and language— those were portable items that one could carry anywhere and pull out when times got tough."

The coming years of tumult for the United States would bring change, struggle, and progress for Latino communities across the country. A people was coming into its own. Down on the border with Mexico, out on the Pacific, back in New York, Latinos would come into the inheritance that was theirs . . . as Americans.

A migrant worker family in the fields.

5

WHO'S "IN"?
WHO'S "OUT"?
WHOSE AMERICA?

MOST AMERICANS only occasionally travel outside the region where they live and work. When they do, it is rarely with the express purpose of digging down deep into the way life is lived day to day by unfamiliar people. Instead, we form impressions. Each person carries a map around in his or her head—a map of places unfamiliar and well-known, desirable and best avoided. We also have a kind of people map, a grab bag of impressions and ideas and conclusions that help us to "know" a place we've never been, and people we've never met. One of the most potent tools for sketching in the details of that mental map is television.

So it was important that on the evening of September 13, 1974, a network audience watched actor Freddie Prinze start drumming a Latin rhythm on a gas pump in an East L.A. garage. The shop's owner, Jack

Freddie Prinze. Born Frederick Karl Pruetzel, the Nuyorican comedian became a situation comedy star as Chico in *Chico and the Man.* CREDIT: © BETTMANN/CORBIS

Albertson, not only tells him to cut out the drumming, but adds for good measure, "Go back to your own neighborhood."

No drumroll. No fireworks. No sudden swell of violins to signal to the audience that something important is about to happen. Prinze's character, Chico, replies, "This is my neighborhood. I grew up watching your garage run down. You need me."

Albertson is puzzled. "For what?"

Prinze answers simply, "I'm Super-Mex."

All right, it's not the Treaty of Guadalupe Hidalgo. It's not the Bill of Rights. But American television audiences had not seen anything like it before. Here was a Latino character telling a mainstream American one:

- That the Anglo is in *Latino* space, a place that is populated, defined, possessed by Latinos rather than a place where they are strangers, foreigners, intruders, or visitors.
- That the Anglo *needs* a Latino for something more than *bracero* labor. Not just a strong back and two arms, Chico is a skilled mechanic, offering to help save a failing business.
- That the relationship can be multidimensional. Over the course of the series comic situations are drawn from more than ethnicity.

There is a wide difference in age between Albertson and Prinze at a time in America when the generation gap yawned like a canyon, after the struggles for civil rights, the Vietnam War, political assassinations, and Watergate. Albertson's character is older, traditional, and occasionally cranky. His hardness is confronted by Prinze's exuberance, humor, and decidedly different worldview.

Some might say, "Big deal." By the Nixon years, Chico was hardly the first Latino leading character on network television. In 1974, however, *Chico and the Man* took a mainstream audience places it had never been taken by a Latino character before.

I Love Lucy's Ricky Ricardo, played by Desi Arnaz, is not a migrant farmer or a manual worker. He's a talented musician and entrepreneur, a nightclub owner. Earlier TV characters, like the sombrero-topped Cisco Kid (1950–56) (played by Duncan Renaldo, ethnic background ambiguous) and his brave and comic sidekick Pancho (played by pioneering Mexican-American actor Leo Carrillo, whose great-great-grandfather sheltered Apolinaria Lorenzana) are as much Mexican as American, expertly riding horses back and forth over the borders of nationality, culture, and sovereignty in the mid-1800s American Southwest. At home, and skilled in navigating both cultures, Cisco Kid can speak with credibility to both Anglo and Latino, and became a go-between in a rapidly changing cultural and political landscape in newly American territory that was once Mexico. Not a sworn peace officer or member of the new American governing apparatus, Cisco is a kind of Mexican border knight-errant, finding bad guys, righting wrongs, and defending the weak.

Also signaled by the pounding of horses' hooves and a flash of glinting sword was Zorro (a character who first appeared in a serialized magazine in 1919 and who was played from 1957 to 1959 on television by the Italian-American Guy Williams). Zorro was Robin Hood with a Spanish accent and a high-class pedigree. The masked enforcer lived in colonial California, battling corrupt, lying, abusive (and occasionally feminized) Mexican bad guys. It was a weird show, featuring as it did a skillful, brave, and strong Mexican hero, the aristocrat Don Diego de la Vega, while at the very next moment indulging in the worst set of Mexican stereotypes to define his adversaries. The soldiers, aristocrats, and landowners of the Zorro stories are cruel, venal, and stupid.

Springing from the same stereotypes while in a different category from all these Latino characters populating the black-and-white television screens of my youth was Baba Looey, the sombrero-wearing burro

Guy Williams as "Zorro."
CREDIT: © BETTMANN/CORBIS

who was the cartoon sidekick of the self-deluding, clumsy, but well-meaning horse/lawman Quick Draw McGraw (1959–62). While identified as "Mexican" in the near-empty deserts of the American West through his hat and his accent, Baba marries the best traits of the Cisco Kid's Pancho and Cervantes's Sancho. Like Sancho Panza who keeps his wary eye on his "master," Don Quixote, only the little burro appears to know what is really up. Baba breaks down the "fourth wall" of the TV screen and occasionally speaks directly to us, his audience, with a running commentary on his efforts to save his boss and friend from his own worst impulses. When Quick Draw dons a mask and channels his own Zorro fantasies by becoming a cartoon Zorro, "El Kabong," Baba follows, in sombrero and mask and cringe-worthy "Mexican" accent, to narrate the goings-on.

Freddie Prinze's Chico is different. He is confident, secure, and doesn't get his status or his sense of himself from Jack Albertson's "Man," an ethnically undefined character known as Ed Brown. Prinze challenges his would-be boss, "Ask anybody in the barrio about Chico Rodriguez. You know what they'll tell you? 'Oh, yeah! Chico can take apart an engine and put it back together blindfolded.'"

Again, this is not some great cultural milestone. But it's something. Albertson becomes a kind of West Coast Archie Bunker, occasionally mining the same kind of stereotypes as Carroll O'Connor's sitcom New Yorker, to both serious and comic effect. Remember, Prinze is asking Albertson for a job, but Chico believes his skill allows him to be an easygoing wise guy rather than a subservient petitioner. The garage owner hands his visitor a wrench:

> Prinze: "You want me to fix something?"
> Albertson: "Yeah, tighten up your tongue before it flaps out of your mouth."
> Prinze: "Amigo!"
> Albertson: "Don't call me amigo!"
> Prinze: "It means 'friend.'"
> Albertson: "I don't care what it means. Talk English."
> Prinze [adopts his version of an upper-class English accent]: "Very well, friend. I would like to be the first Chicano associated with this floundering enterprise."

Like Chico Rodriguez, Freddie Prinze was an invention. He was born in New York in 1954 as Frederick Pruetzel, to a Hungarian father and a Puerto Rican mother. After his start in stand-up, Prinze moved first to late-night television appearances, then to his groundbreaking sitcom. In 1977, he was at just twenty-two in the third season of his NBC show. He had performed at preinaugural festivities in Washington for Jimmy Carter and Walter Mondale at the request of the incoming president, and vice president. Prinze's press agent, Paul Wasserman, told the *New York Times*, "It was a great thrill for Freddie. It symbolized that he had made it. Professionally, he was at his peak."

The tremendous success of *Chico and the Man* and Prinze himself was short-lived. Just weeks after the performance at the inauguration, after a history of depression, he shot himself in the head.

THE UNITED STATES in the 1970s was faced with major challenges. People who were held back by prevailing prejudices in the years after the Second World War were, one by one and often together, demanding a new kind of society in their country. They learned from one another, made strategic alliances, and banged on the door of the "people in charge"— politicians, business owners, the courts, the schools—for thirty years.

In the late 1960s and early 1970s, you might have plopped down your schoolbooks, as I did, and around dinnertime watched as all the world's sorrows were delivered fresh and piping hot to your TV screen: the Vietnam War and the struggle at home to end it; school strikes over control of administrations, who taught, and what was taught; sit-ins; street riots; assassinations; and the persistent demands for rights from blacks, women, Latinos, gays, people with disabilities, and others.

These extraordinary times also forced people who thought of themselves as ordinary into action. Confronted with the injustice, suffering, and struggle of the workers who picked the crops that ended up on America's dining tables, Dolores Huerta could not sit still.

She was an interesting mix. Her mother was descended from Mexican-Americans in the United States for many generations; her father was the son of Mexican immigrants. As a young schoolteacher in central California, Dolores saw the living conditions and ill health of the youngsters whose parents worked the fields. Maybe half were American citizens; the other half were not. Huerta remembers that they shared the dangerous poverty that handicapped their todays and burdened their tomorrows. "They were so poor, and almost always sick. They came to school in rags, often without breakfast. Most had never seen a doctor or dentist."

Huerta's mother, Alicia, and her father, Juan, had split when Dolores and her siblings were young. Her mother took the kids from New Mexico to Stockton, California, and burned with the desire to get ahead. "She would work two jobs—in the cannery at night and waitressing during the day—to save enough money to open a restaurant, and later a hotel."

Her father stayed back in New Mexico, and became a union organizer and state legislator. You might say Dolores incorporated both examples in her own life—of labor leadership and politics—and she was the model of an ambitious, hardworking, and independent woman.

Standing before her class at Brown Elementary School in Stockton, Dolores realized she could do little to change the circumstances of her hungry kids. Change had to come in the fields, where their parents worked to give Americans cheap and plentiful food, while getting paid a pittance and going hungry.

"The work was hard and dangerous. Crop dusters sprayed pesticides on the fields while people were working. People got really sick, and some died. So many babies were born with brain damage. I remember seeing

Dolores Huerta as a young organizer. CREDIT: © 1976 GEORGE BALLIS/TAKE STOCK/THE IMAGE WORKS

children with the most horrible birth defects. The growers, the business owners, the government: nobody did a damn thing."

Dolores Huerta left the classroom and headed to the fields after concluding, "I couldn't stand seeing kids come to class hungry and needing shoes. I thought I could do more by organizing farmworkers than by trying to teach their hungry children." She became the cofounder of the Community Service Organization's Stockton chapter. In a way she never stopped being a teacher. To the most neglected and mistreated workers in America, she helped teach the techniques of organization and resistance that would help migrant workers stand up to growers with greater resources and contacts.

In the early 1960s, today's common ideas about the rights and abilities of working women were not as widely accepted. As Huerta's devotion to advocacy and the labor movement grew, she was also a young wife who went on to have eleven children. "I was always pregnant. But I cared more about helping other people than cleaning house and doing my hair, and this didn't go over well at home.

"It ended up in my second divorce. Every day in 1961, I drove to Sacramento to lobby the legislature to pass laws for poor people. Meanwhile, my husband was trying to take my kids away from me in court. Hard times."

Where does the mother end and the citizen begin? If you knew Dolores Huerta and her work during these years, would you have thought of her as a hero, or a neglectful mother? She ended up raising her kids alone. "I don't remember anything about my daughter Alicia's childhood except nursing her in the ladies' room during breaks in city council meetings."

In between nursing breaks, Huerta was making her mark. In one year she helped get fifteen bills passed in the California legislature. Poor children would now get free breakfast and lunch in school.

In 1962, Huerta met a young organizer who was already developing a growing reputation in California's agricultural heartland. His name was Cesar Chavez. "I had heard a lot about him. Cesar this and Cesar that. But he didn't make much of an impression on me. I forgot his face. He was very unassuming. He had a reputation as a great organizer, but I found it hard to believe."

History is full of teams that go on to build enduring reputations and accomplish great things: Lewis and Clark, Watson and Crick, Lennon and McCartney. Their first meetings have often been uneventful, even hard to remember for the partners themselves. In Huerta and Chavez, the farmworkers had organizers, leaders, and allies who would eventually pull them from the shadows and ask Americans to think about how food gets from the soil to their table.

Chavez's grandparents came to Arizona from Mexico in the 1880s. His family started a freight business, bought land, and began farming. Chavez's family did not stand still. His father added a grocery store, a pool hall, and a garage to the family holdings.

When the Great Depression hit, it wiped out all the businesses, and the state of Arizona repossessed the family home. Like millions of other Americans, Chavez's family hit the road. They worked the fields and lived in camps. By his reckoning, Cesar and his brothers and sisters attended some thirty different schools in those years. Later, he recalled how Spanish was forbidden. "The teacher swooped down on us. I remember the ruler whistling through the air as its edge came down sharply across my knuckles. The principal had a special paddle that looked like a two-by-four with a handle. It was smooth from a lot of use."

As an adult he could speak to illiterate farmworkers as a peer and friend, and to the powerful and influential as an equal. He was soft-spoken, erudite, sophisticated. Chavez left school after the eighth grade and headed into the fields.

"It was a hell of a life. Working in the fields in the scorching hot summers. Living in a broken-down car, or else in the dark, overcrowded shacks without toilets, electricity, or running water.

"Farmworkers were in a uniquely bad position. After decades of struggle and bloodshed, unions were established in other industries. But there were no farm unions."

The men, women, and children who made Americans' food were very different from other workers. Many had no permanent home, simply following the seasons, arriving in a state or county around the time the lettuce, broccoli, strawberries, tomatoes, apples, or grapes were ready to be picked. When a crop was in, it was time to move on. A worker could labor for the same grower for years, only to be a stranger to him if the two passed on the street. It was hard to make a life in one place, because before long, it would be time to leave again.

To the end of his life, Cesar Chavez insisted that his union members be regarded as human beings, invested with the dignity that is the right of workers anywhere, in any industry. "I have been driven by one dream, one goal, one vision: to overthrow a farm labor system in this nation which treats farmworkers as if they were not important human beings, to see my people treated as human beings, and not as chattel."

Chattel is property. A system had grown up over the years that allowed growers to regard workers as just another machine. They had become something like temporary serfs. While serfdom around the world had taken on an implied, if small sense of obligation from master to worker, America's serfs seemed to deserve nothing. Even if their well-being was ignored, they would be back in another year, when the fruit began to ripen.

At twenty-five, Chavez began doing social work with Mexican-American migrant farmworkers. Nine years of that work had brought little tangible success. When Chavez met Huerta, a partnership began that would remake the struggle in the fields, shake up the labor movement in America, and bring a new kind of attention to Latinos in America. Another part of the story, less noble perhaps, can't be denied: Dolores Huerta moved into Cesar Chavez's shadow, and would never emerge from it.

Yet that does not appear to bother Huerta. When asked about her role and reputation, she replied simply with a story: "One day Cesar called me over to his house and said, 'You know, farmworkers are never going to have a union unless you and I start it.' There was no disagreement that he would be the leader. I didn't mind. In those days, even woman reporters didn't report on what women did. I always say, 'Men want to see who gets the blame and who gets the credit.' Women say, 'Let's get the job done. Who cares?'"

Cesar Chavez, on a hunger strike, with Senator Robert Kennedy. CREDIT: © BETTMANN/CORBIS

Remember, it was the 1960s. Though Dolores Huerta was one of the creators of the United Farm Workers, it was Cesar Chavez who became the hero, the symbol, the name attached to *la Causa*, the Cause. In the early 1960s, what would eventually become the women's movement was just gathering steam. Women working the same jobs as men were routinely, and legally, paid less money for the same work. In offices, men made decisions and women made coffee. Across the professions, in colleges and universities, in industry, women were discouraged or barred by custom from the upper reaches of leadership, responsibility, respect, and pay.

Add to women's unequal status in American society the prevailing ideas about gender in Latino cultures, and Dolores Huerta already had plenty in her path. Maybe you've heard the term *machismo* to refer to ingrained male dominance in Latino attitudes about gender. The term has passed into common use among Americans, usually to refer to an abusive, oppressive kind of masculinity that involves unquestioned male authority and even tolerates physical abuse. The code of the *macho* is a little more complicated than that.

It is true that exaggerated masculinity and male dominance have been features of Latino life in America and back in the home countries of Latin America. Along with the less savory notions, there is a broader definition of *machismo* lost in its migration to the United States. Part of that male pride traditionally came from dignity, responsibility, and self-control. A man with little money or education would still gain social status from handling his affairs, and *being seen* to handle his affairs with dignity, like an adult. A man who was seen out of control in the public sphere, being made to look like a fool, or making a fool of himself, lost status in his community.

A *macho* may seem like an anachronism after long decades of growing opportunity for women, and legal recognition of the rights and equality of women. Once upon a time, he made sense to his town, village, or neighborhood . . . and most of all, to himself.

But times were changing. Dolores Huerta moved into Cesar and Helen Chavez's house with six of her children. Huerta traveled with Cesar to the migrant camps at the edges of the fields, while Helen Chavez cared for fourteen children, hers and Huerta's. It was a bold move for a Mexican-American woman. Raised in a community that valued women for their skill in keeping a home and raising children, Huerta was taking a radically different road. She created an identity for herself separate from family and home. She traveled with a married man for days at a time, trying to persuade men to take a risky, even dangerous step: defying the bosses to form a union.

"The organizing work has always come first with me," Huerta said, "and I just tried to catch up on the other things as well as I could. Because I felt that for every unmade bed and for every unwashed dish, some farmworker got one dollar more in wages somewhere."

Huerta's campaign for workers' dignity was also advancing the cause of women. "I did see in the union a lot of the women that were doing all the work and going on strike and going to jail. Taking the kids out to the picket line and then afterward, when the dust settles, then all of a sudden the women are not in the . . . they're not in the decision-making positions.

"I even told Cesar, 'You know what? There's just a lot of chauvinism here in the union,' and I told him, 'I'm not going to take it anymore from anybody.' It was mostly from the other guys, not from Cesar himself. I said, 'I just want to let you know that.'

"When I negotiated my contracts I always had the same wages for men and women. It didn't even occur to me that they should be different. Whenever we elected a ranch committee to the contract, I made sure we had women on it. Sometimes I had to really argue with the husbands to make sure that they let them, wouldn't stand in their way. But that's something you have to work at. The chauvinism unfortunately is very instilled in our society. And not just with farmers. I think it's just part of society."

The union formed by Huerta and Chavez came to be called the United Farm Workers, the UFW. In 1965, the young union began a defining confrontation with the grape growers in Delano, California. Filipino workers had walked off the farms, the grapes still on the vines. Huerta led the negotiations with the growers, and made an audacious demand: She wanted to bring farmworkers' wages up to the federal minimum wage. It was not a promising situation. No growers had ever signed a union contract.

The farmworkers did have some leverage. Grapes were rotting on the vines, but the growers were determined not to let a woman get the better of them. They brought in workers from Mexico and continued the harvest. Neither side could have known a war had begun that would last five years.

The growers began this battle with considerable advantages. They had money, property, political connections, and the support of the wider business community. In many ways, it is hard to think of a worker with less power, less leverage, less influence than a farmworker. Even though they were paid little money, there were always more people willing to plant, tend, and pick crops. That reality put steady downward pressure on wages. Eight out of ten farm families earned less than the federal poverty-line wage of $3,100 a year. By the 1960s the life expectancy of farmworkers was decades less than that of the average American.

Bracero labor, once contemplated as a temporary measure to fill labor shortages created by World War II, had never gone away. The growers' ability to bring up poor Mexican workers had created new expectations among growers for a steady supply of low-cost labor in the fields. "The *bracero* period had a big impact on agricultural practices," Huerta recalls. "When we first started organizing there were probably more families. But the trend had gone more to hiring single men. It became more of a speed-up, taxing people to the maximum of what they could produce. So it became brutal labor."

Chavez and Huerta began to build a movement that brought sympathy, interest, and solidarity from Americans of all walks of life. I shouldn't get ahead of the story. The pair had to create a crusade with, and for, poor workers that pulled in many others.

The UFW had a potent set of symbols: a red flag with a black, geometric Aztec eagle; the patron saint of Mexico, Our Lady of Guadalupe; the people's theater and stunning political organizing of the Peasant's Theater, El Teatro Campesino; and the handsome brown face of Cesar Chavez.

Culturally, it was a perfect storm. The power of political graphic art, perfected earlier in the twentieth century in Mexico, shaped the visual language of posters, picket signs, and banners. The explosive talent of young Californian Luis Valdez created theater pieces for and about the men and women in the fields. Sympathetic artists created stunning visual and musical works, like (National Medal of Arts winner) Lalo Guerrero's *corrido* for the farmworkers, "Corrido de Delano."

The farm owners did not stand still as the UFW charged ahead. The growers hired strikebreakers, who charged the picket lines and beat the strikers. Shocking film from the confrontations shows tough guys driving pickup trucks into groups of workers, spraying their faces with pesticides as police stood by, simply watching. The strikers did not fight back. Chavez and Huerta, like Mohandas Gandhi and Martin Luther King, insisted that if the workers' struggle turned violent, that violence would all come from the other side.

Huerta moved women to the front of the picket lines, ordering them to kneel on the ground to pray when police charged in to drag them

An elderly marcher carries the Aztec eagle of the United Farm Workers. CREDIT: WALTER P. REUTHER LIBRARY, WAYNE STATE UNIVERSITY

away. Several farmworkers were killed in shootings and beatings. Many more were clubbed by sheriff's deputies and strikebreakers. Dolores Huerta said she and Chavez watched the early struggles of Filipino farmworkers in Southern California and worried for their members' safety. "There was a lot of brutality against the Filipinos. They were beaten up. Beaten at their labor camps. The growers shut off their gas, water, and lights."

It may sound funny to say, but it is important to remember an important reality: Everybody eats. Autoworkers had a union, and while their product was an important one, not everyone bought or drove automobiles. Carpenters, miners, and electricians all had unions, but many Americans did not see themselves as conscious consumers of those workers' output. But everybody eats.

At the same time, the production of food for human consumption had become separated from most Americans' daily lives. The vast human migrations from farms into metropolitan areas meant the tempting mounds of low-cost food in a typical urban or suburban supermarket was ever more removed from the land used to grow it, the hands used to plant, tend, and weed it, and the strong backs that toiled in tough conditions to get it out of the fields and on its way to a kitchen table.

The fight in the fields did not yet generate that kind of attention. In March 1966, Chavez led a group of strikers on a 230-mile walk from Delano to the state capital of Sacramento, a pilgrimage that drew national press coverage. Huerta and Chavez made a direct public connection between the struggle against the grape growers and the black struggle for civil and human rights and the Christian religion. Chavez declared, "This is both a religious pilgrimage and a plea for social change for the farmworker. We hope that the people of God will respond to our call and join us for part of the walk, just as they did with our Negro brothers in Selma.

"The time is now for people, of all races and backgrounds, to sound the trumpets of change. As Dr. King proclaimed, 'There comes a time when people get tired of being trampled over by the iron feet of oppression.'"

As the march headed north it grew in size. Less than a month after he set out, on Easter Sunday, Chavez and his pilgrims reached the steps of the Capitol in Sacramento. Around the same time, the first company gave in to business pressure and bad public relations, as the UFW's hardnosed negotiator, Dolores Huerta, had secured a collective bargaining

UFW picketers. The workers and their supporters around the country took their struggle far from the fields where food was grown to the supermarkets where it was bought.
CREDIT: WALTER P. REUTHER LIBRARY, WAYNE STATE UNIVERSITY

A flowered cross and the Virgin of Guadalupe lead a farmworkers' march. CREDIT: WALTER P. REUTHER LIBRARY, WAYNE STATE UNIVERSITY

agreement with the Schenley-owned wineries in Delano. It was a major breakthrough for the fledgling union.

The strike started to attract national attention. Across the country, black Americans were confronting violent resistance from white Southerners who shot them, beat them, and turned dogs and fire hoses on them. The eyes of the world were fixed on Montgomery, Selma, and Birmingham as segregationists dug in their heels and U.S. presidents struggled to balance difficult politics and clear constitutional requirements. The Cold War meant problems in the South were going to become the subject of newsreels and television programs in the Soviet bloc, as America's original sin of racism became a propaganda failure in the superpower public relations race.

As long as the fight for a farmworkers' union pitted poor, powerless, and exploited workers against growers, an essential combatant was missing, and that was the public. Buses loaded with strikebreakers rolled through picket lines to bring in harvests far from the public gaze. The substandard shacks provided by growers to house workers and their families would never be seen by the shoppers who inspected a pint of strawberries or a bunch of grapes picked by those workers. Even Huerta, a relentless optimist, started to get discouraged.

"I was running my picket line and it was about the second week of the strike. The fields were full of strikebreakers, because we were so close to the Mexican border it was really easy for growers to bring them in. I put someone in charge of my picket line and went into the office.

"And I said, 'Cesar, the fields are full of strikebreakers. We're not going to win.' And he said to me . . . and I'll never forget it, 'You go back to that picket line. The only time we ever lose is when we quit. You've got to go back, and don't let me ever know that you left your picket line. Go back right now.'

"So I ran back to my picket line right away because [Cesar] had told me, 'Something's going to happen in that field and those workers are going to walk out.' The conditions were so bad that some worker was going to get insulted or mistreated inside and sure enough that's exactly the way it happened."

La Huelga, the Strike, was gathering momentum in the fields in the spring of 1966, but the UFW was still largely a California movement and a California story. Chavez and Huerta concluded that the only way to pull the rest of the country into the struggle in the fields was to take the conflict to their neighborhoods. Eating crops from the growers' land and the farmworkers' hands was going to be turned into a political act. Until the growers did business with the union, and signed contracts, the UFW would urge Americans to boycott their products, first grapes, and then lettuce. Huerta was coordinating the boycott in the whole country east of Chicago. "People didn't know who Cesar was, didn't know what the union was, who the farmworker was, what we were fighting for.

"We were selling the movement and getting people involved. And people in our country are very good-hearted people, and our message was so simple. Just don't buy grapes. Don't eat grapes. It was something that people could do."

The boycott began with young people, political progressives who volunteered as fieldworkers for the UFW, getting the message out among people likely to be in sympathy with the UFW: Democrats, trade unionists, college students. Over time, the message fanned out, percolated through the culture, and became a more broad-based effort to force a change in the fields. The union sent workers to other parts of the country. Huerta said, "They would go to union halls and they would go to churches. On Sundays, everybody had to go to a church. We'd speak, and we'd ask for volunteers to come and help us."

No other growers recognized the union and signed a contract. It was time to raise the stakes. Huerta headed east to nationalize the struggle, urge Americans to boycott table grapes, and deliver a dangerous blow to the growers' business. Huerta later remembered, "We took the fight from the fields of California to New York, Canada, and Europe. I think we brought to the United States the whole idea of boycotting as a nonviolent tactic. We laid a pattern of how farmworkers are going to get out of their bondage."

With the strike in its third year, Chavez began a water-only fast that lasted twenty-five days. The fast, to be followed by many more over the years, burnished the union leader's growing reputation. The fast also highlighted the religious nature of this struggle for civil rights. Americans had long since been accustomed to ministers, priests, and rabbis making overtly religious appeals to the country's conscience. The symbols of the United Farm Workers were Christian, but also something new. The visual language of Latin American Christianity tells the viewer a familiar two-thousand-year-old story of Jesus's life and death, but with different emphasis. In churches from the Andes to south Texas, images of blood, pain, and sacrifice are much more in evidence than in the less ornate, more subdued imagery of familiar mainline Protestant churches.

So the religious icons and the support of Catholic priests associated with the young farmworkers' movement struck a chord with the almost entirely Catholic membership. So did Chavez's own physical self-sacrifice. "A lot of people thought Cesar was trying to play God, that this guy was trying to pull a saintly act," says Dolores Huerta. "Poor Cesar! They just couldn't accept it for what it was. I know it's hard for people who are not Mexican to understand, but this is part of the Mexican culture—the penance, the whole idea of suffering for something, of self-inflicted punishment. In fact, Cesar often mentioned that we will not win through violence; we will win through fasting and prayer."

A Baptist minister who was turning his attention from the fight for new civil rights laws to social and economic justice saw in Cesar Chavez a comrade in the struggle for a different America. The Reverend Martin Luther King Jr. sent Chavez a message at the conclusion of the fast. "As brothers in the fight for equality, I extend the hand of fellowship and goodwill. Our separate struggles are really one. A struggle for freedom, for dignity, and for humanity."

As Chavez was preparing to break his fast, he was joined in Delano by Senator Robert Kennedy. The New York Democrat and younger brother of the assassinated president was a member of the U.S. Senate subcommittee on migratory labor and a recent convert to the farmworker cause. During Kennedy's first trip to Delano in 1966 he held a hearing on the conditions in the fields and the struggle to build a union. During one exchange with a local sheriff, the lawman admitted to arresting farmworkers who looked "ready to violate the law." An angry Kennedy shot back, "May I suggest that during the luncheon period of time that the sheriff and the district attorney read the Constitution of the United States?"

In the coming years the politician from the world-famous political family drew closer to the leaders of the farmworkers' nascent union and to the workers themselves. Kennedy returned to Delano in 1968, and RFK fed a weakened Chavez at the close of another hunger strike and told reporters, "I am here out of respect for one of the heroic figures of our time—Cesar Chavez. I congratulate all of you who are locked with Cesar in the struggle for justice for the farmworker and in the struggle for justice for Spanish-speaking Americans."

Robert Kennedy news conference in California. With Dolores Huerta at his side, RFK speaks to the national press. The New York senator and presidential candidate brought national attention to the struggle in the fields. CREDIT: WALTER P. REUTHER LIBRARY, WAYNE STATE UNIVERSITY

Kennedy had taken a long personal journey from his days as a hard-hitting counsel on the Senate Labor Rackets Committee. The bitterness and conflict of 1960s America, the killing of his brother, the corrosive effect of the Vietnam War, his tours through intense concentrations of poverty in Brooklyn and the Appalachian Mountains, and his journey to apartheid South Africa had pushed the senator to a new idea of American politics and the struggle for justice.

RFK's friend and biographer, Arthur Schlesinger Jr., said of the unlikely relationship between Chavez and Kennedy, "For all their differences in background the two men were rather alike: both short, shy, familial, devout, opponents of violence, with strong veins of melancholy and fatalism."

This stretch of weeks in early 1968 can only be remembered as a shock to America's system. In a few short months, the North Vietnamese and their Viet Cong guerrilla allies in the south launched the stunning Tet Offensive, a series of surprise attacks on the U.S. military and its South

Vietnamese allies. In the same period, the incumbent president, Lyndon Johnson, withdrew from the Democratic primaries and RFK announced he would run for president; Cesar Chavez launched his hunger strike; student strikes against the Vietnam War escalated in size and intensity, and both Martin Luther King and Robert Kennedy were murdered on the front edge of what would become a summer of urban riots, fires, and destruction on a breathtaking scale.

As Chavez grew in stature and renown as the public face of the UFW, Huerta was the organizer and negotiator who took the boycotts nation-wide and hashed out contracts with the growers. Dolores Huerta was also religious, and revered the place of the Church in Mexican-American culture. It turned out even the Church was not entirely ready for Huerta's expansive view of the role of women in the farmworkers' movement. "This priest I had worked very closely with when we were organizing the Agriculture Workers Association told me, 'You know what? You just need to stay home and take care of your children.' And I was so devastated. This is a person I had been working with very closely. I had a lot of faith. I was in my mother's house at that time and we had a meeting at my mother's house, and after [the priest] walked out the door my mother handed me a glass of tequila because I started crying. And she said, 'Don't listen to him.' And we both had a shot of tequila.

"But the farmworkers themselves, I never got that from them, ever. They knew what we were doing was so important and it was our only way to change things. So they really respected me a lot."

The success of the boycotts gave power to the last push for recognition. The struggles, the sacrifice, the violence endured, ending with a union that bargained with the growers. Not long after came a series of historic contracts and a state law making the fertile soil of California, into, in effect, a closed shop. The growers had to negotiate with the union.

Huerta, Chavez, and the workers had won. They had done it without resorting to the tactics others had used to stop them. A prayer from Cesar Chavez shows that for him, staying true to oneself was a victory. "It is how we use our lives that determines what kind of men we are. I am convinced that the truest act of courage, the strongest act of manliness, is to sacrifice ourselves for others in a totally nonviolent struggle for justice. To be a man is to suffer for others. God help us be men."

. . .

NOT EVERY LATINO struggle took the same road. Black Americans won major legal and constitutional victories in the 1950s and 1960s using the courts and nonviolent civil disobedience. Latinos had to fight many of the same battles, even as they benefited from the new civil rights laws. It did not matter whether it was an aging building in a teeming urban neighborhood in the Northeast, or a one-story frame "Mexican school" next to a dusty play lot in the Southwest: Latinos went to terrible schools.

It did not matter whether a substandard house stood in sight of the U.S.-Mexican border or in view of the Manhattan skyline, a lot of Latinos lived in aging and unhealthy homes. It did not make much difference whether they were farmworkers, city or county employees, or were crowded into vast urban barrios; Latinos were not heavily represented in city and county councils, state legislatures, or the Congress of the United States.

From Crystal City, Texas, in the Rio Grande Valley this time of breathtaking change had not changed much about daily life. In 1968, José Ángel Gutiérrez was twenty-four, bilingual, and restless. "At the end of the day, the Anglos went to their side of town and the Mexicans went to their side of town, across the railroad tracks. The gringos owned almost everything and controlled everybody. Anglos *worked* Mexicans, but no Anglo *worked for* a Mexican."

José Ángel's father died when José was a young teenager. The elder Gutiérrez, a physician, had fought alongside Pancho Villa in the Mexican Revolution. José Ángel Gutiérrez explained it this way: "My world had three spheres—a parental Mexican world, an Anglo school world, and my Chicano [U.S.-born Mexican] peer world. Every day I had to make choices: Do I eat in the school cafeteria with most of the Anglos but few of the Mexican kids?

"And if I bring lunch to school to be with my Chicano kind, will it be a white-bread sandwich or tortilla tacos? Which kind of tortillas—corn or white flour, that is, real Mexican or Chicano tortillas?" The duality—or, in young Gutiérrez's case, a *three-part* identity: American, Mexican, and Mexican-American—is one many Latinos will recognize. For this Rio Grande Valley kid the questions went much deeper than the mundane details of today's lunch to core notions of identity. "My feelings were all jumbled with regard to who *could* be my friends, who *should* be my friends, and who *were* my friends. My Chicano friends started calling me '*agachado*'—trying to be white."

Gutiérrez made a fateful step across the boundary line between accepting the way things always were and demanding they be different by making speeches at Chicano voter-registration rallies. One day he was hustled into a car by a man with a gun and brought to a private home filled with local police, the Texas Rangers, and representatives of the Anglo power structure in town. "I'd heard stories about how the sheriff and the Ranger captain had shot Mexicans in the back. This wasn't an urban legend—both of them had made frequent declarations to the press about how many men they'd killed, not counting Mexicans. I was convinced I was to join that list—of Mexicans not counted."

The men tried to muscle Gutiérrez into renouncing his public speeches, interrogating him for hours at gunpoint. He did not give in. "I began to realize the extent to which these men would go to keep things in *cristal*, as they were, to keep Mexicans in their place. It was a transformational moment in my life. I went from naive Chicano to militant Chicano. Fear of gringos in me was replaced by rage."

Gutiérrez turned his rage into political action. In 1967, in San Antonio, he and some friends founded MAYO, the Mexican American Youth Organization. The group took off, with more than forty chapters in Texas alone after just two years. The young political party devoted its attention to one arena where it was badly needed: schools. MAYO brought the mass walkouts called "blowouts" in East Los Angeles to small-town Texas, starting in Gutiérrez's hometown of Crystal City. While sixty percent of the students were Mexican-Americans, almost all the teachers were Anglos. "The only Chicano teachers were an assistant football coach and the Spanish teacher," Gutiérrez recalled. "The whites dominated the faculty, school board, and the curriculum too. They taught us that Davy Crockett and Jim Bowie and the other illegal aliens at the Alamo were heroes, and the Mexicans were bloodthirsty and brutal.

"The students couldn't even vote for their own student representatives. It was strictly prohibited to speak Spanish at school. The cafeteria serviced only Anglo food. All but one of the cheerleaders were Anglo. All this in a town that was eighty-five percent Chicano."

Gutiérrez and MAYO were learning by doing. They organized students from the ground up, and learned to talk to those in authority, pressing their grievances. "The superintendent said, 'Take the demands to the school board.' The school board said, 'Take the demands to the superintendent.' So a student leader printed up the list of grievances and passed it out at school. For which she was suspended."

The walkout began in the high school, and spread to the junior high and grammar schools, keeping some seventeen hundred students away. Three student leaders took their first airplane trip, to Washington, D.C., to meet with three U.S. senators. Before long, the U.S. Department of Justice pressured the Crystal City school board to negotiate. On January 9, 1970, the school board approved most of the demands of the striking students. Gutiérrez liked the taste of victory. It would encourage him to push the reluctant American Southwest even harder, as one of the activists who began attracting followers, imitators, admirers . . . and enemies.

The fight for Latino self-determination began to take many forms in many places. The crusaders had to decide for themselves how they would frame their demands, whom they would be willing to take on, and whether they would fight from inside or outside the established order.

In New Mexico, a former preacher named Reies López Tijerina insisted the Southwest had been taken illegally from Mexico in the nineteenth century, and should be returned to the Mexican-Americans of the region. In 1967, López Tijerina went as far as to lead an armed raid on a New Mexico courthouse. He was captured and sent to prison.

In Colorado in 1969, another preacher, Rodolfo "Corky" Gonzáles, hosted a youth conference in Denver that produced a document still used as ammunition by nativists and anti-immigration forces: "The Plan of Aztlán." The name is Aztec, for "a place in the north," and the document advocated the creation of a new Latino nation on the Mexican lands that became part of the United States after the Treaty of Guadalupe Hidalgo in 1848. What is now California, Arizona, New Mexico, Colorado, Texas, and Oklahoma was Aztlán, a country for Chicanos. The manifesto said, in part, "We are a Nation. We are a Union of free pueblos. We are Aztlán. *Por la Raza todo, Fuera de la Raza, nada.* [For *la raza*, the race, everything. Outside of *la raza*, nothing.]

"Something stolen can never be made legal property," said José Ángel Gutiérrez. "We did not want to assimilate with Anglos; over one hundred years of assimilation had not brought justice or anything like equality." Gutiérrez's words reflect a new lack of apology for simply being who you were. Other activist groups were starting to arrive at a similar idea.

"Even the idea of assimilation was offensive. Hey, we were here first. How come the Anglos didn't assimilate with us? We wanted our own homeland back. An independent Chicano homeland." Read a quote like that in the twenty-first century, and it seems a little far-fetched. It might sound different when placed in the context of Malcolm X and Stokely Carmichael demanding a black homeland, the American Indian Movement reviving ideas of Indian national sovereignty, and Puerto Rican activists demanding American withdrawal and an independent nation. Aztlán is rooted in its time.

Gutiérrez committed to playing an inside and an outside game. In south Texas, he tried to use the ballot box to capture political power, but he rejected the Republican and Democratic parties. La Raza Unida, the United Race, registered voters, ran petition drives, and got on the ballot for a range of offices in the counties bordering Mexico. In 1970, "La Raza Unida captured majorities in two school boards and two city councils, and elected two new mayors," said Gutiérrez, but he was not finished. "The next year we won more local elections. I was elected head of the Crystal City school board."

La Raza Unida now brought Gutiérrez into conflict not only with the Texas white power brokers and political establishment, but with one of the leading Mexican-American politicians in America, whose base was also south Texas. Henry B. González was the anti-Gutiérrez in generation, tactics, philosophy, and style. When La Raza Unida was racking up its first victories, "Henry B." was in his mid-fifties, a veteran member of the U.S. Congress, a legislative tactician, and a political warrior for the Mexicans and Mexican-Americans of Texas. His view of his people's place in America was the absolute opposite of Gutiérrez's.

Like many other families in Texas, González could trace his lineage back to sixteenth-century Spanish settlers in Mexico. Henry B.'s family came to the United States fleeing the tumult of the Mexican Revolution of 1910. His father became the editor of *La Prensa*, a prominent and historic Spanish-language newspaper.

González went to college, then to law school. He became the first Mexican-American in modern history elected to the San Antonio City Council. In 1956, he headed to Austin as a member of the state senate. In his first full year as a senator he tried to head off ten bills that would allow Texas to resegregate its schools, getting around the U.S. Supreme Court ruling against separate-but-equal schooling in *Brown v. Board of Education of Topeka, Kansas*.

Congressman Henry B. González of Texas. CREDIT: GONZÁLEZ FAMILY

The stylishly dressed freshman senator took the floor to push back against the tide of anti-integration sentiment across the South. He challenged his fellow Texans to examine their prejudices against the black and brown citizens who had been part of the state's history from its earliest days. "Why did they name González, González if the name was not honored in Texas at the time? Why did they honor Garza along with Burnet?" Then he burrowed in further, invoking some of the most revered events in Texas history.

"My own forebears in Mexico bore arms against Santa Anna," González said, reminding his audience of Texas's battle against the Mexican president. "There were three revolutions against Santa Anna—Texas was only one of its manifestations. Did you know that Negroes helped settle Texas? That a Negro died at the Alamo?"

He spoke, he said, to "register the plaintive cry, the hurt feelings, the silent, the dumb protest of the inarticulate." He went on for twenty-two hours straight, the longest filibuster in the history of the Texas legislature. To his colleagues in the Texas senate who argued that the bills were necessary, he thundered, "Necessity is the creed of slaves and the argument of tyrants!"

In the early hours of the morning in his second night holding the floor, González's colleagues were asked whether he would relent and sit down if his opponents agreed to withdraw four of the ten bills. He stopped the filibuster. Eventually, nine of the ten bills were withdrawn or declared unconstitutional.

In 1960, González headed to Washington as a member of the 78th Congress. He came to Washington with President Kennedy, and González's legislative agenda was very much in tune with the New Frontier. He fought for civil rights and affordable housing, improved education and better wages. The congressman was fighting for an America that would accept him, and his people in Texas, as part of the American whole. The young firebrands like Gutiérrez and López Tijerina had given up on that project, despairing of ever being accepted as full Americans instead of a racial and ethnic "other."

While activists in the younger generation were talking about Aztlán and a Chicano nation, González voted against including Mexican-Americans in the legislative language of the Voting Rights Act. He opposed the formation of MALDEF, the Mexican-American Legal Defense and Educational Fund, which spearheads the legal struggle for Latino civil rights. He even refused to become a member of the Congressional Hispanic Caucus, formed by Edward Roybal, a young congressman from Southern California.

He saw the rising militancy in the Southwest as unlikely to advance the fight for equal rights. In a 1968 speech on the House floor, he said, "We see a strange thing in San Antonio today. We have those who play at revolution and those who imitate the militancy of others. We have those who cry, 'Brown Power,' only because they have heard, 'Black Power.' And we have those who yell 'oink' or 'pig' at police, only because they have heard others use the term.

"We have those who wear beards and berets, only because they have seen it done elsewhere. But neither fervor nor fashion will bring justice."

This was, after all, the late 1960s. Fervor, as Henry B. put it, was the background music of American culture. Almost everything shouted across the various divides in our national life seemed to be followed by exclamation points.

José Ángel Gutiérrez set a fire that still smolders more than forty years later when he told a San Antonio news conference, "MAYO will not engage in controversy with fellow *Mexicanos* regardless of how unfounded and vindictive their accusations may be. We realize that the effects of cultural genocide take many forms—some *Mexicanos* will become psychologically castrated; others will become demagogues and gringos as well. And others will come together, resist, and eliminate the gringo. We will be the latter."

A reporter for the *San Antonio Express-News*, Kemper Diehl, followed up with Gutiérrez immediately after the incendiary statement. His paper printed what Gutiérrez calls "Diehl's version" of the exchange. "What do you mean by 'eliminate the gringo'?" Gutiérrez answered, "You can eliminate an individual in various ways. You can certainly kill him but that is not our intent at this moment.

"You can remove the base of support that he operates from, be it economic, political, social. That is what we intend to do." Diehl recounted, "Gutiérrez was again pressed as to intentions of killing gringos 'if worst comes to worst.' Gutiérrez replied, "If worst comes to worst and we have to resort to that means, it would be self-defense."

Congressman González wanted Mexican-Americans to succeed as Americans, as U.S. citizens, in a country that sometimes regarded them with condescension and scorn. Gutiérrez and other political organizers were in no mood to beg for acceptance from Americans they felt would not accept them even when they had, as Gutiérrez had, risked their lives for the country fighting in Vietnam.

To the political establishment in Washington and back home in Texas, Henry B. González was "that Mexican." To Gutiérrez, and Southwest Voter Registration Education Project founder Willie Velásquez and Corky Gonzáles, the *congressman* was the establishment.

Henry B. gave as good as he got, calling the younger generation of more militant leaders "professional Mexicans" and demagogues, who were "attempting to stir up the people by appeals to emotion [and] prejudice in order to become leaders and achieve selfish ends. They represent the politics of hatred, a new racism [that] demands an allegiance to race above all."

The conflict made enemies of Americans who should have been allies, and were struggling to get their people a better life in the United States. The fiercely independent congressman who had fought to abolish the poll tax and improve access to small business loans and affordable housing was now dismissed as someone with "gringo tendencies" by Gutiér-rez, who said, "The fighter for the underdog was now fighting those who fought for the underdog. . . . Henry B. made it safe for the gringo racist to be against us."

Four decades later it is easier to see how both approaches, working from inside established political institutions and pushing from outside them, were necessary ingredients of the fight. Ironically, one of the stron-gest validations of the inside game is the growing reach and power of the Congressional Hispanic Caucus that Henry B. González did not want to join. With almost two dozen members it is an important group inside the caucus, a go-to caucus for coalition building inside the House of Repre-sentatives.

The organizational children (and grandchildren) of the vanguard generation of Latino civil rights organizing are now organizing, and su-ing, and registering voters, under the umbrella of such organizations as the National Council of La Raza, the Mexican-American Legal Defense and Educational Fund, and the regional voter registration projects.

What the young radicals in the Southwest appeared to underestimate was the strong and persistent conservatism of many Mexican-Americans.

Then as now, turnout is a challenge for organizers urging Latinos to flex their political muscle. Getting numerically potent Latino communi-ties to punch their weight politically has been a challenge since the first voter registration drives of the postwar period led by the likes of the American GI Forum. As the Latino civil rights movements of the 1960s and 1970s tried to mobilize Mexican-American towns in the border states, the first heavy lift was registration. The next was convincing the newly registered to appear at the polls on election day. In many commu-nities what seemed an unassailable Anglo power structure and a reluc-tance to believe things could be otherwise made many Latinos partners in their own disempowerment. Then the idea of a Latino political move-ment roared out of Texas to other Southwestern states, but rarely had high impact outside of school boards and other local and county offices.

The tug-of-war over models of assimilation would continue over the coming decades: Did Chicanos want to become fully vested Americans, acculturated and accepted in mainstream culture, or hold on to a dis-tinct and separate yet very American way of life? It turned out Mexicans and Mexican-Americans did not have to make that stark choice. Willie Velásquez offered a third way.

Velásquez was a Texan. Early in his career as an activist, he coordinated farmworker strikes in the Rio Grande Valley. He sought the support of his mentor Henry B. González as the UFW tried to move out of its Southern California base. González was wary. He kept his distance from the farmworkers, saying the strike "was out of my district."

Velásquez teamed with José Ángel Gutiérrez to found MAYO and La Raza Unida. If González's careful calculation and arm's-length distance from the UFW pushed Velásquez left, Gutiérrez's hardening political stances and "kill the gringo" rhetorical bomb throwing pushed Velásquez to the right. He ended up splitting the difference politically, to conclude that Latinos would realize their full power and influence in society once they started to vote in greater numbers.

For his success in registering millions of voters and inspiring regional voter education projects in other parts of the country, Willie Velásquez won the Presidential Medal of Freedom, America's highest civilian honor, in 1995. The honor was accepted by his widow, Janie. Velásquez died at just forty-four years old, of kidney disease, in 1988.

THE DEBATES ABOUT assimilation or separation took place in the multiplicity of environments that Latinos inhabited. Between the end of the Second World War and 1960, an estimated one million Puerto Ricans moved to the United States, most to the New York metropolitan area. The unique constitutional status of Puerto Ricans did not make their struggle for acceptance any less profound.

Juan González was born in Ponce, Puerto Rico, in 1947. His father had served in World War II with the 65th Infantry Regiment, the "Borinqueneers." His family moved to New York in the early 1950s, where Juan attended New York City public schools in Spanish Harlem and East New York. From Franklin K. Lane High School, González headed to Columbia University. Assimilation was a goal: ". . . at one point the U.S. seems foreign; then it seems like home. Or you want it to be home, at least."

González was part of a big cohort of young Puerto Ricans in 1960s New York, born on the island, or born in New York of newly arrived parents, who wrestled with whether their new "home" really wanted them at all. González explains that time this way: "I think in the 1960s some Puerto Ricans suddenly realized who we were. We were not real Americans. We were economic refugees from the last major colony of the

United States. We were different from European immigrants, who came from independent countries like Italy and Ireland."

That realization—that a typical immigrant path led to an eventual emergence as a "100 percent melting pot American"—led many in González's generation to reject that view. "I dropped out of school, and I thought, 'We have to start something that will change the world.'"

The *something* was the Young Lords.

A Chicago street gang led by José "Cha-Cha" Jiménez morphed into a social movement in 1968, pushed by police brutality, urban renewal, and deplorable schools into challenging the government of Mayor Richard J. Daley. Led by González, Felipe Luciano, Pablo Guzmán, Denise Oliver, and others, a Young Lords chapter started in New York in 1970. Now Denise Oliver-Velez and a writer and college professor, then the Young Lords Party field marshal, Oliver said there was plenty of work to do. "I can tell you having lived in El Barrio and the South Bronx, it was like the armpit of humanity in terms of sanitation and all the issues we took on. Lead poisoning was widespread. The schools didn't have breakfast programs at the time. They had a lot of hungry kids. So for Puerto Ricans particularly, as the new wave of urban poor, and the existing position of African-Americans, there was a perfect opportunity for a movement for social change. Particularly because there was also the influence of the civil rights movement."

There was also a strong identification with, and affinity for, the work of the Black Panther Party in urban ghettoes across America. "Our offices were located right in the heart of every community we organized. So we had access to regular folk in the community." Oliver said the Young Lords were beloved by the people whose children got breakfast and new school outfits from clothing drives, by the renters whose complaints about poor garbage pickup had been ignored for years.

"We occupied a church for eleven days," said Juan González, "while we provided free breakfast and clothing programs, health services, a daycare center, and a liberation school, all inside the occupied church. We seized hospital equipment and took it where it was needed. We did what we did because we felt our people should not have to live like that."

An important part of the Young Lords' political program was the liberation of Puerto Rico from U.S. rule. Independence for the island was always asserted as a crucial goal right along with improving the lives of Puerto Ricans living on the mainland. The revolutionary fervor, the berets and fatigues, the combat boots and marching drills fused with increasingly assertive rhetoric about a free Puerto Rico.

In time, the leadership got older. Puerto Rican populations were dispersing from New York City throughout the rest of the state, and into New Jersey, Connecticut, and Pennsylvania. A wing of the anticolonial movement turned to armed resistance and guerrilla action against the U.S. government. As an organization, the Young Lords Party waned. However, its legacy is strong. Juan González has won the most prestigious awards in American journalism for his work as a reporter, columnist, and author. Felipe Luciano and Pablo Guzmán have also made names for themselves in New York media.

Celina Sotomayor's daughter, Sonia was roughly a contemporary of the Young Lords, but she went a different way. She was born in New York in 1954 to parents who met after leaving Puerto Rico and settled in the Bronx. Sonia's father, Juan, died when she was nine, leaving her young mother to raise two children on her own. Born in Lajas on Puerto Rico's southwest coast, Celina had served in the Women's Army Corps in World War II, worked in New York as a telephone operator, and earned credits for a nursing license at night school.

Celina took her children out of their Bronxdale housing project as the complex fell into the grip of gangs and drugs. Like many aspirational families across America in those years, the Sotomayors bought a set of encyclopedias. Celina insisted her children work hard in school and assured them education would pave the way to a better life.

When Sonia Sotomayor was in the academically selective Cardinal Spellman High School in the Bronx, the Young Lords were operating just a few miles away, blockading East Harlem streets with bags of trash and teaching Puerto Rican history. Juan González dropped out of Columbia University, but just a few years later Sonia Sotomayor headed to Princeton University on a full scholarship. "At Princeton I felt like a visitor landing in an alien country. I was too intimidated to ask any questions the first year. I felt there was a chasm between me and my classmates. I really only knew the Bronx and Puerto Rico, while my classmates spoke of European vacations and skiing."

Her mother's struggle had given the young Ivy Leaguer options none of her ancestors, and only a few of her Puerto Rican peers in New York, could have imagined. She made choices that reflected insider and outsider status at the same time. Sonia Sotomayor was still every bit as Puerto Rican as the Young Lords working in the Bronx. She led a Puerto Rican students' organization at Princeton, challenged the school's pitiful record in minority hiring, and wrote her senior thesis on the island's first elected government and the struggle for self-rule. Sotomayor closed her Princeton career by winning the highest academic honor conferred on undergraduates.

Sonia would attract attention for her academic prowess, and find powerful mentors who helped her rise in the legal establishment. She was often the first and often the only Puerto Rican to hold the positions she gained as she climbed the legal ladder. At every step she remembered whom she came from, where she came from, and tried to use increasing clout to improve the lives of Puerto Ricans in New York.

In the decades after World War II, Latinos found they could construct their American selves in a way not possible in early eras. The struggles for civil rights, school desegregation, and equal protection of the law manifested themselves differently across the United States. Some individuals plunged into the work of lifting up the poorest and most powerless of their people. Others took advantage of new opportunities for schooling and political access that would make power and influence possible in a whole new way.

While the idealism and anger of the postwar decades mellowed in some activists, it was very present and carefully channeled in others. González became a leader in his profession and a mentor and guide to subsequent generations of Latino journalists.

José Ángel Gutiérrez became a county judge, an administrative law judge for the state of Texas, and a law professor. When the other side changed, so did he. "A lot of gringos stopped being racist. Most people now are at least civil and polite. It's not politically correct to be a bigot in public anymore. So I still maintain optimism. I think we can make it better."

Sonia Sotomayor became the first person of Latin American descent to sit on the United States Supreme Court. Her high court career is still young, but a wealth of experience in the rough-and-tumble world of New York law is serving her well. In her early terms of argument at the court, she is a persistent, and creative questioner. She is more than holding her own among the brightest minds in her profession.

Henry B. González served in the U.S. House of Representatives for almost forty years, and was succeeded by his son Charles, who retired after seven terms. Father and son served the San Antonio region in Congress for more than half a century.

His health broken, Cesar Chavez died young, at sixty-six, in 1993. He had watched as the American food industry went through decades of consolidation, mechanization, and heavy downward pressure on wages. Toward the end of his life he worried about the challenge of illegal immigrants to the UFW's attempts to guarantee a fair wage to its members. He predicted—and was proven right about—the threat to the health of American farmworkers posed by the increasing use of herbicides and pesticides in American fields.

Dolores Huerta carries on the fight into her eighties. She crisscrosses the country to lecture, rally, and organize. In 2012, President Obama gave Huerta the country's highest civilian honor, the Presidential Medal of Freedom. After everything she has seen over a long career, she said she is sure better times are ahead for American working people. "It's in the wind. It's almost like in the sixties and all these young people are out there. People know how to do the work and they can do it even more rapidly with the Internet, with things like MoveOn."

By the end of the 1970s the Vietnam War was over. The Young Lords were in decline. Richard Nixon and J. Edgar Hoover were out of power or dead. The burst of organizing and demands for equality and freedom had succeeded in many places in many ways. A new sense of Latinos as a people would emerge from these struggles. A substandard school was not that different in Los Angeles and Chicago. Lousy housing in Brooklyn or in the Rio Grande Valley created a cause for new alliances, rather than an old debate about whether Mexicans and Puerto Ricans would, or could, make common cause.

Mexican farmworkers in the California fields.
CREDIT: © BETTMANN/CORBIS

**New citizens taking their
oaths in Los Angeles.**

WHERE ARE
WE GOING?

(¿ADÓNDE VAMOS?)

LEO MANZANO was born in Mexico in 1984. He moved to the United States with his parents at four years old, and was raised in little Granite Shoals, in central Texas. What distinguishes Manzano from many other immigrants to the country is simple: He runs fast. At the 2012 London Olympics, wearing the uniform of his adopted country, he won the silver medal in the fifteen-hundred-meter race.

Manzano draped the Stars and Stripes of the U.S. flag over his slim shoulders and smiled as the enormous crowd cheered. Then he was handed the red, white, and green of the Mexican flag, and held that aloft too. The Mexican tricolor definitely played second fiddle, held by a corner in his right hand as the American flag stretched across his shoulders.

Many of his fellow Americans were not happy. Syndicated columnist Ruben Navarette, calling the gesture "misguided and ill-mannered," concluded that Manzano put his ego above his U.S. team. "Manzano wasn't there to compete for himself but to represent his country. All he had to do was decide which country that was. He chose not to choose."

The elite runner seemed perfectly at peace with his decision, and clear about why he did what he did. "Standing on the podium has been a dream of mine and I share it proudly with my family, friends, coaches, and all my supporters from Austin, Marble Falls, and Granite Shoals, Texas, as well as Dolores Hidalgo, Mexico."

Manzano was undocumented, living in the country illegally as a youngster. Today he is an American citizen, and a Mexican citizen. A dual national. For a few weeks after the summer games, it was an Internet sensation, bringing vitriolic criticism and tepid praise. At a time of severe economic distress and rising anxiety about America's place in the world, Manzano's flag-waving was treated very differently from exuberant displays of Irish pride at St. Patrick's Day celebrations across the country, or the proud declarations of Polish identity by large civic organizations in Chicago. The difference is easy to understand: No one worries about Polish supplanting English as the language of commerce, or having to supply Gaelic-speaking teachers in local public schools.

We Americans often forget history. That makes whatever happened today the best and the biggest and the worst . . . and the first. So, people on all sides of the argument acted as if Leonel Manzano were the first American to bring another flag onto the playing field. Just twenty years earlier Oscar De La Hoya, born in East L.A. to Mexican-born parents, was preparing for his Olympic moment, a gold medal fight against Marco Rudolph of Germany. He was getting ready to bound into the boxing ring, small American flag in his hand, when, "My aunt handed me a Mexican flag as well. 'Hold this in memory of your mother.' Of course I would do that. But a U.S. official blocked my path. He said, 'If you take that up there, we're gonna disqualify you.' Still, I did it anyway."

The two very different reactions, Manzano burning up the Internet chat rooms and a ho-hum after De La Hoya, may be in part the product of changing technology that allows people to join in pitched verbal battle across the globe in an instant. It may also be a product of the mood of the United States in the second decade of the twenty-first century. The optimism that ended with the September 11 terrorist attacks has carried over into discussions of American culture, nationhood, economics, and our shared future.

Ricardo Jiménez, for one, has never accepted the idea that he is an American. Brought from Puerto Rico as an infant, Jiménez was raised in Chicago's Humboldt Park neighborhood. While agitating for a Puerto Rican studies course at his dilapidated and overcrowded neighborhood high school, he started asking tougher questions about the status of Puerto Rico and the circumstances under which the Stars and Stripes flew over the island. He began to dig deeper, and what he unearthed radicalized him.

"I realized that this is what it is to be Puerto Rican; this is the rich and glorious history that we have had and that I don't know about. I found out that we have a father of our country, and we have authors, that we have painters, that we have poets; I mean, we have all these things that I didn't know, that I never knew were in existence. I said, 'Why is this happening?' On my quest for information I got involved in the Puerto Rican independence movement and realized who I was as a Puerto Rican. I realized the circumstances that were happening here and understood why people would leave Puerto Rico. Then I found out the reasons and the whole colonial status and that became my passion."

Jiménez said the isolation and segregation of Puerto Rican Chicago made the experience there very different from that in New York. The Puerto Rican population of Chicago was and is much smaller than that of New York. Yet Chicago played an enormous role in Puerto Rican politics on the mainland. It was the place the Young Lords was born before coming to greater prominence in New York. It was the home of many of the men and women who would be arrested and sent to federal jail for violent conspiracy against the U.S. government in their quest to make the United States leave Puerto Rico.

The Chicago members of the Fuerzas Armadas de Liberación Nacional—the Armed Forces of National Liberation, or FALN—were highly educated. Many had been born on the mainland, but grew up steeped in Puerto Rican culture. At the time of their arrest in Evanston, Illinois, in 1980, they were in their twenties and thirties. When asked whether he fully understood what he was getting into when he joined the resistance to U.S. rule, Jiménez said, "The reality was that anybody that fights for Puerto Rican independence, you can assure yourselves that you're going to be . . . there's going to be repression. You're going to be sure the FBI at one time or another is going to bother you; you're going to be watched.

"So it's when you decide that you're going to defend our country that you have found that reality, the history of Puerto Rico. You know why it is the way it is, and you decide that you're going to dedicate your life to the Puerto Rican independence movement; it is without a doubt that you're going to face repression; you might face prison or death. That's a reality in the Puerto Rican independence movement, because the United States has made that very, very clear."

Federal prosecutors linked Jiménez and eleven others to some one hundred bombings or attempted bombings since 1974, none of which was connected to loss of life. He was charged with seditious conspiracy, interference with interstate commerce by violence, interstate transport of firearms with intent to commit a crime, and other felonies. The prosecution never directly linked Jiménez and the others with the actual placement and detonation of the bombs, a much harder case to prove in court. He was sentenced to ninety years in prison. He does not see the decision to confront the United States as a fateful one. "We didn't decide to confront the United States; it decided to confront us. They're the ones who invaded our nation. We didn't invade the United States. So the initial confrontation and the initial persecution come from the United States, not from the Puerto Rican people."

President Bill Clinton offered clemency to the FALN inmates not directly connected to violent acts and loss of life. The president was accused of making the offer to the Puerto Rican nationalists as a boost to his wife Hillary's electoral prospects as a candidate for U.S. Senate in New York. The blowback from the president's decision was so severe that a few weeks after the clemency offer was announced by the president, his wife the Senate candidate denounced it.

In 1999, Jiménez was released from federal penitentiary after serving nineteen and a half years. He publicly denounced the use of violence, and supported utilizing the democratic process to end what he calls Puerto Rico's colonial status. When asked about the decisions he has made, and the life he led, Jiménez has steadfastly refused to express regret. One exception is the sadness expressed over the loss of his mother during his long prison sentence. "I never got to see my mother again. I was never able to have closure. I was never able to say good-bye. I was never able to give that last kiss. I was never even able to comfort her and help her for all the sacrifice she did.

"Yes, you sacrifice a lot. But it's a decision that I made that I felt was the correct decision, not only for my family but for the nation of Puerto Rico, for all Puerto Ricans.

"There cannot be any regrets for something that is a just and noble cause for the freedom of our country. You know when people understand what freedom is, when people understand what the nation of Puerto Rico has gone through, they will understand why we have sacrificed our lives in order to see it free."

Ida Luz Rodriguez was caught in the same dragnet as Jiménez, and spent the same nineteen and a half years in prison. In her few interviews since clemency, one gets from Rodriguez more of a sense of regret, and a more skeptical look at her own youthful passions. When asked shortly after her release about how she looked at her past, she said, "I would say there was an evolution on my part. I saw that in countries that won political independence, there's so much more they have to do to gain their freedom. There was a lot of pain and injury caused on both sides of the struggle, and when you look at it, you say, 'I'm sorry that has happened.'

Yes, I have regrets. I think every single human being has done things in their lives that they regret, but if we carry the past, it is much too heavy, and we can't go forward."

Supreme Court Associate Justice Sonia Sotomayor is a generational peer of Ricardo Jiménez and Ida Luz Rodriguez. Journalist Juan González is just a few years older. Veteran congressman Luis Gutiérrez is a Chicago-born peer who grew up a short drive from Jiménez's boyhood home, and was active in the Puerto Rican independence movement in college. All understood and were shaped by the Puerto Rican predicament, the economic struggles on the island and the mainland. All made different decisions about how to be a Puerto Rican living in the United States in the second half of the twentieth century.

The poet Tato Laviera tried to define the ambiguity for Puerto Ricans in his poem "commonwealth," in which he writes that both he and his island are in the same commonwealth stages of their lives. The state of semi-limbo that Laviera describes gave Puerto Ricans what other Latinos would see as a gift: the ability to move to the United States whenever they wanted. From inside the Puerto Rican diaspora, that "gift" looked different. They came from a country without sovereignty, to live in the nation that claimed them, but did not seem to want them.

Born in Puerto Rico, raised in New York, journalist and historian Juan González finds that ambiguity easy to understand, and perhaps harder to explain. "Puerto Ricans can come back and forth and as a result the identity is a lot more fluid and the sense of place becomes a lot more fluid. You can go back and forth because you have citizenship wherever you are. For immigrants from Mexico, or Guatemala, or El Salvador, when they go back to visit family they really are entering a different nation.

"Puerto Ricans don't feel they are entering a different nation, but they are. What you have to deal with is much more complex, psychologically, socially, politically." Through the Supreme Court rulings that came to be known as the Insular Cases, González said, American law affirmed again and again that Puerto Rico belongs to, but is not part of, the United States. "So no one born in Puerto Rico, including me, could ever be president of the United States.

"Puerto Ricans who are born in Puerto Rico as U.S. citizens have a different set of relationships and a different set of rights from other U.S. citizens. The Supreme Court has also ruled in other decisions that not all of the protections of the Constitution are affordable to Puerto Rico as they are afforded to other parts of the country. It is not part of the United States. It belongs to the United States."

Back on the island, the two big political parties representing pro-statehood and procommonwealth forces command a stable mid–40 percent support. The proindependence party bumps along at less than 10 percent approval in opinion polls and in repeated plebiscites on future status. Despite this lack of success at the ballot box, it is no exaggeration to say the leaders of the most nationalist tendency are still widely admired as defenders of Puerto Rican identity and culture, as men and women brave enough to push back against the giant United States. One recent example was the successful struggle to get the U.S. armed forces to stop using a small island that is part of Puerto Rican territory, Vieques, as the site of live-ammo target practice.

For Cubans, the push and pull factors of identity and nationality were utterly different. At the same time Jiménez and his young radical friends in Chicago are nursing a deepening anger about U.S. involvement in their island, Cubans are in the midst of their transformation of a booming regional capital. Miami became a bilingual city as Cubans grew in cultural influence and economic clout, but also as Miami became an offshoot of Central and South America. Instability elsewhere in the hemisphere made Miami attractive to the wealthy and mobile in Spanish-speaking countries. Miami was easily accessible by jet, had a Spanish-speaking business community, and had bankers more than happy to deposit the money they were pulling out of their turbulent and inflation-ridden homelands.

Cuban refugees and their U.S.-born descendants were perceived by other south Floridians as largely white and middle-class in values and outlook. While other Floridians did not share the passionate interest in exile politics and the political state of play in Cuba, they did share their Cuban-born neighbors' interest in housing values, new shopping centers, and foreign investment.

In 1978, Emmy Shafer of Miami Beach went on a frustrating march from one office to another, trying to find a public employee who spoke what she thought was good enough English to help with her problem. Nearly two decades after Cubans fleeing the Communist revolution poured into Miami, it was possible to get along pretty well speaking only Spanish. What bothered Shafer was how difficult she thought it was becoming to speak only English. She had spent part of World War II in a

German concentration camp, came to Miami as a teenager, and learned English. Now, she figured, it was the Cubans' turn.

"How come the Cubans get everything?" Shafer asked. "This group of people gets one hundred percent and everything their way because our local politicians are for sale. It's a disgrace when you sell your own heritage and your own language for a dollar. They forget that the English people are the ones that vote." That is a stunning—and very American— statement. A Russian-born Holocaust survivor moves to Miami Beach, becomes an American, and gets to team up with "the English people" in unhappy solidarity over the new guys' refusal to learn the language.

Shafer led a successful petition drive, gathering more than twenty-six thousand signatures, but the push to turn back legal bilingualism languished until 1980. Then Shafer got an unexpected assist from a surprising place, and an unexpected politician: Havana. And Fidel Castro.

El Jefe's intention was clear. Castro took an opportunity to give Washington a poke in the eye, while at the same time getting rid of inconvenient Cubans. Mirta Ojito was sixteen when the knock on the door came at her family's apartment in Havana. "They asked for our names. But then they asked something strange. They asked if we were ready to 'abandon' the country. Yes, we were ready to leave. My father never believed in Fidel's promise of a better society. We wanted freedom. We wanted to go. And a lot of other people did too."

It started when a bus carrying half a dozen people rushed through the gates of the Peruvian embassy, followed by people just running off the streets onto the embassy grounds and asking for asylum. The idea spread to the Venezuelan embassy, with cars simply crashing the gates to get into the compound. Thousands of people crammed onto the embassy grounds, a humiliation for the Castro regime. Pictures were beamed around the world that showed dense crowds standing inside the gates. Fidel got an idea. He could turn this around, end the diplomatic standoff, and end up with far fewer mouths to feed all at once.

When Castro announced that Cubans who wished to leave the island were free to do so, that was all the encouragement many needed. Hundreds of boats streamed toward Florida, loaded with everyone they could carry. Ojito would have help. "My uncle was an exile in Miami. He always promised to help my father get out. So my uncle left his family and his job, and without knowing how to swim, knowing nothing about boats, he chartered this boat and came to get us out of Cuba."

Between April and October of 1980, about 125,000 Cubans reached south Florida. This refugee flow came to be known as the Marielitos, after the main point of departure, the port of Mariel. Cuban community groups frantically began to place the new arrivals, but even their considerable organizational heft was overwhelmed. Marielitos ended up in armories and recreation centers, churches and even the Orange Bowl. Some were airlifted to military facilities in Arkansas, Pennsylvania, and Wisconsin.

For Fidel Castro, Ojito said, the opportunity to cause mischief was too delicious to pass up. "Imagine you're the leader of a country, and a hundred and twenty-five thousand people want out. Fidel wanted to turn it around, to punish the U.S. So he tainted the process. He ordered Cuban police to take patients from hospitals and inmates from jails, then *forced* them to board boats."

Only a small fraction of the Cubans streaming into Florida, 4 percent, were mentally infirm, but twenty-five thousand had criminal records. After twenty years as Latino America's "model minority," Cubans were getting an unwelcome makeover. In the 1983 movie *Scarface*, Marielito coke smuggler Tony Montana, however dodgy his Spanish accent may have been, put a new face on south Florida Cubans. Beginning in 1984, the television hit *Miami Vice* gave Latino actors work by parading a weekly perp walk of prostitutes, pimps, drug dealers, and money launderers across the small screen.

Election Day, 1980, followed the end of the boatlift by just a few days. Shafer's proposal banned the use of county funds for messages in any other language but English and blocked expenditures to promote "any culture other than that of the United States." Shafer's plea to return Miami "to the way it used to be" found a receptive audience among English-speaking Dade County residents, though black Miamians wondered aloud what United States culture might be.

Latino leaders carefully pointed out that Miami had changed in a way that permanently altered it, meaning it could never be "the way it used to be" again. Silvia Unzueta of the Federation of Hispanic Employees of Metropolitan Dade County told the *New York Times*, "We are aware that a lot of people would like to erase Cubans, Haitians, Nicaraguans, Hondurans. But with or without the ordinance we're not going away. To go back to the 1950s would be an impossibility. The county has changed and, I argue, for the better."

Shafer's proposal to "de-bilingualize" Miami got nearly 60 percent of the vote. A majority of the English speakers who voted for the ordinance said they would be pleased if passage of the proposal made Miami less attractive to Spanish speakers. It didn't. The Latino community of south Florida continued to grow in numbers, and in political and commercial clout. In 1993, a now Latino-majority Dade County Commission threw out the 1980 ordnance, and returned county government to supplying services and information in Spanish and other languages.

In his eye-opening book *The Nine Nations of North America* (1981), journalist Joel Garreau broke the continent into regions that crossed state and national borders, and grouped people by who they were and how they lived rather than the jurisdiction listed on their driver's license. Garreau argued that farmers in central Illinois had more in common with their peers in Missouri and Iowa ("the Breadbasket") than they did with their fellow Illinoisans up in Chicago, who in turn shared a "nation" ("the Foundry"), with Ohioans, Michiganders, and the people of industrial southern Ontario.

MexAmerica was a nation that joined both sides of the U.S.-Mexican border, running from south Texas west through New Mexico, southern Colorado, Arizona, and Southern California. Its "capital" was Los Angeles. A multinational "nation" identified by Garreau was called simply "the Islands." It joined together Central America, Cuba, Puerto Rico, Haiti, and the Dominican Republic, the English-speaking island nations of the West Indies, and south Florida. The capital of Garreau's island nation? Miami. It may be securely attached to North America, but it is where the continent dips its toe into the warm waters of the Caribbean and the Gulf of Mexico.

An economic study of Miami in 1980 found Cubans owned eighteen thousand businesses, including sixty car dealerships, five hundred supermarkets, and two hundred and fifty drugstores. After Mariel, those paled next to Al Pacino's M16 military rifle and the challenge, "Say hello to my little friend!"

A backlash was under way. So was a demographic revolution.

THE 2010 CENSUS counted almost forty million residents of the United States having been born in another country, more than twenty-one million of them from Latin America and the Caribbean. Forty million people represents a near tripling of the share of foreign-born since 1970, and a doubling since 1980. That means one of every eight Americans started life somewhere else on the planet. It is a share of the national whole we have not seen in a century, and has launched a debate with wide-ranging consequences that demands answers to so-far unanswered questions:

Is there a limit to the number of people the United States can admit?

Does a high level of immigration complicate the task of creating one people with a common culture . . . and is that goal even desirable?

Are there costs and consequences to taking on millions of new people that we have not yet reckoned with?

And finally, what kind of peace have these millions of new residents made with taking on American identity, with accepting the acculturation and entry into the mainstream that other immigrant groups have done for centuries?

Everywhere you look, there are different answers, different examples of how Latinos have replied and will reply to those questions. Perhaps now more than ever there is also a wide range of responses you would get from other Americans, standing outside the Latino community and looking in at it. There are two enormous groups of people asking the flip side of the same question: Are we *them*? Are they *us*?

Linda Chavez is a descendant of an old New Mexico family. Her father's ancestors were seventeenth-century Spanish settlers. Her mother was an English-speaking American, not of Latino ancestry. From her work with the United Federation of Teachers and its longtime leader, Albert Shanker, Chavez became the editor of *American Educator*, a quarterly publication of the AFT focusing on educational issues. "It was clear that under my direction the *American Educator* had become a conservative journal of ideas. We had William Bennett, Jeane Kirkpatrick, and Robert Bork writing for us. Not only did we promote Shanker's hard-core anticommunist views with articles critical of China, Cuba, and the Soviet Union, but we also took on affirmative action, ethnic studies, and radical feminism."

From her time at the magazine Chavez caught the attention of President Ronald Reagan. She became director of the United States Commission on Civil Rights, and then White House liaison director. She was the highest-ranking woman in the Reagan White House. She moved from the Reagan administration to become president of U.S. English, an organization critical of bilingualism, multiculturalism, and any efforts to adapt to large numbers of non-English-speaking residents. Immigrants, in the view of U.S. English, should acquire English as quickly as possible, rather than trying to make it in America using government-supplied translations for applications, driver's license exams, and voter registration materials. The organization supported state drives across the country to establish English as the official language of the United States.

The national face of U.S. English was S. I. Hayakawa, a Canadian-born Japanese-American and a respected linguistics scholar, who had served in the U.S. Senate. Standing behind Hayakawa was the less well-known cofounder, Dr. John Tanton. The organization attracted positive press coverage, well-known supporters among intellectuals and immigrants like Alistair Cooke, Arnold Schwarzenegger, Walter Cronkite, and Saul Bellow. Linda Chavez backed the broad goals of U.S. English, and was particularly distressed by what she saw as the failures of bilingual education in U.S. schools. "Our specific purpose was to convince the country to adopt English as the official language. This would mean that schools would only use English in the classroom. I was concerned with the effects of bilingual education on young Hispanics. In California and elsewhere youngsters were learning to read and write in Spanish instead of English when they entered first grade. Once enrolled in bilingual programs they could be stuck there for years."

There was a strong appeal in U.S. English's pitch to common sense and American ideas about assimilation. State after state placed official English referendums on the ballot. The organization found a supporter in conservative champion and U.S. English honorary chairman Senator Barry Goldwater. "You live in this country, you speak English. You live in Mexico, you speak Spanish. You live in France, you speak French."

Marielito Mirta Ojito did her modest part. After months of dreaming of returning to Cuba, she crossed a threshold. "I went to the movies. I was watching, and for the first time I understood a complete sentence in English. 'It seems you are coming down with a cold,' one actor said. The sentence is etched in my memory. It marked the moment I began to feel the possibilities of life in the United States. It felt like I'd been handed a key that could unlock the door into my new world."

Language was a hot topic. The air was thick with recollections of immigrant ancestors who seemed to have learned English quickly and competently forty, fifty, and sixty years earlier. The newsstands of the Ellis

Island generations stuffed with foreign-language newspapers; scenes of grandchildren translating their grandparents' negotiations with store-keepers; German-language classrooms in the Midwest and Plains states disappeared down the memory hole, replaced with angry anecdotes about retail clerks and lunch counter waitstaff who had trouble taking orders in English.

In the late 1980s, the backlash escalated from Miami to Los Angeles, when debates over the official language emboldened businesses to order Spanish-speaking employees not to speak to one another in any language other than English, with the added threat of suspension and firing. In 1987 a Tucson, Arizona, Ramada Inn forbade employees to speak any language other than English, and in that same year an Arizona Pepsi bottling plant fired Rafael Lugo after sixteen years on the job because he could not speak sufficient English.

Then Dr. Tanton's wider interests became better known. He was an advocate of official English, and a strong supporter of ending not only illegal but also legal immigration to the United States, with the eventual goal of stopping population growth in the United States. In a private memo in 1986, he wondered whether Latinos would ever get the hang of being American: "Will Latin American migrants bring with them the tradition of the *mordida* [bribe], the lack of involvement in public affairs, etc. . . . What are the differences in educability between Hispanics (with their 50% dropout rate) and Asiatics (with their excellent school records and long tradition of scholarship)?"

Tanton wondered who would come out ahead in America, groups that limited their fertility, or those that went ahead and had more children? "Can *homo contraceptivus* compete with *homo progenitiva* if borders are not controlled? Or is advice to limit one's family simply advice to move over and let someone else with greater reproductive powers occupy the space?"

Tanton saw a grim future for a "minority-majority" California, likening it to apartheid-era South Africa, as long as Latino birthrates remained high. "Perhaps this is the first instance in which those with their pants up are going to get caught by those with their pants down!"

When the note was made public in 1988 it brought a storm of bad publicity and criticism. Walter Cronkite publicly resigned from U.S. English's board, as did Linda Chavez. "I firmly believed that learning English was the only way to succeed in America, that it was the key to opportunity. But how could I continue to represent an organization whose founder and cochairman harbored such unsavory views? I also discovered that the umbrella organization NumbersUSA, controlled by Tanton, had received donations from a foundation that contributed to eugenics research and advocated forced sterilizations—views I considered beyond the pale."

Chavez had been caught by an enduring truth of more than a century and a half of debates about immigration and acculturation in the United States. While many sincerely asked tough questions about the ability of a society to welcome, settle, and support large numbers of newcomers, others denounced America's historic open door out of xenophobia and white supremacy. The two critiques of American immigration policy constitute a persistent strand in the country's politics going back to the panic over large numbers of central Europeans and Irish in the mid-nineteenth century.

U.S. English was only the best-known of the groups that emerged in this era to question, and militate against, the growing accommodation of foreign languages in American life. There were widespread complaints—and more substantially, campaigns against—such government services as driver's tests, election materials, and public school instruction in foreign languages. Because of prevailing immigration patterns, one language, Spanish, got more attention than any other.

In 1988 voters headed to the polls in Arizona, Colorado, and Florida, all once parts of the Spanish Empire where the language was still widely spoken, and passed English-only laws. Eventually, fourteen more states did the same. In context, this anxiety should not have been surprising. The decade that shaped the country's self-concept as a nation of immigrants, 1900 to 1910, saw more than eight million legal immigrants come to the United States. Those numbers plunged in succeeding decades (but, of course, the impact was proportionally even greater in a country that had, in 1910, just over ninety-two million people).

Those huge numbers of new immigrants were not reached again until the 1980s, when just over six million immigrants entered the United States (similar to the decade of 1910 to 1920), but this time the 1990s followed with more than nine million, and the 2000s with more than nine million. Even with a much larger-based population of more than 250 million people, these were stunning numbers of new people. Add in millions of illegal immigrants to that total and more than thirty million people came to stay in thirty years.

Since the 1830s, Latinos in the United States could say to America, with some justification, "We're *here*, because you were *there*." The United States had been deeply involved in the rapid increase in residents with roots in the Spanish Empire through purchase, war, and conquest. Mexicans, Puerto Ricans, Dominicans, and Cubans could point to eras in history when Uncle Sam reached into their home countries and began encounters that ended with large numbers of people from all those places living in the United States.

In this new era, there would be similarities and differences. Many left economically moribund regions of the hemisphere hoping to find more opportunity in the United States. Others lived in countries whose recent histories had been deeply marked by occupation, influence, and outright meddling in their domestic affairs in either economic or political realms. Often both. The superpower confrontation between the United States and the Soviet Union would have a lasting impact in Central America and cause a poignant brand of migration: Hundreds of thousands fled Central America to a country some saw as deeply involved in their country's troubles.

Carlos Vaquerano was a teenager in the late 1970s, as the rising tide of political violence in El Salvador pitted conservative, pro-Western, Catholic Church–aligned forces against anticapitalist, antiestablishment groups armed by the Soviet Union and its allies. One of eleven children, Carlos joined an antigovernment organization with some of his brothers in 1979. The killings reached his small hometown of Apastepeque, more than thirty miles from the capital, San Salvador, in 1980.

"I graduated from high school in 1979, and became involved in antigovernment organizations. Some of my brothers did the same. On July 12, 1980, a death squad found its way to Apastepeque. I remember that day well. I was at my brother's house when we saw a group of men dressed in paramilitary gear pass by. All heavily armed. All wearing masks. Like evil spirits."

Just an hour later, word reached Carlos that his brother Marcial and his cousin Luis had been taken away. He fled to the capital. "When we arrived, our neighbor from Apastepeque told us that Marcial's body had been found, with six others. The death squad had pulled off their fingernails, beaten them severely. They'd been burned with acid, then shot in the head. And then six of them were laid out in a row for public display. They left the body of my cousin Luis hanging off a bridge."

The death squads were often comprised of current and former mili-

Carlos Vaquerano back in El Salvador. As the tensions rose in the small country, Vaquerano decided he had to flee his small hometown, Apastepeque. After a flight to Mexico and a bus ride to the border, he crossed into the United States stuffed under the hood of a pickup truck. CREDIT: CARLOS VAQUERANO

tary officers, out of uniform, schooled in the use of weapons. It would be an exaggeration to say the United States supported these extrajudicial killings, but no exaggeration at all to say Washington supported the governments and political parties from which these squads grew.

In El Salvador, the Nationalist Republican Alliance—Alianza Republicana Nacionalista, or ARENA—rose to oppose the FMLN, the Frente Farabundo Martí para la Liberación Nacional, or Martí Front for National Liberation, a Communist-inspired, Cuban-supported left-wing alliance trying to overthrow the Salvadoran junta. ARENA death squads killed Catholic priests and nuns, trade union officials, and left-wing sympathizers. In tiny El Salvador, smaller than the state of New Jersey, more than eighty thousand were killed in the civil war that raged throughout the 1980s, and almost ten thousand simply vanished.

During the years when similar wars engulfed Nicaragua, Guatemala, and Honduras, almost a million people left Central America. Their number one destination was the United States. Vaquerano was one of them. "I was faced with a dilemma: Should I stay in a country that had murdered two of my brothers, my cousin and my friends? I couldn't go back to my mother's home without the risk of being tracked down. My sister Lupita had gone to Los Angeles and had a job there. She offered to help me come live there."

Whether you left Dublin in the 1840s, Poland in the 1890s, or Sicily in the 1910s, what often determined whether you went to Australia, Argentina, South Africa, or the United States was whether a relative was already established one place or another. An advance guard of Salvadorans had already taken root in the city that would attract more than half the Salvadorans heading north: Los Angeles.

The United States supported the Salvadoran government under José Napoleón Duarte, and was helping it fight the FMLN. So Vaquerano could not enter the United States as a political refugee, even though he believed the death squads roaming Apastepeque constituted what U.S. law required, "a well-founded fear of persecution." If he could not reach *el Norte* by the front door, he concluded, he would have to figure out a way through the back.

"I had little money, but I was able to fly to Mexico City and take a bus to Tijuana. From there I knew I would have to enter the United States illegally. Two coyotes took me and another Salvadoran man, heading for the border around midnight in a GMC pickup truck." Coyotes are people smugglers. They stashed Vaquerano under the hood, atop the truck engine, protected only by a thin towel.

"It was unbelievably hot. Burning. We were getting desperate. I almost started screaming. Then, finally, I heard the signal—tapping on the dashboard. Thank God, we made it through. When I got out of that engine cabin I treasured every breath of fresh air my lungs could take in."

The smugglers celebrated their successful crossing by taking Vaquerano to eat at a place whose red sign and golden arches symbolize America to the far corners of the earth, McDonald's. At that moment the newly minted illegal immigrant had to confront the ambiguities of refugee life. "To me McDonald's was a symbol of U.S. cultural and economic domination of the world—the country supporting a government that killed my brothers and other innocent people. So I was very angry at this country. But I was also very hungry. So I ate the Big Mac. And I knew what I had to do. So I started taking English classes right away."

When Ronald Reagan signed the Immigration Reform and Control Act in November 1986, it had several goals. It would first and foremost put the enforcement burden for hiring workers who were not authorized to live and work in the United States squarely on employers. Second, but far more noted by the general public, it would open the path to legal residence to millions of people who had come to the country illegally and begun to make lives here. The thinking was simple: The United States would give people who had cheated under the old system a chance to get legal, and then slam the door behind them. Hundreds of thousands of off-the-books and underground workers would now pay taxes, have Social Security numbers and their equivalents, and the new

President Ronald Reagan signing the Immigration Reform and Control Act in November 1986. The law required employers to verify their workers' legal right to be in the country, and gave amnesty to people who entered illegally before January 1, 1982. Millions of undocumented people have come into the country and gone to work since the act was signed. CREDIT: RONALD REAGAN LIBRARY

system would work to ensure that millions more would not come illegally to work.

The first half of that idea worked. More than two and a half million people who had been living and working illegally in the United States became legal residents. The new law put enforcement pressure on employers, who would be fined for hiring undocumented workers, penalties that would double with each new infraction.

The years that followed presented an interesting mix of American hunger for low-wage labor, constant complaints about IRS enforcement from employers, and surplus labor in Latin America looking north for opportunity. The result? After years of steady economic growth, there were an estimated twelve million people in the United States by the 2000s who did not come here legally. Though the lack of enforcement ended up giving "amnesty" a bad name in American political debate, the Immigration Reform and Control Act ended the hiding and lying for millions of people.

Carlos Vaquerano became a legal resident of the United States in 1988. In 1992, when the main combatants in the Salvadoran civil war signed a peace deal and promised to do their fighting at the ballot box, Vaquerano did not go home. "Like a lot of Salvadorans, I began to realize that my place in this country had begun to change. No longer were we short-term asylum seekers, but a growing and permanent community in the United States."

At the end of the Central American civil wars and the Cold War, there were large and growing communities of Guatemalans, Salvadorans, Nicaraguans, and Hondurans in New York, Washington, D.C., Miami, Houston, Los Angeles, and elsewhere. During the 1980s the Latino population of the United States had grown by a stunning 53 percent, to more than twenty-two million.

Cities and counties outside the Western and border states or Florida and New York now saw things they had never thought about before: barrios and bodegas, demand for teachers of English as a Second Language and Catholic priests able to say the Mass in Spanish, and social workers and cops who could find out what they needed to know from clients. New Latino residents revived sagging commercial strips, took seats in post–baby boom elementary schools, and helped the high school soccer team suddenly become a contender.

Omar Vasquez became part of the new wave of immigrants moving to places unaccustomed to immigration. For most of American history the states of the old Confederacy were the most uniformly native-born of all the states. With the exception of Louisiana and Florida, the American South had not been home to large ethnic communities, had not been a place accustomed to the sounds of foreign languages on the street or on the radio. Vasquez left Los Angeles, a place he found tougher to work in and growing steadily less safe, and headed east to Dalton, Georgia. Since the Immigration Reform and Control Act, he had a green card in his pocket, and the carpet mills were hiring.

"The mills were going day and night. There was lots of overtime. The very next year lots of people started to come from Los Angeles, Chicago, Texas, and Mexico." Along with the work, Vasquez said, he found security. "When we arrived here it was strange, but I found out that it was different than California. Dalton was safe, not like Los Angeles. There were no gangs. It was family friendly. People don't rob you here."

By the 2000 census, Vasquez had plenty of company. Dalton was 40 percent Latino. They made up a third of Whitfield County, where Dalton was the county seat. A third of Mexican immigrants were no longer heading to the big metropolitan areas that had been destinations since the Mexican Revolution. Now they were going to Georgia, Alabama, Nebraska, North Carolina, Iowa, and New York.

No longer confined to agricultural labor, Latino workers have spread to every part of the country and many different sectors of the economy. Latinos are heavily represented in the South's carpet industry, as in this factory in Dalton, Georgia. CREDIT: AP PHOTO/JOHN BAZEMORE

Professor Rubén Hernández-León of UCLA's Center for Mexican Studies said a look at multiple factors makes it easier to understand why Mexicans in particular have moved well beyond traditional areas of settlement. The Immigration Reform and Control Act and continuing illegal immigration brought the number of Latino workers seeking jobs in the Southwest to the saturation point.

"There were, in essence, too many immigrants, too many conationals competing for the same jobs in the same labor markets, in the same industries. At the same time, the quality of life was actually deteriorating for many families, and those conditions actually propelled many of these immigrants to look for alternative destinations in places like Dalton and other cities and states in the Southeast. More recently, of course, the recession has had an important severe impact across the country for sure, but in places like Dalton that are essentially one-industry towns."

So, has dispersal worked for the new migrants? Enrique Pumar, the chairman of the Sociology Department at Catholic University of America in Washington, D.C., has found in his research into the new Latino suburbs that, on balance, it has. "It's a good thing for them. They are out of the way. They are not as visible and not as exposed to anti-immigrant politics. They do very well in these new communities.

"For a century this model, the University of Chicago school of urban sociology, was based on the assumption that newly arrived immigrants would settle in the city. Today that model is upside down. It's no longer viable. Center cities are becoming very attractive. So the price of housing has increased and immigrants don't feel as welcome anymore."

However, that old immigrant model existed for more reasons than just the price of housing. An immigrant arriving at Ellis Island in, let's say, 1905 would have headed to a place where already settled immigrants had begun to build a place where he or she would feel welcome. A place to buy a newspaper or bread for Sabbath blessings in Yiddish, a place to hear Mass in Italian and live among people who come from not just your country, but your own hometown.

Suburbanizing immigrants pay a price, according to Pumar. "There is a loss of social solidarity, because the barrio is disintegrating and people are taking advantage of opportunities outside the barrio. The old immigrant neighborhood was a place where people had a grocery store and a local bank that knew them.

Even as Latino trailblazers move into professions where they once were rare or that were even closed to them, they are still disproportionately represented in blue-collar work. CREDIT: AP PHOTO/CHATTANOOGA TIMES FREE PRESS, DAN HENRY

"There are effects on mental health. Low social solidarity means greater social problems. We have to be compassionate. Individuals left their families behind, and now find themselves in the United States without neighbors who can show them around. They have to acquaint themselves with a new environment, and it can be very difficult."

In the first decade of the new century, many Americans were not feeling particularly compassionate, or seeing any upside in what some were now calling an "invasion." Who were these people? Where did they come from? Latinos, legal and illegal alike, were not prized workers and much-needed customers; they were a drain on the public finances. They arrived at hospital emergency rooms with critical needs and no health insurance. They gave birth in county hospital maternity wards and the public picked up the tab. Their kids arrived in kindergarten unable to speak English, not just taking up a classroom seat and costing the school district money, but also needing expensive supplementary help while pulling down test scores and driving other families away. All this, it was alleged, while giving back "nothing" to the community and paying nothing in to defray the added costs caused by their arrival.

Governor Pete Wilson of California figured he had taken his citizens' temperature, and saw an opportunity. "For Californians who work hard, pay taxes, and obey the laws, I'm suing to force the federal government to control the border. And I'm working to deny state services to illegal immigrants. Enough is enough!" Governor Wilson said cash-strapped California could no longer afford to pay to educate and provide health care to more than a million people living in the state illegally. The state's ballot initiative Proposition 187 asked Californians to give state government the power to withdraw public services to people living in the state illegally.

In the 1994 election, the measure passed with a seventeen-point majority. The ballot measure won support throughout the state, except for a cluster of counties around the liberal bastion of San Francisco. Proposition 187's supporters called the initiative "Save Our State." Its opponents called it racist and unconstitutional and headed to federal court.

Just weeks after a majority of voters said Proposition 187 should become California law, a federal appeals court judge, Mariana Pfaelzer, said it would not, issuing a permanent injunction against 187. Part of Pfaelzer's legal reasoning was that California could not regulate immigration through state legislation, a responsibility reserved by the federal government. Remember that argument; it will come up again.

Sociologist Marta Tienda of Princeton University has said the panicky political rhetoric about an immigrant "invasion" was out of date anyway. It was natural growth of an already present population that was driving Latino numbers. "Immigration was not the problem. It was merely a smoke screen. By the nineties most of the Latino population growth was in fact due to birthrates. If you look at the census numbers there was a dramatic shift in the population. But most of the growth was in the number of children born to legal and American-born Mexicans."

President George H. W. Bush had negotiated and pushed hard for the ratification of the North American Free Trade Agreement, NAFTA. The treaty created a three-nation free-trade zone among Canada, the United States, and Mexico, a common market for goods from the Arctic Circle to the Guatemalan border.

Henry Cisneros became Mayor of San Antonio, Texas, in 1981 and joined the Clinton Administration as Secretary of Housing and Urban Development in 1993. CREDIT: AP PHOTO/SUSAN RAGAN

Attorney and public servant Maria Echaveste rose to become deputy chief of staff to President Bill Clinton. CREDIT: MARIA ECHAVESTE

Apart from changes in the labeling on manufactured merchandise, and pressures to move manufacturing and sales staffs for international companies south, Americans didn't anticipate major changes right away. For Mexico, NAFTA brought wrenching transformation, not least in farming. With the agreement to end the *ejido* system of communal lands, with roots going back before the arrival of the Spaniards, Mexican small farmers would feel the chilly blast of competition from the vast mechanized farms of the United States and Canada.

Corn was to be opened to increasing competition from other North American markets. Corn is central to Mexican identity and the Mexican diet, and now thousands of farmers would find they could no longer make a decent living growing it. Eduardo Paz, a Mexican and a Mixtec Indian, was one of them. Two years after the passage of NAFTA, he decided to head north.

"Many people from my village were leaving. We were all working in the traditional way, raising corn on our small plots of land, watered only by rain. The little plot of land could no longer support the family." Eventually, a million farmers gave up. When you look at an economy from very high up, in treasuries and agricultural ministries and international trade talks, these are the necessary compromises needed to modernize an economy, but that did not make it any easier for Eduardo Paz. "Necessity is what drove me to go north. I couldn't make a living. I had to feed my family. So I came to *el Norte*. I came to this country to work honestly and make a little money for my children. It is with this purpose that I came here. We are all the same. We want to help our families."

The original rationale for NAFTA, often heard in the Washington debates over the treaty, said the trade pact would eventually reduce illegal immigration by making work more plentiful and profitable in Mexico, giving people a reason to stay home. All it did was change where Mexicans left to move north in search of opportunity. NAFTA brought new prosperity to metropolitan areas while making it harder to earn a living on the land.

Paz eventually headed to Dalton, Georgia, where Omar Vasquez had relocated. "We have three children—a daughter and then twin boys. They were born in the U.S., so they are citizens. We've lived in Michigan, North Carolina, Kentucky, and now Georgia. I work at one of the factories where they don't check for papers. There used to be so much work that they would hire people without asking for papers.

"But since the economy has slowed down and there is less work, things have changed. Georgia recently passed a law that makes it illegal for me to be here. If I get caught driving without a license I'll probably be deported. My brother-in-law and my friends who have driver's licenses take turns driving me to work."

Like millions, Paz lives in a mixed-status family. He and his wife are in the United States illegally. His children are citizens. If he is caught by immigration authorities in a workplace raid, or even after inquiries made during a routine traffic stop, he and his wife face deportation.

Minor children who can remain in the country legally cannot save their parents from being sent home. So families face difficult choices: leave young children behind with family or friends, with no clear road to reuniting with their parents, or just take them back "home," to a place they have never been.

Activists working on behalf of these families hope comprehensive immigration reform will find a durable solution for the Paz family and millions of others. Others who lobby Congress look at the current political scene in Washington and put any such immigration bill many years away.

The sudden and devastating decline in new construction ushered in by the housing crisis in 2008 landed like a sledgehammer on Latino

Eliseo Medina was born in the Mexican state of Zacatecas. His parents were farmworkers, and the family headed north to look for work in California. He worked as a grape and orange picker and eventually as an organizer for the United Farm Workers. Medina was a leader in spreading the boycotts and an organizer in the fields. CREDIT: ELISEO MEDINA

Eliseo Medina eventually left the UFW to become the highest-ranking Latino in the history of the Service Employees International Union. He is the international secretary-treasurer of the heavily Latino service workers union. CREDIT: ELISEO MEDINA

employment among the native-born, legal residents, and illegal immigrants alike. Latinos had moved heavily into the construction industry over the previous twenty years, and now saw cratering job markets, spilling over into manufacturing centers and places like Dalton. After all, if people are not building new houses, and losing the ones they already own, fewer carpets will be made and sold.

For Professor Hernández-Leon the resulting suffering heightens the need for a solution to the immigration issue: amnesty, legalization, regularization, a path to citizenship, whatever you want to call it. "Any of those names, any of those labels essentially addresses the very crucial need to give legal status to millions of immigrants who have basically lived their lives or a good chunk of their lives, a good part of their lives in this country—that have purchased homes, that have paid taxes, that have contributed to retirement and Social Security, who have contributed to economic growth and the vitality of their communities through their labor.

"These immigrants are not just workers; they are parents, they are grandparents, they are children and brothers of other people who are in a similar situation, so this issue of immigration regularization is clearly the only way of dealing humanely and practically, in fact, with the current situation."

The professor also argues that such reform is not vital just for Latinos, but for all Americans. "It is not good for any country to have a large population that essentially lives in the shadows of society. These are individuals who are afraid of interacting with institutions in general, who may not be willing to report a crime to the authorities. These are people who cannot make long-term plans, who cannot make the investments that any person makes throughout a lifetime, and who cannot contribute fully to the well-being, the development of the next generation. So it's very important that this population receive some kind of legal relief, so they can essentially get on with their lives and live their lives just like any other human being who not just resides in a place but actually has legal rights and really, ultimately belongs to the place where he or she lives."

Dan Stein does not buy that argument. As president of the Federation for American Immigration Reform, he is one of the highest-profile spokesmen for the proposition that the United States already has too many immigrants and should be very cautious about taking more. In 2011, he told *PBS NewsHour*, "I know some people think we're too hard-hearted. We're truly concerned about a breakdown in the integrity of this country's ability to control its borders and determine who has the right to stay and who doesn't. That is what is at stake here, far broader than the question of the three hundred thousand people now in the deportation queue. . . .

"The American people have a right to have their fiscal integrity secured through border and perimeter controls, whether it's good schools, health care, hospitals, our job market. We have the right to compete in a fair labor market where illegal immigrants are not working."

Before the recent severe recession and continuing problems in the job market, the battle lines were already sharpening. Between 1990 and

2002 the Latino population took another enormous leap, adding ten million. The U.S. Border Patrol and other police agencies were catching ten thousand undocumented people a week trying to cross the border, or in workplace raids.

Tensions grew, and lurid anti-Latino crimes began to be reported in widely dispersed places across America:

- Twelve-year-old Emilio Jiménez Bejinez was killed by a single shot to the head as he crossed the border with family members near San Ysidro, California. Two men in an apartment near the border got out a rifle and took aim after one suggested, "Let's shoot some aliens."
- Near San Francisco, a young white man bludgeoned a Mexican mother and daughter to death on the street, while friends watched from a parked car.
- An arsonist burned an apartment in Columbus, Ohio, killing ten Mexican immigrants.

Then in 2002 came the Minutemen. Across the country local people volunteered to keep an eye on the U.S. border and daily-hire pickup sights in communities far from the Mexican frontier. Their opponents called them vigilantes. The Minutemen insisted they were simply doing their duty as citizens, helping law enforcement at every level of government.

Minuteman Project cofounder Jim Gilchrist said the United States was under threat, and did not have the luxury of waiting for the federal government to act. "The border between the U.S. and Mexico is not a border. It's a wide-open invitation to illegal aliens, drug smugglers, child-sex traffickers, and terrorists! It's a national disgrace—and a huge danger to our country. I finally came to the realization that we were having an illegal-alien invasion crisis."

Veteran Republican Representative Jim Sensenbrenner of Wisconsin caught the spirit of the times. He introduced H.R. 4437, the Border Protection, Antiterrorism and Illegal Immigration Control Act of 2005. It called for up to seven hundred miles of fence along the U.S.-Mexican border at the most popular crossing points. The bill mandated fines for illegal immigrants, made housing one a felony, and redefined being in the country illegally from a low-level civil infraction to a federal crime.

Representative James Sensenbrenner (R-Wisconsin). The veteran congressman sponsored galvanizing legislation that would have made being in the United States without legal status a felony. The Sensenbrenner bill helped drive protests nationwide in support of undocumented workers in 2006—protests that in turn provoked a strong backlash. CREDIT: GETTY IMAGES

H.R. 4437 passed the House with a strong majority. The Wisconsin congressman lit the match, and immigrants of every stripe, naturalized and illegal, longtime and newly arrived, began shouting back. Many of the drum majors leading the marches were radio talk-show hosts on Spanish-language radio. In Chicago, Rafael Pulido, *El Pistolero*, urged his listeners to take to the streets, and they did. In the following weeks and months of 2006, huge crowds gathered in demonstrations in support of immigrants.

The marches got America's attention. Downtown businesses were closed, lacking the workers to make sandwiches, bus tables, take deliveries on loading docks, or staff retail counters. Critics of the first demonstrations were enraged by the Mexican flags carried in the streets of America, heavily critical of the self-confidence the marchers showed in making demands of the United States.

In Phoenix, two hundred thousand came out. In Los Angeles, nearly a million on just one of the May Day marches that snarled traffic in big metropolitan areas from coast to coast. By May Day the streets were full of American flags to accompany the national flags that made so many so angry. The flags carried alongside the Stars and Stripes were not just Mexican. It was a reminder of how many people had come from so many places under a variety of circumstances. In New York, West Indian and West African immigrants demonstrated the diversity of the country's foreign-born. In Chicago, Polish and Irish flags were proudly carried with the Mexican banner. In several cities, Puerto Rican flags, carried by people who had no immigration problems, testified to the solidarity many felt, even if they were in no jeopardy themselves.

"How can a country of immigrants be against immigrants?" asks Mexican-born Juan José Gutiérrez, one of the national organizers of the marches, in a PBS interview. "The truth of the matter is that by the millions, men and women, hardworking men and women that do the tough jobs in America, who pay taxes, abide by the rules, have children, have to work hard to put food on the table . . . they decided to stand up, to do the American thing, you know, to take a page from history of what this great country has had to go through to right the wrongs of this nation: They've said, 'Enough.'"

The marches of 2006 not only got Americans' attention; they showed the immigrants and their allies themselves how much organizational power and economic clout they really had. For years before 2006, Republican politicians had taken some comfort in the opinion polls among Latinos that showed a split community, not necessarily supportive of an easy path to legal status or citizenship. Polls earlier in the decade had shown that many longer-term residents were no more sympathetic to the aspirations of illegal immigrants than their non-Latino neighbors.

The vehemence of the attacks of 2005 and 2006, the harsh rhetoric that surrounded the debate over H.R. 4437, convinced many Latino onlookers that the debate had long since stopped being just about illegal immigrants. In the tone of the attacks, Latinos heard a distaste for their community writ large.

Univision news anchor María Elena Salinas, born in the United States and raised in Mexico, says Latinos now saw themselves in the immigrants they were defending. "The majority of Latinos in this country are U.S. citizens or residents, and many feel that attacks against immigrants are attacks against their own parents, siblings, cousins, neighbors, or friends. Among the hundreds of thousands who participated in immigrant marches in the spring were legal residents and U.S. citizens. Many carried signs that read, 'Today we march; tomorrow we vote.'"

The Sensenbrenner bill may have sparked an explosion in immigrant activism, but it died after the House vote, when it could not be reconciled with a much less stringent Senate bill. There would be no comprehensive immigration reform in 2006, or 2007, or in the years that followed. There was clear interest in both the Democratic and Republican parties in solving the challenges posed by an immigration system that was not making anybody happy.

By the 2010s, it was hard to remember that just a few years earlier there were bipartisan bills meant to address the widespread complaints about border security, the sclerotic legal immigration system, family unity, and the challenges of the twelve million illegal immigrants already living in the United States. Representative Luis Gutiérrez (D-IL), Representative Floyd Flake (R-AZ), Senator Edward Kennedy (D-MA), and Senator John McCain (R-AZ) drafted bills that aspired to give all the contending groups in the debate enough of what they wanted to be able to walk away from the table thinking they had made a good deal.

As the war between the political parties escalated on Capitol Hill, the idea of a grand bipartisan deal, even with a supportive President George W. Bush in the White House, faded. By the 2008 primary season, John McCain denounced the very version of immigration reform he had helped draft and cosponsor two years earlier.

One influential combatant in the immigration debate was political scientist and historian Samuel Huntington. His book *Who Are We? The Challenges to America's National Identity* was widely quoted by those who saw continued high levels of immigration as a threat to any settled idea of what the country is and what it means to be an American. Huntington was straightforward. "In this new era, the single most immediate and most serious challenge to America's traditional identity comes from the immense and continuing immigration from Latin America, especially from Mexico, and the fertility rates of these immigrants compared to black and white American natives."

While only lightly citing evidence, Huntington concluded that the assimilation "successes" of past immigrant flows was unlikely to be repeated with this latest generation of Latino immigrants. He came to some frightening conclusions, writing, for instance, that if America neglected this threat there was the real possibility that the population would break up into two distinct peoples with two cultures—Anglo and Hispanic—and two languages.

Ominous signs abound: a Spanish-language late local newscast tops the ratings in one city; "José" replaces "Michael" as the most popular boys' name in another. The United States is compared to countries with entirely different histories that have led them to persistent conflict over language and culture: Belgium and Canada.

Huntington conceded that previous immigrant groups eventually set aside their mother tongue and adopted English. Looking at the size and persistence of Latino immigration to the United States, the late historian concluded that the cultural conditions—television and radio stations, cable channels, and big Spanish-speaking neighborhoods—meant Latinos would not have to learn English. The possibility that Latinos might retain some degree of Spanish fluency in subsequent generations while still learning English was rejected, Huntington citing the lack of French ability in Canada's western provinces.

There are few more provocative assertions in the entire book than this one: "There is no *Americano* Dream. There is only the American dream created by an Anglo-Protestant society. Mexican Americans will share in that dream and in that society only if they dream in English."

Huntington died in 2008. Had he lived, he might have had the opportunity to revisit some of the dire predictions he made in *Who Are We?* The Great Recession ended the rapid rise in the number of Mexican immigrants in the United States. By 2012 it was estimated that population flows had reached "net zero," with roughly the same number of Mexicans heading home from the United States as entering the country. He would have had the chance to examine the steady supply of new data from organizations like the Pew Hispanic Center that showed English acquisition taking place at roughly the same speed as it did for other immigrant groups.

A fellow academic, Marta Tienda, looked at the same country Huntington did and reached a very different conclusion: "What we are dealing with is fear. It is fear of a large Hispanic presence in this country. People say that Hispanics don't assimilate like other immigrants, that they don't learn English. If you look at the numbers they're just like other immigrants. By the third generation most have assimilated and are English speaking."

Finally, Huntington might have had a chance to look at the campaigns of Mayor Julián Castro in San Antonio, Governor Susana Martinez of New Mexico, and Congressman Henry Cuellar of the Rio Grande Valley to see lively, hard-fought races contested among voters who are not burdened by some sort of "historical memory" of dictators and military juntas elsewhere in Latin America. Along with those prominent examples there are thousands of school board members, county executives, and state representatives whose very lives disprove the idea that American-style democracy and traditions are something Latinos have no interest in mastering.

The real and passionate arguments about what having so many Latinos in the United States really means continued into the data gathering and tabulation of the 2010 U.S. census. People who watch American demography, politics, culture, and commerce all waited for the new numbers, particularly the new stats on the Latino population.

Over a period of weeks, the Latino numbers were released three states at a time. "And we noticed something interesting," said Mark Hugo Lopez of the Pew Hispanic Center. "In every new data set, every one, the state numbers were coming in higher than the projections heading into 2010." Lopez said there was an office pool, and only one person picked a number over fifty million. "And of course, that's who won."

When the final number was released in early 2011, the number was stunning: 50.5 million people, one out of every six people in the United States, identified themselves as having family roots in the Spanish-speaking countries of the hemisphere and Spain. Hiding inside that massive number were people with a lot of differences. Some had milky pale skin and blue eyes, and others were as dark as their African forebears stolen by Spanish and Portuguese slavers centuries earlier.

Many spoke native Spanish and had only begun to learn English, and many hardly spoke Spanish at all. A portion of that fifty-million-plus were descended from the columns of Spanish soldiers and settlers who headed north four centuries earlier, and many had only just arrived. Their roots were in the Mexican lands that became part of the United States, in the Caribbean, and from Central America clear down to the tips of Argentina and Chile not far from the Antarctic Circle.

The continuing job creation crisis in the U.S. economy fueled the anxiety that powered the continuing debate over immigration. Meanwhile, Latino families suffered mightily, losing two-thirds of their entire accumulated wealth after the collapse of the housing market. The last decade had begun in great optimism and spurred families to buy that first house. The decade ended in foreclosure, debt, and heavy, long-term underemployment.

While it was ravaging the balance sheets of Latino families, the Great Recession was doing the same to millions of other Americans. Rising economic anxiety made it a great time to reopen the argument that never really goes away: If you are not legally in the United States, and not allowed to work, why are you here and why do you have a job? State governments, with an ear closer to the ground of public sentiment, took on the anger over illegal immigration.

More than a dozen states drew up new laws assigning state governments and police agencies more of the responsibility for enforcing national immigration laws. Perhaps the best-known of these efforts was Arizona's Senate Bill 1070, which was signed into law in 2010. The law gave state and local officers in Arizona not just the option, but the obligation to check someone's legal right to live in the United States if they encountered police for any reason. Any police business, from a domestic quarrel to a traffic stop to a murder investigation, could trigger inquiries about the legal status of all the parties involved.

The law's supporters maintained that the state had to take over responsibility because the federal government was not enforcing immigration laws and Arizona was overrun with people crossing the border into its southern deserts. The opponents said S.B. 1070 would open up a legal way for police officers across the state to racially profile suspects, intercepting people going about their business in order to inquire about immigration status. They alleged that police would equate Mexican with illegal status, in a state that is between a quarter and a third Latino.

The Obama administration, fighting to protect its right to be the sole enforcer of national immigration laws, went to court to stop S.B. 1070 from going into effect. The U.S. government won the argument in various federal courts of appeal, while Arizona under the leadership of Governor Jan Brewer continued to fight for the state's right to enforce federal laws.

When the Supreme Court of the United States ruled in 2012, it handed down a split decision, forbidding Arizona from putting several parts of the law into place, while allowing a core provision empowering local law enforcement to investigate any individual's immigration status.

S.B. 1070 was the model for similar laws in a dozen other states. In letters to the editor, television interviews, town halls, and Internet chat rooms, the attitude of many Americans could be summed up in one rhetorical question: "What part of 'illegal' don't you understand?" Efforts to frame legislative fixes that would start collecting income taxes and fines from illegally resident workers were bashed as being insufficiently tough on people who had broken the country's laws when they stayed, and then kept on breaking them every day they went to work.

In the morality play of immigration debates, one more sympathetic group of people were called "Dreamers," after the law popularly called the Dream Act aimed at finding a way to let some immigrants stay in the United States. They were brought to the United States as children, sometimes even babies in the arms of parents, unlike many of their own brothers and sisters who were born in the United States and were thus citizens. These youngsters often had no memory of having lived anywhere else, but were vulnerable to deportation "back home" if caught by immigration authorities.

The Dreamers were sometimes called the "low-hanging fruit" of the immigration debate, an easy sell for advocates of a wider amnesty, hard to disdain by immigration hard-liners, since they took no active role in their illegal migration to this country. They faced a particularly tough set of choices as they reached adulthood, unable to vie for scholarship money for higher education, and legally barred from paying in-state tuition for colleges and universities.

In 2012, President Obama ordered his immigration enforcement agencies not to deport young men and women who would have qualified for legal residence under the Dream Act proposal that was unable to pass Congress at the end of 2010. The new policy required that these undocumented people come forward and give all their personal information. In return, they would be assured of two years of a form of legal residence.

Representative Luis Gutiérrez, who represents a Mexican and Mexican-American majority district in Chicago, insists Americans have been moved by the personal stories and the bravery of the young Dreamers, and deporting them would bring "a political backlash" no political party would court. Others were not so sure, questioning the wisdom of telling the government that has the power to send you out of the country where you are, where you work, and where you go to school. "No one has an answer [to] what it means after the two years," Latino political analyst Angelo Falcón said. "Are these young people who are relishing a victory, or are they turning their families in to the federal government?"

• • •

WHEN CUBAN-BORN AROLDIS Chapman unleashed a screaming fastball, clocked at more than a hundred miles an hour from the Reds' mound in Cincinnati . . .

When New York–born and Dominican-reared Alex Rodriguez of the New York Yankees sent another pitch sailing into the stands, burnishing his credentials as one of the greatest players ever to take the field . . .

When Puerto Rican–born Iván Rodríguez of the Texas Rangers and Florida Marlins read a base runner's lead perfectly, and gunned him down with a precise throw to a waiting infielder . . .

. . . you were seeing the fruits of one of the great transformations in modern baseball—the steady march of players from Latin America and American players of Latin American ancestry to a central role in baseball. Major League Baseball named an "all-Latin" team in 2011, and the lineup shows a fearsome team: along with Iván and Alex Rodríguez, Dominican superstar Albert Pujols; Puerto Rico's Roberto Alomar; Venezuelan shortstop Luis Aparicio; one of the game's earliest Latino stars, Puerto Rican outfielder Roberto Clemente; Mexican-born pitcher Fernando Valenzuela; and Dominican hurler Juan Marichal, among others. This Spanish-speaking dream team would be led by Dominican Felipe Alou, who enjoyed a solid major-league career along with brothers Mateo and Jesús before winning more than a thousand games as a manager.

The time line that culminates in Latin players filling more than a quarter of all roster spots on major-league baseball teams (and making up almost half the rosters of U.S. minor-league teams) starts in the second half of the nineteenth century.

Cubans who came to the United States mainland for an education headed back to their island home with bats and balls. The same cross-pollination that saw Caribbean culture and political movements take root in the United States brought baseball to Cuba. The Guilló brothers, Nemesio and Ernesto, studied at Springhill College in Alabama, and upon their return to Havana founded the Havana Baseball Club in 1868. In 1878, the Guilló brothers' club played the first "away game" in Cuban history in Matanzas, the story goes, against the crew of an American schooner that put in to the Cuban port for repairs. Later, in 1874, again in Matanzas, the Havana club played the first professional baseball game in Cuba.

The Zaido brothers, Teodoro and Carlos, returned from Fordham College in New York to found Havana's crosstown rivals, the Almendares Baseball Club. Almendares played the first game with an American club in Havana in 1878, against the Hops Bitter team from Massachusetts. By 1900, American clubs were playing winter exhibitions in Havana—in that year the Brooklyn Dodgers played the New York Giants and a Cuban all-star team.

For all the history of involvement of the United States in the Caribbean and throughout Latin America, it was not Americans who brought the game to some of its most beloved homes today. The turmoil of Cuba in the nineteenth century sent people fleeing to Venezuela, Puerto Rico, and Mexico. Of all the places Cubans brought *béisbol*, it has sunk no deeper roots anywhere than in the Dominican Republic.

Around the same time as Almendares and Havana were nursing their rivalry as the Yankees and Red Sox of prerevolution Cuban baseball, young men fleeing Cuba's Ten Years' War (the same war that sent José Martí into exile) laid the foundations for Dominican leagues. As in Cuba, young men returning from high schools and colleges in the United States further solidified the game. By the time American troops began the occupation of the Dominican Republic in 1916, the game was already well established.

The first steady exchanges of talent came between Cuba and the United States. Lighter-skinned Cuban and Cuban-American players trickled into the U.S. major leagues, and Afro-Cubans became standout players in the Negro Leagues. After the segregated championship series were played in the autumn, black and white players often spent the winter in Latin America, playing exhibition games against local talent, and being teammates on integrated rosters.

Adolfo Domingo de Guzmán Luque played for Almendares and Havana, and as "Dolf" Luque became one of the early Latino stars of American baseball. Beginning in 1914, Luque pitched for the Boston Braves, Cincinnati Reds, Brooklyn Dodgers, and New York Giants, and managed top teams on both sides of the Florida Straits. Luque owns the curious distinction of leading the league in losses one season (with twenty-three in 1922), and wins the next (when he went 27–8, with twenty-eight complete games, in 1923).

Martín Dihigo would have been a standout player every bit Luque's equal, but as a black man he was barred from American baseball's top teams. Instead, he put together an outstanding career in the Negro Leagues, the Cuban League (as a player for both Almendares and Havana, among others), and the Mexican League that stretched from 1922 to 1950. He is the only man enshrined in the U.S., Cuban, and Mexican baseball Halls of Fame. His plaque was unveiled in Cooperstown in 1977, six years after he died in Cuba.

By the end of World War II, when the draft had depleted many major-league lineups, thirty-nine Cubans played in the big leagues. Many of the greatest Cuban players ever would remain on all-black U.S. teams, like Luis Tiant Sr. and Lázaro Salazar. Over its existence, several Negro League teams had "Cuban" in their name, like the New York Cubans, Cuban X Giants, and Cuban Stars, stocking their lineups with standout players from the Cuban League.

Once Jackie Robinson (who played winter ball in Cuba) broke the major leagues' color barrier in 1947, the gates opened for Caribbean players of all colors. Havana native Saturnino Orestes "Minnie" Miñoso came up to the majors with the Cleveland Indians in 1949, and played for four teams over the next fifteen years. A seven-time American League all-star, Miñoso was a league leader in stolen bases, doubles, and triples throughout the 1950s, and was beloved off the field for the humor and approachability that made him a perennial fan favorite, especially in his hometown during most of his career and his retirement, Chicago. Miñoso played a few games when he was a coach at Cleveland in 1976, and two with the White Sox in 1980, meaning he played major-league baseball in five decades.

The 1950s would raise the tempo of Latino entry to the American major leagues, as big-league scouts fanned out across Cuba, the Dominican Republic, Puerto Rico, Venezuela, and Mexico.

Orlando Cepeda and Robert Clemente headed to the National League from Puerto Rico. Luis Aparicio and Chico Carrasquel joined American League teams from Venezuela. Ozzie Virgil and Juan Marichal arrived from the Dominican Republic, part of a trickle that would become a stampede over the next forty years, with more than four hundred players, far more than any other Latin American nation, putting on a major-league uniform.

Instead of filling a manpower shortage, as in the Second World War, or providing small-market teams with a source of cheap talent, as in the 1950s, Latin players became superstars who thrilled fans across the country with their style of play. They were once seen as down-roster utility players valued for their glove work, but Latinos became power pitchers and power hitters who contended for the game's most exalted records and honors.

Catching has long been a path to managing and coaching careers after a player's time on the active roster is over. Scouting and player development have created two generations of outstanding catchers who have led teams to World Series and will likely lead teams in the United States and in Latin America in the years to come: Panamanian Manny Sanguillén and Dominican Tony Peña, and a who's who—or *quién es quién*—list of outstanding Puerto Rican catchers, including Iván Rodríguez, the Yankees' Jorge Posada, the Atlanta Braves' Javy López; Benito Santiago; Sandy Alomar Jr.; and the incomparable Molina brothers, Bengie, Yadier, and José, who have all been outstanding backstops at the major-league level. All three Molinas have World Series rings in their jewelry collections.

More than a dozen Latinos have been enshrined in the Baseball Hall of Fame, the first being the incomparable Clemente, the first Hispanic player to reach the three-thousand-hit plateau and win an MVP, and the latest being Roberto Alomar, inducted in 2011. Many latter-day players are among the game's biggest stars. Alex Rodriguez was the youngest player to reach the five hundred and six hundred career home run marks. The Chicago Cubs' Sammy Sosa's home run heroics and the single-season home run race with Mark McGwire in 1998 enchanted fans who had soured on baseball after the players' strike brought on the cancellation of the World Series. Pedro Martínez of the Dominican Republic played a huge part in classic Red Sox–Yankees rivalries. The Detroit Tigers' Miguel Cabrera in 2012 became the first player since the 1960s to lead a league in home runs, runs batted in, and batting average, the coveted Triple Crown, and he rivals Albert Pujols as one of the handful of best hitters in the current game. When he was named MVP in 2012, Cabrera was the first Venezuelan to be so honored.

As America's game steadily internationalizes, with more new players from new places (like Australia, Korea, and Japan), Latin America is still head and shoulders above other regions of the globe in producing major leaguers. Now, along with the hustling children of immigrants who have been taking to the game since the first professional teams stepped onto the diamond in the nineteenth century, American-born Latinos are also making their mark on the game.

Future major leaguers learned their baseball on rutted infields in upper Manhattan, with Little League teams in Florida and California, spurred by parents who brought a love for the game from the Spanish-speaking world or whose families had been here for generations. They include 2001 World Series MVP Luis González, Yankee first baseman Tino Martinez, standout player and successful manager Lou Piniella, six-time all-star slugger Bobby Bonilla, and six-time Gold Glove infielder Eric Chavez.

Boston Red Sox and now Los Angeles Dodgers star Adrian González presents an interesting example: The first baseman was born in San Diego, and raised on both sides of the U.S.-Mexico border. González's father was a member of the Mexican national team. In the international tournament known as the World Baseball Classic, González played for Mexico.

For all the setbacks, Latinos continued to move into the mainstream of American life. In sports, in literature, in politics, industry, and the law, people whose parents and grandparents never could have imagined their success were climbing higher and higher. A high school dropout

The 1980s, the 1990s, and the first years of the twenty-first century saw Latinos moving into new areas of American life. In 1992, Latin pop star Gloria Estefan headlined the Super Bowl halftime show, the height of Americana. CREDIT: AP PHOTO/ NFL PHOTOS

raised in Harlem, Richard Carmona got an equivalency diploma and headed into the U.S. Army. After distinguished service with the Special Forces in Vietnam, he returned to the States and began to make up for lost time. An M.D. at thirty, he put together outstanding parallel careers in medicine, teaching, emergency services, and law enforcement. Dr. Carmona became the surgeon general of the United States in 2002.

Chicago-born Sandra Cisneros grew up lonely and, by her account, a little out of step in a big Mexican family in a small house in a predominantly Puerto Rican neighborhood. She nurtured her talent and willed herself into becoming a writer. She tells of one day sitting in a seminar at the prestigious Iowa Writers' Workshop and realizing her life was a source of material her classmates could not match. "It wasn't as if I didn't know who I was. I knew I was a Mexican woman. But I didn't think it had anything to do with why I felt so much imbalance in my life, whereas it had everything to do with it! My race, my gender, and my class! And it didn't make sense until that moment, sitting in that seminar. That's when I decided I would write about something my classmates couldn't write about."

The novel *The House on Mango Street*, published in 1984, propelled Cisneros to a place in American literature most writers can only fantasize about. The coming-of-age story of Esperanza and life in her Chicago neighborhood brings American youth to a place most of them would never get to know any other way. The book is assigned to middle and high schoolers across America, making Cisneros one of the few Latinas to find a place in the young adult canon. In the quarter century since the book's release, millions of young people have read *The House on Mango Street*.

A century and a half after Apolinaria Lorenzana was brought to the mission in what became San Diego, Ellen Ochoa was growing up in nearby La Mesa, and from her schoolgirl days she showed a special interest and aptitude for science. After a stellar academic career capped by a Ph.D. in electrical engineering from Stanford University, Ochoa led a team of scientists and engineers in developing optical systems for automated—that is, unmanned—space flight. She entered the space program in 1990 and three years later became the first Latina in space, flying three shuttle missions and logging more than a thousand hours in space.

You get the point. A people at times regarded as an inconvenience and a nuisance by English-speaking Americans heading west were now confidently entering fields where they would have been at least unexpected if not exotic and strange.

Y AHORA . . . ¿QUÉ? And now . . . what?

The 2010 census counted more than fifty million Latinos in the United States. Of these, nine million voted in the 2008 presidential election, some twelve million this time around. If that does not sound like a lot, there are some good explanations for why the turnout is still low.

In this country, older people are more likely to vote than younger ones. Wealthier people are more likely to vote than poorer ones. Better-educated people vote at higher rates than less educated ones. Citizens can vote, and noncitizens cannot, under any circumstances. In 2012, Latinos are younger, poorer, and less educated than the rest of the country as a whole, and a large fraction of the population over eighteen, even among legal residents, has not yet naturalized, not yet taken the oath of citizenship.

The median age of Latinos is twenty-seven, meaning half of the community across the country is older, and half is younger. Compare that to the median age of U.S. residents, about thirty-seven years old. That means more Latinos are school age, first-job age, first-marriage age, and so on. It also means far more Latinos than Americans as a whole have not had children, or are still children themselves, than other Americans. In 2008 and 2009, more than one of every two newborn Americans was a Latino, and the youth of the population means that number ought to rise even higher as more Latino teens enter adulthood. Sixteen states counted more than half a million Latino residents, and in twenty-one states Latinos were the largest minority group.

Since Juan de Oñate led his column of settlers through today's El Paso to settle New Mexico . . .

Since a boat put ashore on the California coast carrying Apolinaria Lorenzana and the other parentless children . . .

Since Juan Seguín helped Texas break away from Mexico . . .

Since José Martí dipped his pen in ink and wrote of his own American dreams . . .

And since Isabel González took her fight for Puerto Ricans' American rights all the way to the Supreme Court . . .

. . . the American vision of making many one—*e pluribus unum*—has been made real by people from across the hemisphere who came to the United States. They think of themselves as, and still are, people who have part of the real estate in their head occupied by a slightly different concept of race, identity, and culture. They are Americans who watch football, eat pizza, open Twitter accounts, and vote for America's next Idol. They also carry some inheritance, some self-concept that comes from a steeply sloped farming village in Mexico, a village grocery store in Peru, a communal laundry sink in rural Guatemala.

That young population is going to have to be schooled and get health care, both significant costs downstream. In an aging country, Marta Tienda explains, that is not a bad thing, "The Hispanic population represents a significant dividend not available to other industrialized countries experiencing population aging.

"Given the projected growth of the Hispanic population growth over the next twenty years, if high school and college graduation gaps between Hispanics and others are eliminated or narrowed, by 2030 the majority of the country's labor force could be today's Latino youth supporting the older generation. If we compromise the future economic prospects of Hispanics by underinvesting in their education, we will

Jennifer Lopez is an actress, businesswoman, designer, producer, and singer. She's also one of the highest-paid Latinas in the world. CREDIT: AP PHOTO/MARK LENNIHAN

likely compromise the nation's future as well. *If we ignore the Hispanic moment we do so at our own risk*" [emphasis mine].

Sylvia Puente has spent her adult life as a community activist, educator, and scholar serving Latinos in Illinois. The vast majority of her staff time and resources at the Latino Policy Forum is now devoted to education, a make-or-break issue for Latinos—and the country. "The fate of the nation is tied to the success of the Latino community. Our futures are intertwined."

When she looks at a state labor market where two out of three new entrants are Latino, and a nation whose educational output is lagging behind that of other industrial nations, Puente worries. "Economically this state won't be able to function without a skilled Latino labor force.

"The good news is, when you look at young Latinos, people twenty-five to thirty-five, the numbers that have completed four-year degrees have increased considerably. And recently the data came from Pew that showed there are more Latinos than ever on college campuses, at numbers that outnumber African-Americans."

Enrique Pumar arrived in the United States in 1974, in time to attend his last year of high school. His subsequent work as an academic has led to a large body of published work and his current post as chairman of the Department of Sociology at Catholic University. Pumar is pleased by the signs of progress he sees among Latinos, but also sees a vanguard class peeling away from the rest in places like Washington, D.C. "There are two different kinds of Latino communities: working-class and professional. And the professionals are almost invisible, but they are not a small number." They come, Pumar says, for the opportunities America offers, just like farmers and factory workers. "And they reproduce the inequalities of Latin America.

"If our economy continues to move in the direction of an innovation, knowledge economy, a digital economy, the stratification is going to be very visible. We've seen this stratification, for example, in Miami.

"There are two Miamis. It looks very different if you drive along Brickell Avenue, and if you drive in Hialeah. On Brickell Avenue you have financial institutions that cater to Latin America, and it's a whole different city. This divide is becoming visible in many cities.

"People who are moving here are people who, for one reason or another, can't make it down in Central America. They tend to be working-class. They are likely not to speak English very well, likely not to have a

A busy day at Miami Dade College. With more than 160,000 students, MDC is one of the largest educational institutions in America. Two out of three students are Latinos. Course offerings include a Dual-Language Honors Program allowing top students to study in English and Spanish. CREDIT: MIAMI DADE COMMUNITY COLLEGE

degree, and even if they have a degree they won't be able to convert it in the U.S. They end up in services and low-end jobs."

In the twentieth century, when the United States was the factory for the world, immigrants and their descendants could use manufacturing jobs, often at high wages, to move into lives of middle-class security that could be handed on to their children. The bulk of today's Latino population arrived in the American workforce at a time when manufacturing was in full decline, and trade unionism was in retreat. Moving into the middle class, and staying there, is a much more complicated proposition, as it is for any American.

"The Latino middle class is very fragile." Sylvia Puente points to the economic setbacks of the last several years: "We lost most of our wealth, since so much of it was tied to home ownership, but it's not just this last time. If you look at the last five or six recessions, Latinos and African-Americans came back from recession more slowly than other groups.

"Sure, there's bifurcation. There's a cohort in the population, small but significant, that's doing well, that's living the American dream. That percentage, and the number of families, are increasing. But for a majority of the Latino population, it's a questionable future."

Yet she comes down on the side of optimism. "Latino culture is more of a 'we' culture. Most of American society is an 'I' culture. There are leaders coming forward who've chosen to make a career running non-profit organizations. Individuals step forward to run neighborhood organizations that provide services to families in need. Many of them came out of corporate culture, but success there wasn't enough to fulfill them.

"I think that 'we' culture will prevail."

To hear Angelo Falcón tell it, that "we" culture had better prevail, because the issues that challenge the working-class majority are just not very interesting to most other Americans. The political scientist and activist maintains that things have changed, and not for the better. "Political folks, the users of our research and the focus of our work, they don't want to talk about poor people anymore. It's a constant battle against this idea of a postracial America.

"And it's not just people on the right. When you talk about Latino issues, all you get is a blank stare. Unless you're trying to get their vote! But issues like and wealth and poverty, it's hard to raise them, unlike thirty years ago."

Falcón came to New York from San Juan as an infant in the early 1950s. One of the biggest changes he notices from his childhood and teen years is the visibility of Latinos, but he wonders whether it means much. "When I was younger and coming up, we were having trouble getting visibility. It

"My mom is detained." A demonstrator's sign speaks to an increasingly common challenge in Latino communities. Millions live in "mixed-status" families, most commonly with parents and older children in the country illegally and younger children who are American citizens by birth.
CREDIT: AP PHOTO/JOHN AMIS

was tough to get the media to pay any attention at all to Latino issues. Today, it's the reverse. It's almost overexposure, especially since the 2000 census. I've never seen so much attention by the political parties.

"But all this exposure has led to an amazing feeling of cynicism about the political process. People realize they're not invited to the table when important decisions are being made."

Falcón sees a paradox: tremendous attention to Latinos, increasing cultural awareness of their presence, but an almost total ignorance of anything more consequential. "That's the irony of it all. There's growing nativism in this country, growing xenophobia. I'm constantly getting asked, 'Why do you talk so much about being Cuban, being Puerto Rican, being Mexican? Latinos are doing so well! What's the big deal?'"

In recent years, increasing numbers of Latinos of all national backgrounds have been more inclined to identify themselves as a race, separate and distinct from white and black Americans. A group of Latino scholars looking at the survey evidence from the Latino National Survey concludes that it is isolation, not being welcomed into the American whole, that is pushing Latinos to define themselves in racial terms. Falcón agrees. "I tell them, 'It's your hostility, your treatment, as "others," that creates that nationalism. It's not something that comes from the

The eight members of the Salices family faced the dilemma of millions of other "mixed status" families. After a traffic stop, the matriarch was found to be in the country illegally, and was deported. After a long legal process, the Saliceses are reunited in Dalton, Georgia. CREDIT: JORGE SALICES

community, but from America's reaction to that community. If you had been more welcoming, you wouldn't have had this reaction.'"

To feel more optimistic, Falcón says he would want to see more new leaders, and a national agenda those leaders can use to shape Latino belief in an American future, and the rest of America's belief in Latinos as part of the American whole. "It took time for the Irish and the Italians. They were discriminated against when they came here, but they all became part of the ongoing American reality. Latinos have not been allowed to be a part of that. So you see a racialization of their reality that's become more persistent. It's not clear what it means for the future."

A comprehensive survey published in 2006, the Latino National Survey was designed to lift the lid on Latino public opinion. Researchers concluded a "substantial percentage of Latinos perceive discrimination and one response to this perception of being singled out because of their accent, skin color, immigrant origin or ethnic background is a strengthening of ethnic attachment and a sense that Latinos are a distinct racial group. Thus, the paradox is that even as Latinos Americanize, they may increasingly see themselves as part of a distinct ethnic or racial group."

The Latino National Survey makes fascinating reading, in part because it shows how evenly spread Latino public opinion is across countries of origin, regions, even income and levels of education. It should be reassuring to the rest of the country just how sold Latinos are on the possibility of getting ahead in America through hard work, even in the face of ferocious economic setbacks. The values Latinos told LNS opinion researchers they hold place their public opinion on issue after issue directly in the core of the American mainstream.

Latinos showed the pollsters that with more time in the country, fewer and fewer immigrants report an intention to return to their home countries. As they are in the country longer, Latinos consume a greater percentage of their media diet in English. One thing the data did *not* show was any sign that Ronald Reagan's old line is yet true: "Hispanics are Republicans. They just don't know it yet."

Gary Segura, a professor of political science at Stanford University and one of the lead researchers who compiled the data from the Latino National Survey, reminds leaders of both parties that for now, Latinos are anything but latent supporters of the GOP. "There is no evidence of the claim that Latinos are closet Republicans. There are two things that Republicans look at to make that conclusion. They look at entrepreneurial behavior among Latinos, which is very high; I've never met a Mexican immigrant who doesn't have an idea for a business; it's just . . . maybe it's the self-selection process of who chooses to migrate or whatever, but Latinos are starting businesses left and right.

"The second is that this is a very churchgoing, family-oriented subculture that would appear to be consistent with the family-values segment of the Republican coalition. In fact in neither instance does that represent a core ideological commitment.

"There is very clear evidence that on things about wanting government to do more, versus do less, or thinking government should grow to address problems, versus shrink, or reliance on government versus the free market . . . In every one of those survey questions supermajorities of Hispanics—seventy percent or more—articulate a position in favor of a more progressive government involved to solve social and economic problems.

"So I would say about two-thirds—between two-thirds and three-quarters—of Hispanics are socially, politically, liberal progressive, and that's a real problem for the Republicans, who can't really stop being Republicans in order to appeal to this group. I mean, they are a conservative party and that's their role."

When Segura takes a closer look at the intersection between religion and social issues in politics, he recalls the results of a poll taken by his own firm. "Overwhelmingly Hispanics are churchgoing. Overwhelmingly Hispanics report that religion guides them in everyday life. But when we asked them, 'Should ministers or priests be allowed to direct parishioners or congregants to vote for someone?' they absolutely opposed that. Over seventy percent of Hispanics opposed that. When we asked, 'Is government really about economic issues, gas prices, taxes, jobs? Or is government about family values, same-sex marriage, abortion?' seventy-five percent of our respondents—including seventy-five percent of Catholics, seventy-five percent Protestants, seventy-five percent of self-identified born-agains; there was not variation across subgroups—three-quarters of Hispanics believed that politics is about bread-and-butter issues; it's not about morality.

"So finally we asked the question, 'Should politicians who have strong religious beliefs rely on those beliefs when they are making decisions about policy?' Over two-thirds said no. So they are a religious community. But religion is religion and politics is politics, and they are not dragging one into the other."

For now, with Latinos relying so heavily on public schools, public transit, and other government-sponsored or -supplied services, it seems unlikely a big shift is under way toward a political party that heaps scorn on public services and promises to supply fewer of them. Other immigrant groups in earlier generations moved to the Republican Party once they durably and securely reached the middle class. It will be fascinating to watch whether Latinos do the same, and if so, when. Even as they are less uniformly aligned with the Catholic Church with each passing decade, Latinos still share that Church's disdain for contraception, homosexuality, and divorce.

There is a fascinating "two-ness," the duality that we have witnessed before, now with regards to the conversation inside and outside the Latino community about what the present tells us about the future. A Pew Hispanic Center projection of America in 2050 sees a national population of 438 million, and a Latino population more than twice its current size, of more than 130 million, approaching one of every three Americans.

As we have mentioned, U.S. population growth in the early twenty-first century was driven by young Latinos, and after the 2010 census, half of all people added to the U.S. population in any given year were Latino. This demographic pattern was established at the same time a wave of baby boomers came crashing into their sixties and seventies. In the next thirty years America's population will increasingly feature a growing cohort of young Latinos and a huge population of white elderly.

What is not clear is how these young Latinos will see themselves. "There is a new level of multiculturalism among our youth," says Sylvia

By some estimates, one third of Americans will trace their family history to Latin America and Spain by the middle of the twenty-first century. That would mean by 2050 a tripling of the 50 million Latinos counted in the 2010 census, as the United States grows by about 150 million people.
CREDIT: GETTY IMAGES

Puente. "My daughter's generation doesn't totally get it. The world she and her friends grew up in is totally multicultural, so she can't relate to the struggles she hears about from me and others about how difficult things were for Latinos in the past.

"So youth may not have the same affinity for strong ethnic identity in a country that's not defined by the standard of white American culture."

You cannot forget that Latinos are "marrying out"—that is, marrying people of other racial and ethnic backgrounds—at a very high rate. A quarter of all marriages involving Latinos are to a person of another ancestry. Of the more than 275,000 mixed marriages counted in 2010, more than half were between Latinos and what the census bureau calls "non-Hispanic whites." Play that trend out into the big-number Latino future, and millions of the projected 130-million-plus may be people whose relationship to a Latino "community" may be pretty tenuous. Add the quickening pace of movement away from traditional residential centers into the suburbs, and the gradual abandonment of Spanish, and what does it mean to have a country that is 30 percent Latino at midcentury? Maybe not much. Maybe a lot.

Angelo Falcón has noticed a great deal of attention from people trying to sell things to Latinos, from car insurance and toothpaste to public school vouchers and abortion bans, while at the same time "media and politicians try to deracialize politics and policy questions.

"Yes, it's a paradox, but it does make sense to me. The whole idea is to create a passive, malleable political consumer group. You can get the money out of them. Get the votes out of them, without really having to invest in them."

When Arturo Madrid, a professor at Trinity University in San Antonio, looks back at his family's, and his people's, four-hundred-year history in what is now the United States, he remembers a grandmother's decision to join "an American church," to become a Protestant. A pastor warned, "If they don't let you in the front door, you go in the back door. And if you can't get in the back door, go in the side door. And if you can't get in through the side door, you go in through the window."

To Madrid, it is emblematic "of the experience of most Latinos who have not been able to enter the institutions of American society through front doors, but had to come in through back doors and side doors and some of them even through the window at night."

Even as the holder of an endowed university chair, widely published, traveled, and experienced, Madrid finds not all doors are open in the academy, even now. "It's space that Anglo-Americans feel is theirs, particularly intellectual, academic, cultural space. They own it and we are hard put to penetrate it. We have to be far more prepared, far more intelligent, far more accomplished, far more productive in order to be accepted."

Yet Madrid is sure the grandchildren who carry his name will not be "anomalous," but instead will be "part and parcel of the fabric of this society, where the 'other' is not constructed as a poor, illiterate recent immigrant but part of the fabric of society."

When Gary Gerstle looks at the old Ellis Island requirements of fitting in, he sees "the jettisoning of your immigrant ethnic heritage, and a full-scale embrace of what the people already in America decided an American should be." Now Gerstle wonders if there is a different model that may not demand that people lose their pasts entirely. "Maybe America will be a better and more interesting place if there is more diversity, if they bring their ethnic cultures, if they maintain them, and inject parts of their cultures into the American mainstream.

"In this new style of becoming American, you are not expected to relinquish everything."

Latinos have spent 175 years learning to adapt. Luis Antonio Dámaso de Alonso of Ciudad Juárez, Mexico, became Gilbert Roland, and a Hollywood star.

Jordi Farragut Mesquida of Minorca, Spain, moved to the United States at the beginning of the American Revolution and became George Farragut, and an officer in the young navy. His son, David Farragut, won the critical Battle of Mobile Bay during the Civil War and became an admiral.

One of America's great twentieth-century poets, William Carlos Williams, was the son of an English Caribbean father and a Puerto Rican mother. He rarely referred to this heritage when talking about his life as a poet. When speaking at a writers' conference at the University of Puerto Rico in 1940, Williams said, "We in the United States are climactically as by latitude and weather much nearer Spain than England, as also in volatility of our spirits, in racial mixture—much more like Gothic and Moorish Spain."

It is an old story. But it is also a story that never ends. When the outlines of the modern country were complete—in other words, when America stopped coming to Latinos, and Latinos started coming to

America—a love affair filled with ambiguity began and continues to this day. The United States holds the possibility of a better life, and the pain of exclusion. This amazing country has given more people from more places than any other country in the world a better, freer life, with an even better set of chances for their children.

The people who cling to the tops of railroad cars to make it to the border . . .

. . . who risk their lives sneaking across burning deserts or hide in trucks stuffed with other desperate men . . .

. . . who lash together scraps of wood into rafts to float out of Cuba . . .

. . . who for more than a century have left everything to try their chances in *el Norte* . . .

. . . are nothing more or less than the heirs of mission soldiers, ranchers, nuns, colonial civil servants, miners, farmers, blacksmiths, sailors, midwives, and governors who started writing the story of this country along with the Pilgrims, along with the Jamestown settlers, the Dutch in New York, the French Protestant refugees, the West African captives, and the Portuguese Jews fleeing Brazil.

America belongs to us all. Its history is made by us all, and someday may be written about us all. We are well along a path that will change, over time, what Americans look like, what the food on your dinner plate tastes like, and what music will sound like in your car and in your home.

You have marched across the deserts of the Southwest. You have charged up San Juan Hill with Teddy Roosevelt, sailed into Ellis Island with Isabel González, and walked out of the jungle leading Japanese prisoners with Guy Gabaldon. You have handed out leaflets for the new GI Forum with Dr. Hector Garcia, and stood firm on the picket line with Dolores Huerta. They are all part of your inheritance. They have all contributed DNA to your American present. Latino history in the United States is your history, wherever you're from. And you won't be able to understand the America that's coming, without remembering the history you've just read.

Viva America.

ACKNOWLEDGMENTS

THERE IS ONE byline name on the cover. However, a book, any book, is inevitably the work of many hands. Special thanks go to my trusty research assistant, Michael Melia; my indulgent bosses in this project, Jeff Bieber, Adriana Bosch and Ray Garcia; my editor, Ian Jackman, and my agent, Rene Alegria.

Thanks to all the people who shared their memories and their personal histories for this book and the accompanying television series. They make any journalist's work better and more interesting. Thanks also to Salme Lopez at Bosch and Company, Gabriela Schulte at WETA and Kim Suarez at Penguin for their help in bringing this book to fruition.

Gratitude goes to my encouraging and sharp-eyed early readers, and to my family members who've learned that "book years" can sometimes mean having to compete for my attention. They may be rivals for my time, but never for my love.